CRAFT BEER COUNTRY

CRAFT BEER COUNTRY

In Search of the Best Breweries
from the South Pacific to the Pacific Coast

KIRK RICHARDSON

MASCOT BOOKS | HERNDON, VA

MASCOT BOOKS

Craft Beer Country: In Search of the Best Breweries
from the South Pacific to the Pacific Coast

For more information, please contact:
Mascot Books
620 Herndon Parkway #320
Herndon, VA 20170
info@mascotbooks.com

www.mascotbooks.com

LCCN: 2018907049

CPSIA CODE: PRFRE0918A
ISBN 978-1-64307-167-1

Book design by THE FRONTISPIECE
Typeset by Kevin Barrett Kane in 11/15 Garamond

First Edition – Printed in Canada

CONTENTS

Breweries   vii

   Into Craft Beer Country   1
1   Paradise by the Pint   5
2   Strange Times with Sour Beer   12
3   The Beer Engineer in Barley Country   19
4   Back to Nature in a Beerhive   29
5   The Flavor Technician from Great Britain   37
6   Caught in a Downpour of IPAs   45
7   Catch of the Day   53
8   Heading into the Heart of Hops Country   58
9   Bringing It All Together in Boise   67
10   Beer and the Lost Art of Conversation   74
11   Adventures in Beer Tasting   80
12   Nerding Out on Craft Beer in P-town   88
13   From Start-up Blues to World Cup Gold   97
14   From Black Butte to Deep Dark Abyss   104
15   The Beer-Brewing Lawman in Lederhosen   110
16   Stumbling on Old Crusty in Rogue Nation   116
17   Taking Craft Beer to New Heights   123
18   Chilling Out at an Aussie's Beer Oasis   133
    Photographs   137
19   Bahl Hornin with a Brightlighter   153
20   Racing Through Beer in Wine Country   162
21   Celebrating Beer with Brew Free! or Die IPA   169
22   Beer Sanctuary by the Bay   177
23   Now You See It, Now You Don't   182
24   Getting a Good Buzz on Avocado Honey   190
25   A Pleasant Surprise in Placentia   196

26 Searching for Arthur's Lost Abbey   203

27 Guardians of the Craft   209

28 Smooth Landing in Fightertown   217

29 More Fun than a Barrel of Monkeys   226

30 Soaking up Suds in Sin City   232

31 A Hidden Gem Under the Neon Lights   238

32 Finding Beer in the Last Frontier   245

33 Exploring Craft Beer Country   255

Acknowledgments   277

About the Author   279

BREWERIES

HAWAII
Maui Brewing – Kihei – Maui

BRITISH COLUMBIA
Strange Fellows Brewing – Vancouver

WASHINGTON
Chuckanut Brewery – Skagit Valley
Anacortes Brewing – Anacortes
Reuben's Brews – Seattle
Cloudburst Brewing – Seattle
Freemont Brewing – Seattle
Elysian Brewing – Seattle
Georgetown Brewing – Seattle
Propolis Brewing – Port Townsend
ENine – Tacoma
Rainy Daze Brewing – Poulsbo
Well 80 – Olympia
Fish Brewing Company – Olympia
Bale Breaker Brewing Company – Yakima
Barrel Mountain Brewing – Battle Ground

IDAHO
Sockeye Brewing – Boise
Boise Brewing Company – Boise

OREGON
Barley Brown's Beer – Baker City
pFriem Family Brewers – Hood River
McMenamins Edgefield – Troutdale
Breakside Brewery – Portland
Great Notion Brewing – Portland
Base Camp Brewing – Portland
Ground Breaker – Portland
Burnside Brewing – Portland
Public Coast Brewing – Cannon Beach
Rogue Ales – Newport
Santiam Brewing – Salem
3 Sheets Brewery – Albany
Flat Tail Brewing – Corvallis
Ninkasi Brewing – Eugene
Oakshire Brewing – Eugene
Alesong Brewing and Blending – Eugene

Deschutes Brewing – Bend
Boneyard Beer – Bend
Crux Fermentation Project – Bend
Wild Ride Brewing Company – Redmond
Sunriver Brewing – Sunriver
Klamath Basin Brewing – Klamath Falls
Walkabout Brewing – Medford
Caldera Brewing – Ashland

CALIFORNIA
Sierra Nevada Brewing Co. – Chico
Out of Bounds Brewing – Rocklin
New Helvetia Brewing – Sacramento
North Coast Brewing Company – Fort Bragg
Anderson Valley Brewing – Boonville
Bear Republic Brewing – Healdsburg
Russian River Brewing Company – Santa Rosa
21st Amendment – San Leandro
Faction Brewing Company – Alameda
Half Moon Bay Brewery – El Granada
Corralitos Brewing Co. – Freedom
Firestone Walker Brewing Co. – Paso Robles
Figueroa Mountain Brewing – San Luis Obispo
Island Brewing Company – Carpinteria
Last Name Brewing – Upland
The Bruery – Placentia
Beachwood BBQ & Brewing – Long Beach
Garage Brewing – Temecula
The Lost Abbey – San Marcos
Stone Brewing – Escondido
AleSmith Brewing – San Diego
Green Flash Brewing – San Diego
Karl Strauss Brewing Company – La Jolla
Societe Brewing – San Diego
Coronado Brewing – San Diego

NEVADA
Big Dog's Brewing Company – Las Vegas
Brasserie St. James – Reno

ALASKA
Alaskan Brewing Company – Juneau

INTO CRAFT BEER COUNTRY

EYEBROWS RAISED, Ken Grossman, founder of Sierra Nevada Brewing Co., waited for my reply from across the conference table. We were in the brewery's Chico, California headquarters, where, supposedly, I was the one doing the interviewing. But Grossman had flipped our roles. "What is this anyway?" he had asked. "Another craft beer bible?"

"No," I had answered, explaining that the book would look at the world's favorite adult beverage from a different angle. "This is a chronicling of my journey in search of the best beers in the West! It's a travelogue that includes many of craft beer's most interesting characters—craft beer rock stars and people you have probably never heard of—and their beers." Grossman nodded and smiled, a signal for me to press forward. I've never looked back.

In fact, that has been my "elevator pitch"—how I'd summarize the book for brewers—from stepping into the story with an interview on the side of a dormant volcano in Hawaii, to numerous other adventures in California, Nevada, Oregon, Idaho, Washington State, British Columbia, and Alaska. These are self-contained vignettes (or episodes if you like), filled with anecdotes, humor, and a more than a few misadventures. Like the swelling streams of great lagers, pale ales, abbey ales, sours, IPAS, brown, amber and red ales, porters, stouts, barleywine, and even more styles on the market, there was more quality beer and fascinating information than anyone could digest, even a voraciously thirsty food and beverage writer.

This journalist's account delves into some of Craft Beer Country's most highly decorated beers, from local, state, and regional award winners to medalists at the Great American Beer Festival (GABF)[1] and World Beer Cup,[2] and includes insights from the interesting characters who created them: guys like Tomme Arthur at The Lost Abbey, Fal Allen at Anderson Valley Brewing, Brett Joyce at Rogue, Adam Robbings at Reuben's Brews, Geoff Larson at Alaskan Brewing, and other amazing entrepreneurial brewers that I've met along the way.

Although fabulous books on beer and food pairing have been written by Garrett Oliver (The Brooklyn Brewery), Peter Zien (AleSmith Brewing Company), and others, I will also dabble in more than a few suggested combinations in the chapters ahead. Many of the brewers couldn't resist sharing their own favorites.

But can you really pin down a best brewery or beer from the South Pacific to the Pacific Coast? People I've met along the way have asked me for my own top choice time and time again. I've consistently answered, "You'll just have to read the book and find out for yourself." Even if you think you have my favorite pinned down, it's more important that you try these and other great beers and pick your own winners. What I've written about between the front and back covers is just the tip of the iceberg, and you will undoubtedly discover other noteworthy renditions of beer styles that are worth talking about.

---

1   The Great American Beer Festival (GABF), founded in 1982, has been growing and evolving along with the American craft brewing industry ever since. Each year, this festival represents the largest collection of U.S. beer ever served, in a public tasting event plus a private competition. The GABF, hosted by the Brewers Association, takes place annually in Denver.

2   The Brewers Association developed the bi-annual World Beer Cup Competition in 1996 to celebrate the art and science of brewing. This global competition continues to create greater consumer awareness about different beer styles and flavor profiles while promoting international brewing excellence.

As you pour over the following pages, you'll find beers mentioned not just by me, your tour guide, but personal picks from creative geniuses like Ricardo Norgrove of Bear Republic Brewing, Patrick Rue of The Bruery, and Robert Horner of Propolis. You will also hear from nanobrewers like Sergeant Klint Sheets of 3 Sheets Brewing—relatively unknown characters who are genuinely passionate about making great craft beer in small batches.

One of the beautiful things about craft beer and the dynamic but often down-to-earth people who brew it is that you have the opportunity to visit them yourselves and write your own story of sorts. That doesn't require a degree in journalism or even a pen and paper. You just need a little curiosity and the willingness to check out new places, talk to the guy or gal next to you on the bar stool, and see, smell, taste, and feel the ever-widening range of delicious beer options available nearly everywhere in in the world.

So without further ado, let's begin this adventure halfway across the Pacific Ocean, roughly 2500 miles from the Oregon Coast as the commercial airline flies, hanging loose with Garrett Marrero of Maui Brewing at his production facility and pub on the slopes of Mt. Haleakalā. That is as far as you can go chasing the setting sun and still be in on the western edge of my Craft Beer Country map.

Prost, skol, salud, or cheers, wherever you happen to be toasting with good craft beer!

Garrett Marrero, owner of MAUI BREWING, serves up a cold one in the brewery's beautiful tasting room on The Valley Isle. Photo credit: Maui Brewing Co. Photo by Edward Smith

CHAPTER 1

PARADISE BY THE PINT

Maui Brewing Company—Kihei, Maui, HI

APPROXIMATELY 2,513 MILES NORTHEAST of Kihei, Maui, in frigid Albany, Oregon, I excitedly unwrap a hefty-sized gift on Christmas morning. By its shape and weight, I boldly predict that I'm the newest member of some beer-of-the-month club. But as I tear away the festive paper, what greets me exceeds my expectations. My *wahine* (Hawaiian for "wife") has transported me back to the sunny shores of Hawaii in the dead-cold Northwest winter. At the foot of the tree before me glow twenty-four golden Maui Brewing Bikini Blonde Lagers.

Five months earlier, we sat on the brewery's sun-drenched patio on the western slope of 10,023-foot Mount Haleakalā. Up the incline to the left, the cone of the dormant volcano disappeared above a low-lying ring of foamy clouds. To the right beyond a few swaying palms, the island dropped away into Pacific waters so dazzlingly blue that only a soft-blonde pint of nice cold beer could distract me from the view.

Bikini Blonde, a well-shaped Munich Helles lager brewed with floral hops and Pilsner and Munich malts, is a nice, easy-going complement to a hot July afternoon. Checking in at a mellow 21 IBUs (International Bitterness Units), this malty craft beer leaves a slightly sweet, biscuity flavor on my taste buds that I'd wager the mainstream beer crowd would appreciate. I make a mental note to test its flavor again, offset with a nice, juicy, lightly seasoned steak complemented by a South Pacific sunset.

In the meantime, we're forced to pause our drinking and daydreaming to head inside for a tour behind the scenes with Maui Brewing founder Garrett Marrero.

Back in January 2005, Marrero and his wife Melanie opened the brewery on a tight budget and a lot of faith. Looking at their thriving craft-beer business today, it's hard to imagine that the Marreros haven't always led a charmed life. "We slept on the floor of a really shitty apartment for several weeks, because we couldn't afford a mattress," confides Marrero. "The first mattress we bought was used. We carried it out of a crack house—I'm not kidding you! Sleeping on that floor helped build character. We ran on a shoestring, and we still do. We looked at pennies, not just dimes, to be competitive here. To brew in Hawaii and to manufacture locally, all those things cost a lot more than they do on the mainland. You'd be shocked at what the cost of production here is compared to the mainland."

Pinching pennies while avoiding the constant lure of the nearby surf in lieu of backbreaking work, the Marreros persevered. They eventually outgrew the company's increasingly cramped 13,000-ft.² Lahaina facility. "From very meager beginnings, this was blood, sweat, tears and a lot of hard work on both my wife's part and mine . . . and our entire team," reflects Marrero. "But I keep pointing back to the fact that we had these visions, these dreams for the company of what we wanted to be. We never deviated from our founding principles, and I think that's what's allowed us to become who we are today. We're very proud that we remain authentic Hawaiian craft beer."

Making those uniquely local ales, lagers, and porters isn't as easy as picking pineapples from a local plantation and tossing them into a kettle with a little malt, hops, and yeast. A lot goes into the process that produces consistently good craft beer. Marrero led us on a tour of the 42,000-ft.² production facility that he opened in October 2014. He guesstimated that his company could brew 60,000 barrels of beer in the fifty—and twenty-five-barrel brew systems.

After inspecting the facility's water filtration system, which removes chlorides, fluorides, and particulate, including fine pieces of lava (remember, the brewery is built on a volcano), we get a peek at the brewery laboratory.

"In fairness to other brewers, not every brewery needs a lab this size," observes Marrero. "For example, San Diego has one hundred or so breweries in the county, and they have access to amazing labs. We don't have that access. We can't just drive down the street with a sample and be like, 'What's going on?'" Although Maui Brewing does send samples to San Diego-based White Labs for government-mandated third-party validation of ABV (alcohol by volume) and other requirements, it tries to do as much as possible in-house. "Paying it forward, we can make that available to other brewers here in the state as well, so that we can help them, especially when they're having problems."

The scientist who helps solve those kinds of problems just walked in the door. Marrero introduces us to Dr. Dre, who runs the company's state-of-the-art laboratory. The good doctor is kindly tolerant of the endless stream of questions that start pouring her way. For example: "What exactly are you a doctor of?" asks my inquisitive photographer.

"My Ph.D is in molecular biology and genetics," answers Dre. I immediately think, but suppress the following dumb question: "So with your credentials, what are you doing in a brewery? Shouldn't you be in a top-secret research facility cloning something?"

While my photographer asks about moving to Maui to be Dr. Dre's new assistant, Marrero and I move onto the many interesting gadgets around the room. "There's a shaker table microscope, some water baths, a centrifuge, a laminar hood, an aerobic incubator, autoclave, all the fun stuff," he points out. "We can measure just about everything," he adds. Then turning to Dr. Dre, Marrero mentions, "Kirk was asking earlier how we have 100-plus IBU on the Double Overhead, but technically you can't really taste above 100." We debate humans' ability to detect exceedingly bitter flavors like Dogfish Head's hopped up 658 IBU Hoo Lawd IPA. "Does a swig make your face shrivel up and turn to dust?" I wonder out loud.

Although the lab is all about those kinds of numbers, we get back to the business at hand. "We put quite a bit of money into the lab, just because this is how you ensure the quality of beer," emphasizes Marrero. "The beer might start in the brewhouse, but if this isn't right here, then you're not making great beer. When you go to the volumes we're doing, that's an issue. Brewing five barrels a year is a different thing than brewing 50,000. For consistency and quality control, this is absolutely important.

"When we first started out, no one would call and say, 'The Bikini Blonde is a little darker today,' or 'Are you sure that it's not Big Swell (IPA) that you actually put in the keg?' You can't have that happen at our size because people rely on Bikini Blonde being Bikini Blonde and Big Swell being Big Swell. We have color parameters that we check using the spectrophotometer as well. So we know these beers have this spec, and this is what they need to be. Otherwise, the brewers and cellarmen aren't doing their job.

"At the end of the day, the ROI on the lab is that there is nothing to worry about, and that means the lab is doing a really good job." In fact, the people on the production floor depend on it. "With Dr. Dre looking at the yeast and doing cell counts and viability, that tells them how much yeast to pitch into the beer that they're brewing." By now, it's definitely time to leave the scientist to her devices, so that the microscopic critters and other ingredients continue to behave as expected.

A short stroll from the laboratory, and we find ourselves in front of a massive stainless-steel vessel. "This is our coconut tank," announces Marrero. "There's 500 pounds of coconut sitting in there that are recirculating in beer right now." If we had X-ray eyes, we could watch the process that infuses the unmistakable flavor of dried white palm seed flesh into one of the most distinctive porters in the world. Marrero reports his brewery's demand for coconut actually exceeds what the local supply chain can provide. "We go through about 15,000 pounds a quarter," he reports. "There's not enough coconut here, so we have to bring it in from Guam and the Philippines."

I'm not enough of a purist to fuss about such a technicality, and most palates won't be able to identify the island of the coconuts' origin.

In my mind, discovering Maui's CoCoNut PorTeR (recently rebranded Coconut Hiwa Porter), a World Beer Cup[1] Gold Award Winner, is like being marooned on a desert island, only to learn that it's actually a tropical paradise where palm fruit is filled with a nutty, brown, 6% ABV liquid. *No ka 'oi!*

"The coconut porter is our top-selling beer on the mainland and in most of our markets," confirms Marrero. "That was the one that first put us on the map. It's a robust porter, brewed with hand-toasted coconut. We do an imperial version aged in rum barrels, and we do one aged in bourbon barrels. (In fact, Imperial Coconut Porter won a 2016 Great American Beer Festival[2] gold medal in the Field Beer category.) We are *the* coconut porter guys!"

"Oh, yes you are," I think to myself, then ask aloud, "Can we just stop the tour right here and pause for another pint to confirm that?"

Instead he mercilessly toys with me, sharing a recipe for coconut porter chocolate cake. "I love to cook and bake from scratch, but a lot of times it's Friday and I just want some sweets." That starts with buying a box of high quality organic chocolate-cake mix. "Instead of doing the water or milk, we put in a can of coconut porter. That's the only substitution. If we want to be really good about it, we use applesauce in place of the oil, but usually we just do the oil or butter. But the coconut porter makes all the difference in the world, because the carbonation lightens up that batter and it stays nice and moist." If I were stranded on Maui, I'm confident that I could survive on Coconut Hiwa Porter and an occasional slice of the Marreros' chocolate cake.

1　The Brewers Association developed the bi-annual World Beer Cup Competition in 1996 to celebrate the art and science of brewing. This global competition continues to create greater consumer awareness about different beer styles and flavor profiles while promoting international brewing excellence.

2　The Great American Beer Festival (GABF), founded in 1982, has been growing and evolving along with the American craft brewing industry ever since. Each year, this festival represents the largest collection of US beer ever served, in a public tasting event plus a private competition. The GABF, hosted by the Brewers Association, takes place annually in Denver.

All this talk of chocolate and coconuts has us thirsty as castaways, and I finally convince my host that it is time to head for the bar. "We have thirty-two faucets, but sometimes we double up or we might be between batches, but with so much variety, you can't drink all of them," sighs Marrero. "Some of them are going to be gone before you get a chance to get around to it. I feel like a tourist in our own tasting room sometimes, especially with all my travel. When I come home, the menu board has changed. I'm like, 'Whoa, where did that one go? I didn't even get to try any!' When the first release of Black Pearl was here, I didn't get a drop. Our national sales manager Pete calls Black Pearl the unicorn. It's the white whale, if you will, because it's at 12.3 percent, and it's an imperial coconut porter aged in local rum barrels."

"That'll kick your ass," I say. "It's a beautiful beer," he replies, adding that it will be ready for Pirate Day. "There is a national day for everything," grins Marrero. "Arrr matey!" I fire back.

Black Pearl isn't the only beer the island brewer makes that is powerful enough to wake the dead. Its limited release Doppelshot Doublebock is brewed with MauiGrown Yellow Caturra coffee from Ka'anapali, a spyglass away on the north shore of the island. "The twelve-ounce can has two-thirds of a cup of coffee in it," reveals Marrero. "We like to use local agriculture to influence the styles of beer we do. It's really important to us that when we brew with fruit, spice, ingredients of any adjunct, that it be an authentic local ingredient. So where we could have brought in 10 percent Maui coffee and 90 percent from Costa Rica, Mexico or Ecuador, we opted to purchase it locally. So 100 percent of the coffee was actually grown here in Hawaii, which was a $30,000 coffee bill. It's worth it because we're contributing to the local environment, the farmers, agriculture. Everybody benefits all the way through, and we're really showing our brewery is about integrity before profit. We started out with those principles on a very small scale at our brewpub in Kahana, and staying true to that has allowed us to evolve into this larger company. We're very proud of that."

It's not that Marrero is out to dominate the world of craft beer. "We don't have this dream to be a quarter million-, a five hundred thousand-, a million-barrel brewery," he says. "That's not what we're here for. We want to stay small, efficient, unique, innovative, use those type of words to describe us, not to describe us based on our size. As much as we are Hawaii's largest brewery, that was not our goal. Our goal was to be Hawaii's best and to be the beer of Hawaii."

As the sun sets over the nearby island of Molokai, I bite into a delicious filet that has been marinating in a blend of spices and Bikini Blonde Lager for hours. A glass of CoCoNut Porter has me back in that craft-beer-induced state of nirvana. All that is missing is a little chocolate cake. Aloha!

Garrett Unfiltered

Finding Hops for One of His Favorite Beer Styles
When pressed for his own favorite Maui Brewing beer, Marrero has to think about it a minute. "That's the hardest question I think you could ask," he says. "Right now (late August), I've been crushing all the lagers, just because it's been so hot here. On top of warm and sticky, a 4.8-percent dry-hop pilsner in the tasting room just goes down so nice."

While sugarcane, pineapples, and coconuts love the island climate, the key ingredients in Big Swell and the brewery's other IPAs must be imported. Although Marrero does buy European hops, he purchases most from the Pacific Northwest. "We do work with a lot of different brokers nowadays, because the hop market has gotten so tight that you can't get all of them from one supplier anymore, especially if you want some unique varieties," he notes. "We have quite a bit of Amarillo, Columbus, Citra, and Liberty. We use a lot of Noble hops as well."

Another of Marrero's favorite beers depends on that supply chain. Maui Brewing's Big Swell IPA is a pineapple-kissed India Pale Ale brewed with four different kinds of Northwestern hops, weighing in at a noticeably bitter 82 IBUs and 6.8% ABV. A taste brings waves of pine and citrus across the palate, which then make their way back up through the nose. Each gulp keeps you paddling back for the next ride. If flying to Hawaii for a few pints isn't an option, fear not. Big Swell IPA has made its way onto the shelves of many mainland markets and at least one *haole's* refrigerator here in Craft Beer Country.

CHAPTER 2

STRANGE TIMES WITH SOUR BEER

Strange Fellows—Vancouver, B.C.

VANCOUVER, BRITISH COLUMBIA is like some of today's experimental beers. There are so many different elements thrown together that it probably shouldn't work. With the white-capped North Shore Mountains serving as a backdrop, Canada's third largest metropolis is a place where modern and classic architecture mingle with the natural beauty of glistening Vancouver Harbor. It's a multicultural city with a radical mix of ideas, art, and cuisine. So why should I be surprised to find one of the western masters of sour beer styles, adept at blending sweet and tart with a variety of unique flavors, continuing to hone his beloved craft in an inauspicious little brewery alongside Clark Drive in East Vancouver?

Inside, fellow beer enthusiast and friend Tony Boyd introduces me to Iain Hill, who started Strange Fellows with business partner Aaron Jonckheere in December 2014. Hill is trim for a guy who has been brewing beer since the 1992 and enjoying it even longer. Though it's late in the afternoon and the lines around his eyes hint that he is probably worn out from a busy day running between tanks, he smiles and asks if I want to taste a few samples during the interview. We are off on the right foot as we leave the noisy pub and head through the brewery on the way to his office with a few of his twenty-two-ounce "works of art" in tow.

Once there, we open a bottle of his Foudreyer, a New World wild ale, fill two glasses and toast, "Cheers!" Barely ripe enough red fruit tumbles out of the glass and onto my surprised palate. It reminds me of the juicy sweet-and-sour plums that I used to bite into as a boy, before my cranky neighbor chased me out of his orchard with a baseball bat. Although gorging myself on fresh plums was certainly a treat, this reddish brown 6% ABV liquid fruit brings more to the table (is that a hint of zesty cherry tomato?), and I don't even have to trespass to steal another taste. "This beer is special because it's made with a whole range of organisms," he volunteers. "It's made with a multiculture, with yeast and bacteria, the bacteria being relevant to making sour beer with lactic acid. It's made in this big (6,000 liters) oak tank," he adds, pointing through the wall to the production floor.

Hill leans back on his desk, and we start at the beginning of the adventure that led him here, or at least the fork in the road that ultimately brought about this unlikely meeting. It seems that he was destined to be in the food and beverage business from his university days. Hill attended the nearby University of Victoria, where studied food biotechnology. "I've been interested in those angles—cheese, beer, wine, pickled foods—for a long time" he says. "In my last year of university, I had a professor who wanted to open a company with me making a product called Lang Milk. It's this terrible Scandinavian stuff and makes up about one third of the yogurt market there. It's like slime."

Thankfully for me and everyone else in the brewery's tasting room tonight, Hill ultimately decided that he preferred working with brettanomyces instead of lactobacillus acidophilus. He and Christine, an arts-school student who later became his wife, moved to Vancouver to look for work. "There were hardly any breweries here at that time," he recalls. However, Hill was lucky enough to put his background in science to work as the Quality Control Supervisor for locally owned and operated Shaftebury Brewing. "They were looking for someone to start a little lab—it was incredibly rudimentary," he explains. "A lot of it became self-taught. I got books, and I knew a guy from Molson who was able to guide me. They started to become very busy, and I was able to learn all aspects of production. So my job ended up being in blue coveralls and rubber boots. I was a brewer, cellar man, tank and keg cleaner. I did everything there. You name it."

A few years later, Hill helped a local entrepreneur run the first brewpub in town, the Yaletown Brewing Company. Over time, that venture ended up growing into several pubs and a distillery, all in British Columbia's Lower Mainland. Being able to experiment with a variety of ingredients, both traditional and nontraditional, helped him fuel his desire to learn more about the world's many craft beer styles.

"Getting into brewing, I was reading as much as I could and learning everything I could," he remembers. He was the one of the first brewers in all of Western Canada to play with lambic-like beers. "It's kind of like a band that no one else knows, but you found them and they're awesome! They're extra good because no one else is listening to them. I really did fall in love with sours."

After an inspirational trip to the Belgium, he began experimenting with a particular type of ale that he fell for while visiting the Flanders region. "I started doing Oud Bruin, which I eventually made my name on, I suppose," he notes. Oud Bruin, or Old Brown, is a barrel-aged brown beer that undergoes a secondary fermentation and is subsequently stored away for months so that the yeast and bacteria have plenty of time to give it a nice sour flavor. Hill became so good at it that he ended up selling all of the Oud Bruin he could make at Yaletown. "People loved it," he says.

That gave him the confidence that he needed to launch his own brewery. Now he just needed someone to help. "For about twenty years, I tried to open a brewery," Hill remembers. "I had been friends with Aaron, and he had the same dream as me. He came from a sales background, which is funny because I wouldn't usually be friends with a salesperson. But Aaron was the potential partner who finally panned out, so we opened here in 2014."

"Why did you name it Strange Fellows?" I ask, wondering what mysteries he might reveal.

Although they had an uninspiring legal name for the business, Hill and Jonckheere couldn't agree on a brand name that would draw patrons through the front door. The heated debate would probably still be going on today if left to the stubborn partners, but cooler heads prevailed. "We were having dinner at our house with our wives, and my wife Christine said, 'You guys are just a couple of strange dudes, really strange fellows,'" he laughs. "It wasn't something that we were like, 'Oh yeah that's the name! But it was a name that made it onto this list and rapidly went to the top."

The ever-creative Christine ran with the new brand name, eventually creating "Strange Days," oddball events when everyone at the brewery celebrates a particularly strange theme based on folklore and/or obscure dates in history. "So in December, we celebrate Krampusnacht," Iain tells me with mischievous grin. Krampus is a beast-like anti-Santa creature, who, during the winter holiday season, punishes children who have misbehaved. "We have a staff member who dresses up as Krampus," he continues. "People bring their children to sit on his knee on a gothic throne, and we make several kids cry for Christmas each year. We do all sorts of fun things. I can send you one of our calendars." I agree, as long as another visit doesn't involve meeting Krampus in person. I'm a prime target for his wrath, well-known for misbehaving since early childhood, when I was reprimanded for peeing in the bedroom trash can, among many other offenses.

Before our conversation goes completely sour, I take a nice calming gulp of Reynard, Hill's now-fine-tuned Oud Bruin recipe. He points out that the fox on the bottle label is taken from Belgian folklore, "A particularly evil fox," he says. As the story goes, Reynard is a trickster that "doesn't give a fig what society thinks" and disobeys convention to satisfy his desires, often unveiling a truth along the way. I can relate. The redwood brown 6.5% is the truth as far as I'm concerned. The Oud Bruin has been aged in oak for more than two years, and the slightly tart cherry flavor that the prolonged process brings out is irresistible and lasting. "This is not only the best sour I have ever had in Canada, it is one of the best in the west," I pronounce, then confess: "Well, in full transparency, this is the only sour that I've had in Canada, period."

Hill wrinkles his nose, and I'm certain that the Reynard we are enjoying is not the offender. "I will say that I'm not fond of using the word *sour* all the time," he remarks. "If you go to Belgium, no one is talking about sours. It's a gueuze, it's a kriek, or it's Oud Bruin. I really dislike using the word sour. It's too generic. To a lot of the market, it's not a positive thing. Objectively, it's fine because all wine is sour. Lemonade is sour. But when you say, 'beer that's sour,' inevitably people who haven't been primed wouldn't know. It can be a bit of a turnoff and kind of dumbs it down. But I sometimes use the same term because I don't have a better way of describing it."

As the old saying goes, "If you can't beat 'em, join 'em!" We agree to let the acidic word seep into our conversation until someone comes up with a sharper alternative.

Hill admits that he is not much of a fan of intensely sour or overly bitter beer. "It's like rock 'n' roll music," he suggests. "The new world pushes the boundaries, whether with food or with rock music." He adds that subtle sours are often an acquired taste.

"A lot of times people are fearful of the word sour," according to Hill. "They tar and feather this whole notion of sours, and I say, 'No, no, no!' If people say they don't like beer, I believe that they haven't found the right beer. There are amazing, approachable, complex sours from Belgium—some of those lambics are like bones-good beers that anyone can drink and actually enjoy. I think that not everybody realizes that there's probably a way in for them. There are hard-core aficionado sour beers that ask a lot of your palette, but it doesn't have to be that."

Those who once favored extreme beer flavors often change their tune later on. "In IPAS, we call it the hops arms race," muses Hill. "But sure enough, it's changing. The market is growing up, and the producers are growing up. We're actually stepping back. Now it's like, 'Oh, I prefer the hop flavor, and I'm not about the bitterness. People are stepping away from that now and are much more concerned about the hop flavor. It's just the market getting mature. It's the same thing with new-world sours. You're going to grow up and come back and be like, 'Actually, I do like that.'"

Sometimes, it takes a little bit of Reynard-like trickery to make these edgy styles accessible to the masses. Like its fruity adult-beverage counterpart, grainy beers can be blended to splendid effect. "A lot of the historical Belgian beers are based on blending," Hill points out. "There are a few lambic producers who don't make any beer. They just buy beer from others and blend it. I've learned a lot about what we like to blend and the results we might get. We're also always playing with different cultures, different yeasts, and different bacteria. We'll say the primary fermentation is this yeast, and we'll do a second fermentation with this culture, and it's wonderful.

"We did a collaboration with Modern Times called 'Strange Times for Modern Fellows'—it was great! We fermented with a saison yeast, and we aged it for a long time. We all thought it would be delicious, and it was, but you don't know going into it what the outcome is going to be. That's especially true with these kinds of beers. With the Reynard, I've made this so many times that I have really dialed into how I blend it."

"With all of this mixing, do you ever inadvertently comingle yeast, bacteria, and other bugs between your beers?" I ask, finishing off the last precious drops from the bottle of Oud Bruin. It's a nice segue to a tour of the brewery, and Hill takes me outside for a quick look.

"When you're trying to do it all in one facility, by and large, some of the beers aren't sours," he observes. "We make a variety of things. We also have our ISA (India Session Ale) and many others. When you're trying to do both of those things in one facility, you have risk of cross-contamination because you're playing with particular strains of yeast. Now we have some separate equipment for things, but we do have some tanks that are in common between sour and not-sour beers, so we have to be extremely careful about use and cleaning. We do have different sets of gaskets, valves, and everything."

"Is it worth the effort?" I wonder. "Why not just stick to the sour styles?" Then I remember my buddy Boyd back in the brewpub and hundreds of other hop-crazed friends in Craft Beer Country.

"Look back twenty years ago, and most of the market share was with the big guys," Hill reminds me. "It was a small group of people drinking craft beer, and ultimately IPA. Now young people graduate immediately to drinking craft beer, rather than what their dad drank. With some of these sour beers, I'm not sure if they will ever become widely accepted.

But I do think that some of the more approachable sour beers will have a really good opportunity to go that way. People will stop calling them sour beers (or so he hopes), it will just be beer and its name." If and when that day arrives, these Strange Fellows with their clever concoctions and fabled brands might just be one of the hottest tickets in Craft Beer Country.

Iain Unfiltered
The Old World Art of Matching Beer with Stinky Cheese
Sour-flavored beers aren't always the easiest styles to pair with food, as I learned trying to wash down jalapeno-spiced pizza one particularly uncomfortable night at another brewery. Hill has a much more sensible suggestion. "One of my favorite things to do is eat a plate of beautiful cheeses, beautiful bread, beautiful pickles," he says. "You could be having some aged gouda. You could have some type of stinky surface-ripened cheese." Now *I* wrinkle my nose.

"A lot of times on a weekend, my wife and I will just tear up bread and olives and pickles, and I'll have pickled herring," he shares, admitting, "She won't kiss me after that! I like having a table full of cold, delicious things. Sour beer is ideal for that. Actually, there is a Flemish Renaissance painter, Bruegel, and there's peasants partying in one of his pictures with a jug on the table. It's been said that beer expert Michael Jackson thought that may well have been a lambic, and he was probably right!"

CHAPTER 3

THE BEER ENGINEER IN BARLEY COUNTRY

Chuckanut Brewery—Burlington, WA

BACK IN THE STATES, an hour south of downtown Vancouver, I stop for the night in Bellingham, Washington. I pick this coastal city, due west of snow-capped Mt. Baker, because I've heard good things about Chuckanut Brewery. In the local Native American language, Chuckanut means "long beach far from a narrow entrance," but I learn that founders Will and Mari Kemper named their business after a beautiful local seaside drive that was probably named after a local mountain range (and so on). Regardless, to craft beer nerds like me, the name has become synonymous with malty Old World style ales and lagers.

Although the Kempers aren't at the brewpub this crisp, cold evening, their German-style beers are, and I order a flight of options to pair with the Brewmaster's Meatloaf, an all-beef recipe accented with beer bacon gravy and a hint of tomato sauce, served with garlic-mashed russets. My favorite "partner" beverage tonight is the Rauch Helles Lager, a bready, golden beer that complements the hot, crumbly meat entree. At a gentle 18 IBUs, the faintly smoked Helles goes down so smooth that I order a pint for dessert.

Chuckanut's full-bodied comfort beers are so memorable that I arrange a special meeting with the Kempers months later. This time, they direct me to their new Skagit Valley "South Nut" location in the fertile countryside of a town best known for its spring Tulip Festival. This is also big-time barley country and home to Washington State University's Bread Lab, with the web of agricultural enterprises that feed it. While they may not be as fragrant as the local flowers, the mountains of grain harvested from the area's other growingly dominant crop are definitely more versatile and arguably taste better in beer.

It's everywhere as I roll through the fields then into a driveway surrounded by kelly-green grass next to a brand new barn-red building with a corrugated roof. After a ninety-minute drive from downtown Seattle, I've finally arrived at the brewery and tap room. It's time to meet the couple who built this welcoming place, a dynamic duo who have been married for more than forty years and perfecting craft beer together since the 1980s.

I gravitate to the bar, pulled by some unseen force. Wooden signs hanging above the ten tap handles on a copper backsplash list today's menu of beers, making me anxious for a taste. That will have to wait. The Kempers come in from the brewery and greet me in the warm tasting room, and I compliment them on their choice of a second location. There was strategic thinking in planning "South Nut," which opened in December of 2016. But it doesn't take a rocket scientist to figure out why the Kempers chose this scenic rural setting (roughly four miles west of Interstate 5) to expand production and help quench the thirst of an ever-growing fan base.

"It's so incredibly fertile here," points out Will. "They have the world record, as far as barley grown, in this area here." Of course, that would be music to almost any brewer's ears, save those filling mash tuns with corn and rice adjuncts or making sorghum-based gluten-free beer. A good portion of those precious barley grains don't have far to travel afield when it is time to roast them for Chuckanut's impressive lineup of ales. We're officially in what the Port of Skagit calls its "Innovation Zone," an area where agriculture-related products add to the viability of farming in the area, according to the environmentally friendly Mari.

"Skagit Valley Malting is right here," she notes, pointing through the east wall. "That's what brought us here to this site." That makes sense because the most of the beers on tap here are more malt-heavy than hop-heavy. It also makes sense/cents (pun intended) for the brewery's local partners. "Malting barley gets a lot more money than feed barley," according to Mari.

The malting house has invested big money to be able to supply top-quality product to the baking industry and brewery customers like Chuckanut. "They created the most sophisticated computerized malting operation in the world, right here," adds Will. "Instead of the concept of the barley conforming, they've broken that concept, so now they can adjust the malting process, and it creates different flavors. It's using new technology, and this could not have been done ten or even five years ago." This is the kind of innovation I can get my taste buds around.

Will is familiar to me, and not just because I found an old, amusing, '80s video of him and Mari on YouTube chronicling their early days in brewing, when the US craft-beer movement was just picking up steam. In 1984, the pioneering couple started Thomas Kemper Brewery, one of the first craft breweries in the Northwest. Back then, that required working with any viable resources that you could get your hands on—in this case, cobbling together a brewery with old dairy equipment.

That is hard to imagine as we move from the brewpub into the shiny stainless-steel guts of their brewery. My balding, grey-bearded tour guide begins by describing everything from valves to tanks in great technical detail. He is a thinker. I've spent a career working with some of the world's best engineers, so I know one when I see and hear one. Will admits to being a little shy, but talking about beer gets him to open up like carbonation bubbling forth from a newly opened growler. "In a baking class, I was petrified to go up in front of the class," he smiles as we wander through production.

As it turns out, I don't know the half of it. After earning a degree in Chemical Engineering from the University of Colorado, Will completed the very first Master Brewers Program offered by the now-renowned University of California at Davis. Ever fascinated with beer, the home brewer took his training a step further, studying brewing microscopy and microbiology at the Siebel Institute of Technology, then sharpening his expertise at the Institute of Brewing and Distilling in London, England. Will even taught brewery engineering for the American Brewers Guild in Davis for a while during the '90s, and his video lectures are still used for professional training courses. Mari points out that her husband hasn't slowed down much. He continues educating others and learning new tricks of the trade as an active member of the MBAA (Master Brewers Association of the Americas).

This appears to be *the* place to come to work if you are an engineer hell-bent on doing something other than fighting corrosion at a refinery or building commercial airplanes. In addition to Will, the technically trained staff includes Head of Operations Michael, an electrical and computer engineer. "So, we're the nerds in the beer industry," laughs Mari. Will adds that Chuckanut is built on a solid, proven foundation, using sound engineering concepts, considerations, and controls just like some of the biggest breweries in the world.

In fact, he custom designs the brites and other tanks specifically for what he envisions getting out of the beers. This is not a cookie-cutter, off-the-shelf approach to building a brewery. "These are 304 stainless steel," Will says as he points to the brites that are part of the new twenty-barrel system. "We supply the engineering drawings for the vessels," he says, adding that they were built by DME in Canada. "All the other pipes and stuff, we do in-house. So they supply the tank, and we make the other connections to make it work." That includes everything around us, right down to the steps, the railing, and the work station in the control room we are now entering.

"The one thing that we use is computerization," says Will. He points out that he and his team of brewers can open and close valves throughout the brewery with a single click. The monitors display graphical depictions of the different steps in the fermentation process. "Everything we do is within a decimal of one degree of Fahrenheit," he explains. "Right now, it's set to 30.1°F. After fermentation, you like to increase the temperature just a little bit to get rid of the diacetyl, which is a butter-type of flavor." I don't remember chemistry class being this much fun, although I did burn a few things in class on my way to a rock-solid D+.

"Then we go into lagering—gradually reducing the temperature at 1°F per hour," continues Will. "Instead of shocking the yeast, which is impacted by severe temperature differential, we're very gentle on it. Once you get down here, you get stratification around freezing. What that means is to bring it down to true lagering temperature. For example, we lager at 30°F. Why it's difficult is the temperature changes based on the density of the solutions in the closed system. We're basically talking water, and the properties of water are such that right around freezing is when the density is actually lowest. That's why ice floats. It's because of that circumstance and peculiarity of water that once you start working in low temperatures, you have conflicting changes as far as trying to reduce the temperature, so you can have squirrely situations." But Chuckanut's clever engineers have harnessed the power of programming to keep those gremlins and their brewing temperatures under control.

"I'm surprised how precisely you can control your equipment," I observe.

"We can actually program the system to a hundredth of a degree Fahrenheit," replies Will. "It is absurd to get to that level. In terms of a decimal or degree, it doesn't make that much difference, but it is a philosophical approach. For us, when we see things that are .3 or .2-degree difference, we say, 'What is going on with that?' If you don't have such quality controls, people could be two, three, four degrees off and say, 'Well, it is only a few degrees off.' But it makes such a difference!"

"Hmmm, German-style beers requires precision, German-style engineering," I say as I connect the dots. Will's innovative operation also includes a spunding device used to control flow rates and shear forces that can have a negative influence on its naturally carbonated beers. The system's valves automatically seal (*spunding* in Deutsche) the giant fermentation vessels just outside the control room window and allow pressure to build inside the liquid. The brewers monitor a pressure gauge and release unwanted excess pressure as needed.

"It needs to be so exact on the CO_2 contents," he emphasizes, adding you don't want variability. "When you manufacture beer, it ferments out. In most beer, there will be five to seven times more CO_2 produced and generated than is required in the final beer. So during the fermentation, we seal it off. The purity of the CO_2 is best because it comes from the fermentation process itself.

"Secondly, a slighter consideration is the aesthetic of the product, because you are dealing with foam. What happens with foam is you are dealing with positive and negative foam agents. The foam agent's negative agents want to defeat the foam. The positive agents are the CO_2 bubbles (usually the proteins). If you keep stirring it, the foam will dissipate much quicker because you're denaturing the foam-positive agents. So by doing natural carbonation instead of forced carbonation, you are lessening the foam-creating properties as well." By now, there is smoke coming out of my ears as I try to keep up. That is really saying something, since I've written more than a few challenging columns for *Chemical Engineering Progress*, the journal of the American Institute of Chemical Engineers.

The wheels are spinning, and I ask Will and Mari if they have spent time in Germany. You don't just magically acquire this high level of industrial knowledge during four years studying the science of heat exchangers and the art of keeping them running at university. Some of his practical knowledge had to have been absorbed elsewhere.

As it turns out, Will has been connected with the Master Brewers Association since 1990. "I used to go the meeting back then, and there were all these old-school brewers in Philadelphia," he recalls. "There would be about fifteen to twenty brewers, and I would be the youngest and only small craft brewer there. I remember sitting with the brewmaster at Stroh, and he said, 'Will, look around you, there are twelve brewmasters here, and only four of them are practicing their craft.' This went back to the consolidation. That was the nature of the industry then, and it wasn't a good time." He pressed on anyway, driven by his fascination with brewing.

Back in the '90s, the Kempers built their expertise by helping to design breweries all over the world. After he and Mari sold Thomas Kemper, Will consulted for a host of other brewers across the country. "We were providing equipment for small breweries across the nation," remembers Will. "We had a brewery that shut down, and I went in with a car, and I'd see things that I would like. I would fill it up, and they would weigh my car, and sell it to me by the pound," he laughs. When that got old, he, Mari, and the couple's twin daughters sought even grander adventures, moving to Mexico first, then to Turkey to open breweries for others. Ultimately, the whole family got so homesick that they moved back to the Pacific Northwest in 2008 to build their own brewery a second time around.

That turned out to be a pretty good decision. "In 2009, the first year we entered the GABF, Chuckanut was named the Small Brewpub of the Year," reports Mari. "In 2011, when production increased, it was named Small Brewery of the Year at the GABF."

Having spent the past hour soaking up the smell of malt and hops as well as Will and Mari's many stories, I am desperate for a cold pint to cool down my "hard drive." We sit at a table with Dave Green, CEO at Skagit Valley Malting. The guys like to come over to the pub and enjoy the rewards of their hard work. Evidence of the meticulous attention to detail that I've witnessed here at South Nut is staring up at me in the form of a bubbly, golden-blonde, light-bodied ale. Even though it is lagered, Kölsch uses ale yeast and is top fermented, so technically it is an ale.

"When we were in Istanbul, my assistant who is from and trained in Cologne, Germany, brought a yeast strain, and we used it to make Kölsch," recalls Will. "We loved it!

"When we moved back to America, I contacted the group from Germany that had the strain, and we never were able to fill out paperwork, and we just gave up."

A year later, during a visit to Europe, Will made arrangements with a contact to bring him two agar slants (small tubes containing growth media and a low number of yeast cells) of this particular strain. "I carried one in my suitcase, making sure we could get out with it," he shares. "Once we got back here, we sent it to the laboratory to contain it, and that's a proprietary strain now. We are probably the only people in the United States doing that particular strain." By my palate's reckoning, the naturally fermented treat in front of me was worth the considerable effort.

Following the traditional recipe for Kölsch, developed in the style's hometown of Cologne, Kemper brews this well-balanced, award-winning beer with two other critical ingredients: pilsner malt, and the noble hops that give it just a hint of fruit. A mouthfeel of grainy goodness is present in every gulp below the creamy, colloidal head. This light, bready three-time GABF gold medalist (including 2017) is too tempting to simply sip. I learn that the sessionable 4.5% ABV, 20 IBU beer has even earned accolades from the judges at the prestigious World Beer Cup, in the land whence the style originated. But I don't need anyone's second opinion to call this low gravity, high satisfaction beer a winner.

"We are excited about Chuckanut," says soft-spoken Will, his tone at odds with the emotion that should go with that statement. "We had been so constrained to getting the brewing going. We use a lot of European Hops, and you can't grow those here properly. For the last two years, they have been horrendous. But the harvest for the 2016 crops was back to normal. The beer we had been making was with inferior hops. The beer was still pretty good, but it is just the nature of the game."

There have been other hurdles to cross on the road to success. The new, full-scale brewery and pub we are relaxing in on this overcast afternoon took $2 million to set up, according to Mari. "The financial part of this is frustrating," she shares. "It is the hardest part for us, even in our relationship. A lot of people end up in divorce and a lot of brewers end up in divorce. It is a very expensive industry for someone starting out, especially if they don't have the money and the knowledge."

But there is a sense of calm after the storm at the table this evening, perhaps because they know they are over the hump and have pretty much made it. Almost everything that they need to brew the exquisite Kölsch we are enjoying is right outside the door of their new beer hall. There is enough laughter in the tasting room that we need to raise our voices to be heard, and that is a good sign too. The somewhat stern, hardworking Will is even cracking a smile now and again. After all, the barley is plentiful, the hop harvest has improved, and life is good here at South Nut.

Will Unfiltered

Beer's Underappreciated Magical Ingredient
"When it comes to beer, everyone I know talks about the hops, and those outliers who don't are all about the malt." But Will says that you really have to respect the yeast, its vitality, and how it works. Matching the right

strain with a style of beer it complements is just practicing good chemistry in this pragmatic brewer's book. "If someone says I am going to make a lager, how are you going to do it?" he asks, eyebrows raised. "You can call a dog a cat, but is it really a cat?"

Brewer-artist Robert Horner displays his seasonal herbal ales inside the "beerhive" at PROPOLIS BREWING in Port Townsend, Washington. Photo credit: Propolis

CHAPTER 4

BACK TO NATURE IN A BEERHIVE

Propolis Brewing—Port Townsend, WA

FROM THE BARLEY FIELDS and breweries of Burlington, Washington, I make my way through a labyrinth of country roads and bridges to the Coupeville–Port Townsend Ferry. After twiddling my thumbs in the car queue for about an hour (okay, texting), I drive onto the massive black, white, and green-trimmed boat and make the scenic thirty-five-minute inlet crossing to the quaint little seaside town hugging the northeast tip of the Olympic Peninsula.

My blood pressure drops as I maneuver out of the ship's hollow hull, across the dock and into tranquility. Port Townsend has several cozy lodging options, and I choose the Tides Inn & Suites, a few blocks down the street from the ferry terminal. Just outside my sliding glass door, a group of kayakers ripple through the calming waters, and a salty sea breeze relaxes me to the point of needing a quick nap.

When I wake up, it's time to take a brisk early-evening walk to a small local brewery that is making some waves in the Washington beer scene. Propolis, a brew house just a shade lighter than a golden Belgian tripel, is tucked in among a hodgepodge of small businesses on a rock driveway off of East Sims Way. A honeybee sign flies high above the doorway of what must be one of the best kept secrets in the west, although from what I hear, buzz is building.

Inside, the hive is humming with soul-soothing instrumental music. A few patrons chill out on a cushy couch, enjoying half-full tulips of honey-colored liquid. I make my way to the black slate bar and meet brewer Robert Horner, who wears a cool cap and a warm smile framed by a bushy brown beard. It feels like I have wandered into some kind of beer spa, where I'm going to be pampered with enlightening conversation and my taste buds will be massaged with tantalizing ales for the next few hours.

Horner is an old spirit walking around in a young guy's body. As young lad, he had the opportunity to develop an appreciation for beer styles overseas. Horner learned to love English ales during frequent visits to the United Kingdom. "I'd even say that I've been inspired by the Real Ale movement," he notes, but adds that he prefers the dryness and the complexities of wild ales like those brewed in Belgium. "I like herbs, making teas, things like that," he says. "Most of the history of brewing is without hops. It was with different herbs. So once I started exploring that, it's a bit open-ended. I like the acidity our beers have, and they're drier. It's great for pairing with food for that reason."

The soft-spoken beerologist (Horner studied microbiology at the University of Iowa, before completing a degree in Architecture at Ball State University) pours me a mesmerizing selection of his handcrafted old-world ales. The colorful half-moon arc of glasses that he arranges on the bar includes: Cedar, an imperial golden saison made with honey; Sigrid, a rustic juniper Belgian quad; Oceana, a petite saison with brett and spruce; Litha, a saison brewed with chamomile, sage, and lavender; Fennel, a saison seasoned with fennel, clove, and orange; Salmonberry, a saison aged in syrah barrels with wild salmonberries; and Sahti, a dark amber saison. These and Propolis's other beers are blended to perfection, a harmony of natural ingredients inspired by the farmhouse traditions of Europe. "We do about anywhere from twenty to thirty different beers a year," he tells me. "We have them all on the website."

Preferring the real thing, I reach for a wine glass of the imperial saison. In addition to honey, Cedar is brewed with two-row, wheat, spelt, specialty malt, noble hops, herbs, fruit, and you guessed it: cedar. "It tastes like champagne," I volunteer.

"It's aged for about six months in a wine barrel," notes Horner. "It's 9.5%, but doesn't drink like it. It's young, too, and nice to age in the bottle."

I imagine this crisp, slightly citrusy golden ale cutting through the rich, fatty flavors of fresh-caught pink salmon from the nearby Puget Sound. My stomach growls at the thought of bringing the saison and a filet together in a backyard barbecue.

The microbrewery meticulously crafts Cedar and its other fine ales in small batches—bottling, corking, capping, labeling and waxing each by hand. "I really stand by the bottle conditioning," states Horner. "We don't force carbonate anything. So our kegs are conditioned like our bottles. I just think it's a better product—tighter carbonation. You said that the Cedar has a champagne quality, so that quality comes through."

As I move on to the next sample, we are joined by Robert's lovely partner, Piper Corbett, who helped him launch the brewery back in 2012. Piper is a charming artist/actress/writer/businesswoman/God-knows-what-else, and the "yin" who markets their intricately spun ales while the "yang" brews them. "It's just the two of us," shares Horner. "I do the production work and business side, and Piper is on the marketing and sales. She also helps out with some production stuff here and there." Most importantly tonight, she delivers dinner, unleashing the aroma of a combo pizza from a box behind the counter.

They kindly offer me a piece, but I'm in tasting mode and don't want anything to compete with the subtly spiced beverages before me. As they eat, I break my from my usual tasting strategy and skip past some of the lighter SRM-scale options to the molasses-colored Sigrid, which has been cellared for more than two years. This is one strong, complex beer, with the hallmark raisin, dried fruit, and spice and tart characteristics of Trappist beers.

"How did you come up with the name Sigrid?" I ask.

"She is a Scandinavian Viking queen," explains Horner. "She torched the mead hall of her enemies in order to maintain her pagan beliefs."

So "she" is not so subtle after all, I think. Maybe it's the burnt toffee I pull from the glass that earned this dark beauty its name. "You know, Sigrid is a character in the History Channel show *Vikings*," I contribute.

"It's what I like to drink when I watch *Vikings*," he smiles.

It appears I have stumbled on another kindred spirit in the witty brewmaster. Still waters run deep in these fjords. Maybe the ferry sank, and I've gone to Valhalla, where all Viking warriors go to drink horns full of mead when they die. This won't be the last time that the alcohol-loving ancient raiders and their thundering gods come up in conversation in the northern reaches of Craft Beer Country.

However, we have more important things to discuss this evening than battle-axes and flaming funeral pyres—topics like bee glue. "How did you come up with the name Propolis?" I inquire, clued in to the connection with the insects, having googled the term. "Beerhive" may be clever, but it seems too easy for this brewery's contemplative founders.

Horner explains that *propolis* was derived from the Greek words *pro* (before) and *polis* (city). An ancient Greek student of nature apparently came up with the term for the sticky resin that honeybees borrow from tree bark to narrow the openings into their hives (or cities) in order to discourage unwelcome intruders. Detecting no stingers in my backside, we continue with the interrogation.

"Propolis is also an antiseptic," he points out. "A lot of the herbs were antimicrobial and preserved the beer for a long time. Juniper is a good example. At first, on the front end, you're like, 'Oh this is a nice aromatic,' and then two years later, you're like, 'What is this? Is this thyme or something?'"

The aging process turns the mix of ordinary ingredients into ethereal saisons, like Oceana, Litha, and Fennel. "They ebb and flow like a wine," observes Corbett. "In the springtime, certain barrel-aged beers open up in a particular way. Later on, they're a little more fruity, and then they diminish and go to sleep like a wine. If you get a cherry beer, you should enjoy it when the blossoms come out, and it's opening up. It's cyclical."

The queen bee here is also a gardener and gatherer of local berries and other bounty. "I was raised here," she shares. "These are all plants I've picked every year since I was little. That, for me, is what keeps it exciting. I'm always looking under trees. They're pulling up all these nutrients and minerals from the ground, anything that's growing around it, any plant.

It's pulling up what's happening in the woods, where you have cedar, alder, and moss. It's more specific to the place." She and Horner are in sync with their community and surroundings, and maybe that is why this place feels so peaceful.

Ah, the Salmonberry! I had locked in on the name when I scanned the list of beers on the black chalkboard behind the bar, sixty seconds into my visit. A half hour later, and it's time to taste the seasonal ale made with the fruit of the Rubus spectabilis bramble. Nothing seems more in tune with this hip hideaway than the brewery's seductive, barrel-aged 7.5% ABV saison. Corbett picks the raspberry-look-alike fruit from wild vines in the area, and then Horner blends it with elderflowers and brett, creating a hazy beer with a fuzzy peach hue. The salmonberry is easy to detect, from the first whiff of the ale to the tail-end of each taste. It's a marriage of red and dark fruit flavors, which reminds me of Oregon Marion berries spliced with the addictive wild blackberries that ripen in thorny northwest bushes during the summertime (like the prickly flesh-ripping vines that reach out and snag my jeans every time I work in the yard). It's a gentle reminder that there are other plants growing in the west that are suitable for flavoring beer.

"We get people who walk in here and walk back out because I don't have an IPA," according to Horner. "That's fine. There's plenty of places to go and get a good one." He even likes a hoppy beer on occasion. "I'm not trying to push people away, but we celebrate what we do. We're not going to make a particular beer just to appease someone who expects it. We want to bend minds and explore different areas of the palate. A lot of the beers are about ingredients that we forage or pick. There's a lot of bounty here. There's a lot of health here, like indigenous herbs with tremendous amounts of antioxidants."

One of the beers that drew me to this artistic outpost on the Olympic Peninsula is the mystical Osoberry, an American wild ale made with plump, health-enhancing blue fruit plucked from a wild shrub. There are elegant wax-capped wine bottles of the ale in the refrigerator to my right, and I plan to acquire a few for the road. "The Osoberry is conditioned nicely," Horner teases me. "It's an Indian plum with an interesting, bizarre flavor. It's like plum, strawberry, and tomato in this tart, brett, amberish saison. It's strawberry-jammy." This is almost sadistic. I briefly imagine raiding the icy treasure chest and dashing out the door with everything I can carry.

As if Robert's mouthwatering descriptions weren't enough, Piper decides this is a tag-team thing and jumps in. "Osoberry?" she chimes in. "It's a Willy Wonka berry. It's almost like a plum fruit leather. And it's got this wild watermelon note to it, like a candy that you remember having as a child, but you can't put your finger on it. It's a really unique beer." Mercifully she stops, and I make a note to post my own impressions on the dark-blue, berry-infused ale on my blog at some point.

In the meantime, I'm beginning to wonder where the heck I've ended up tonight. I don't remember finding a sparkling gold ticket inviting me to visit this quirky but wonderful brewery. I half expect to plunge into a chocolatey stout river on my way to the bathroom.

When I return, parched and a little disappointed that there is no room for cocoa rapids and osoberry waterfalls in this compact factory, I reach for the Sahti. The 7.5%, dark-amber saison is made with 2-row barley, oats, wheat, caramel, toasted and roasted malts, Noble hops, juniper, clove, and ginger. It's the last beer that I plan to have tonight in this potent lineup, lest I spend the night sleeping with a grain sack for a pillow. Like all Propolis beers, aromatic Sahti offers a glimpse of its fruit and nut flavor at first sniff. It's lightly acidic, but that little bite of lemon melts away into a grove of sweet fruit and nuts and a slightly spicy finish. You can taste the unadulterated indigenous wild ingredients in these artisan ales.

"We do lots of rustic beers, but our brewery is very clean," emphasizes Horner. There is nothing wild about this fastidious brewer's fermentation process. "There aren't crazy bugs running rampant here," he looks around, as if to be sure. "It's very intentional, the way we inoculate. We allow an expression to occur that's very local. At the same time, we're not just at the whim of the wind or whatever flows over here. It keeps up that dialogue." In my state of inebriated enlightenment, I just nod my head and agree. At this point in the evening, I'm just one of the worker bees, in perfect harmony with the colony. I turn my attention back to the queen.

"It was always about quality over quantity," reveals Corbett. "We are very strict. We just want to make beer that is good and good for you. You just drank several different beers. Your belly is calm, relaxed, digesting. It is a beer that resonates." I've noticed that my belly is also getting bigger and is threatening to turn my belt into a tourniquet. It's a good thing that I have such strong willpower and skipped wolfing down a few slices of pizza.

After a lull in the conversation, I ask the couple how they met. Like the berries and other perfectly matched ingredients in their saisons, it's obvious these two belong together. Pure kismet! They met here in town while celebrating the opening of a local tavern. That led to a date. "Robert invited me over for curry on February 13th, and the curry wasn't ready until after midnight, which was Valentine's Day," laughs Piper. "It didn't actually occur to either of us. Robert opened an elderflower mead, and we were drinking that together. And there is a little folklore that if you drink that with your partner, you'll be married within a year. We were engaged about seven or eight months later."

"It was about a year," protests Horner.

"It wasn't too much later," she wins. "That was serendipitous on another level because the first beer that we won a major award for was the Elderflower Saison Brett." Indeed, Beltane won gold in the American Style Brett Beer category at the GABF in 2014. Even with that and other awards, the road to success has been challenging for the determined artisan brewers.

"We were brewing for three-and-a-half years on a one-barrel system," recalls Corbett. "It wasn't until this year that we went to a fifteen-barrel system. We didn't have an overhang for the first year, so he was there with a rain jacket, hovering over this pot. There were days up there that absolutely broke us. Things happen. You learn in a small space. Then you get through it, and then something else happens. We just had a one-year anniversary here, and we're very tired. Now we have this moment of peace where we're like, 'Damn, we're doing it!' That is the sweetness after the hard work—when you're completely exhausted, and you feel like you can't believe you just did that.

"We don't take anything for granted," reflects Horner, finishing a glass of the honey-laced Cedar. "That's what having dreams is about. If you have everything given to you, you don't get to dream so much." It's the way of the bee. Work for the good of the hive to the betterment of craft beer and the delight of its welcome guests. And when the busy brewers at Propolis finally find time to let their imaginations soar, they transform those sweet dreams into something really special.

Rob and Piper Unfiltered

Foraging for Enchanting Flavors

Propolis focuses on traditional European ales and has dabbled in at least one style that isn't technically a beer at all. Gruit, an herb mixture used for flavoring beer, was popular in the Netherlands and Germany prior to the blossoming use of hops for bittering. "I wanted to create an ale that my ancestors might have been drinking—more than likely soured and aged in oak," explains Horner. "It's leathery, tobacco-y, and aged with all these beautiful notes. It's a real ale with no hops and lots of herbs in it like yarrow and rosemary. We aged it in Malbec barrels for a year."

Horner says that gruit showcases malt in a different way. "Some of the herbs, like mug wart, are bittering herbs. They're much more potent than hops. But it's a different type of bittering—it's aromatic, creaminess. A different flavor that comes through. You get a lot of sweetness that comes through—lots of backbone, too."

Piper adds that foraging for herbs and turning them into old world potions has drawn attention to Propolis. "A blogger from Los Angeles wrote a story about gruit, and it's called, 'Don't Drink Beer,'" she relays with a wry smile. "He accuses us of having multiple tarot decks and burning sage." Maybe that's the case around the witching hour, but in my book, it's the brewery's handcrafted old-world beers that are most enchanting.

CHAPTER 5

THE FLAVOR TECHNICIAN FROM GREAT BRITAIN

Reuben's Brews—Seattle, WA

REJUVENATED BY THE PUGET SOUND salt air I enjoyed during the Port Townsend, Washington ferry crossing, I pull away from the dock and make my way south toward Seattle. About an hour later, having navigated early rush-hour traffic, I'm entering the city's Old Ballard neighborhood. I deftly dodge a delivery truck, hazards flashing as it unloads in the middle of the street, and squeeze into a parking space on 14th Avenue NW. There is no yellow brick road to follow in this light industrial section of the Emerald City, but I still manage to find the glass door that opens into Reuben's Brews.

Inside I meet the brewery's founder, Adam Robbings, who formerly worked in finance for T-Mobile in the United Kingdom. Already bitten by the notorious British travel bug and yearning for a new adventure, he set out for the United States in 2004 and went to work at a Seattle-based electronics firm. "My plan was to go back after two years, but I liked it, so I extended it a bit," he says. "Then I met Grace, my wife-to-be, so I extended it further." Like a sweet American brown ale and salty British Stilton cheese, the two were just meant for each other.

Yet Robbings admits that coming to the United States exposed him to what craft beer could be. "My beer palate was exposed when I came here," he recalls. "The flavor profiles are so much more different than the UK. When I came here, I cooked quite a lot, so I was getting into flavors and how to mix/match things from cooking. This was a logical extension. I got to the point where I'd find different hop profiles, and even though I didn't brew, I'd say to my wife, 'It would be good to change it this way or that way.' Graciously, she listened.

"Then, when my son Reuben was born in 2009, she bought me a home brew kit to sort of 'Put up or shut up!' That's how I got started on this path. I got interested, and we were lucky enough to pour at the Phinney Neighborhood Beer Festival, a commercial beer festival, as home brewers.

"In November 2010, we won the People's Choice at that festival. There were almost a thousand people at this place. We were in the paper. We were having emails asking for our beers. I was literally just in the garage and had only been brewing for a year." All the accolades inspired him to enroll at UC Davis to take his newfound passion for beer to a whole new level. While studying at the agriculturally oriented Northern California university, Robbings took a plunge into the science of brewing. He was deeply fascinated and started dreaming bigger.

Still operating out of his tiny garage, Robbings parlayed that classroom knowledge and a knack for finding and mixing complementary ingredients into silver and gold. In 2011 he was one of the top homebrewers in the state of Washington and was a silver medalist at the National Homebrew Competition in 2012.

The escalating success was enough to convince the couple that they needed to launch their own brewery, and they found a small commercial space a block from their current address. "We were at capacity within six months," he groans. "So it was, 'What are we going to do now?'

"It took us another two years to find this location." The new 4,000 ft² brewery and taproom has been open since May 2015, and Robbings is about as excited as a composed Brit can be about his new digs. I ask him why, with so many obvious signs that he was on the right path, it took him so long to jump in with both feet.

"When we started up the street, we had scoped it so that we wouldn't lose the house," he answers. "The mistake we made was that we were dipping our toe into the water, but falling into the pool. We had done this, and we were committed and should have realized up front that we were committed. That was our biggest mistake."

Maybe, maybe not. Robbings doesn't appear to be the impulsive type. He thinks before he jumps. "My wife is a teacher, and both of us wanted to get into this," he shares. "I think you should be pulled into something. You shouldn't try to push yourself into something. When people are asking for our opinion, there's that pull, that's 'the ask.' I've met David Walker (co-founder of Firestone Walker, see Chapter 23), and he made a very good point: 'You want to be in the business of brewing. You don't want to be in the business of selling.' That's getting away from what we're really about. That's not what I got into this for." Robbings is wise beyond his forty-three years.

"Want to try some stuff?" he asks, as if on cue.

"I thought you'd never ask," I answer.

"We have won a number of medals for our pilsner," he continues. "It's a good one to start with: nice, spicy, crisp, and light." He introduces me to the bartender. "This is Thor," he says, nodding the bartender's way.

"Are you a Viking?" I ask.

"I come from a long line of Vikings!" says stout and bald but full-bearded Eugene Thor Stoddard as he juggles glasses between tap handles. It dawns on me that I might end up getting hammered if Thor pours me too many 8%+ IPAS, so sticking with this bready, 5.4% Czech pilsner is not only a delicious decision but strategic. The spicy noble and bittering hops bump the IBUS to a comfortable 35. It's easy to see why judges at three different beer competitions have put his well-balanced lager on the medals platform. Like a dry sense of humor, Reuben's pilsner sneaks up and unexpectedly tickles you if you are paying attention to the details.

Not so surprisingly, Robbings looks around the world for the ingredients he puts in his lagers and ales. "This is 100 percent German pilsner malt," he tells me. "It's about nuances. Those nuances, when you add them all together, are exponentially bigger than what you add individually. This is a German yeast strain, German pilsner malt, a water profile that I've been trying to keep soft, and traditional Czech hops. What we're about is,

'What do we want the beer to taste like?' We're going to brew it that way, unconstrained. US pils is different than German pils and Belgian pils. If you start from a position of not wanting to respect those differences, you end up in a spiral."

"You're a perfectionist about this," I interject.

My eyes start to spiral as Robbings continues on about malts. Thor steadies me by placing a taster of Reuben's gose on the table so I can focus. This traditional German sour ale has attracted my undivided attention. Robbings can't help but notice me staring at the glass after enjoying a taste. At an unintimidating 4.3% ABV and bitterness that is barely detectable at 6 IBU, this lactobacillus-soured GABF gold medalist might work for my cider-loving friends who are feeling adventurous enough to try a beer. It's a moderately tart, slightly salty ale with mild herbal and lemon hints.

"We use a certain vendor that we think gives us the most lovely dry coriander, and we crush it during boil so it's as fresh as it can be," he explains. "Over time, it can get musty if it's already crushed. It's pretty obvious which one is the brightest when you go to the store and smell them."

Robbings has an uncanny ability to weave delicate flavors and aromas into his beers. "My wife is half Korean, and I joke her taste buds have been half burned out by kimchi." He pauses and cracks a little smile. "Mine has been neutralized by British food, so anything is extreme to me. The only thing I've got is I can taste something and know how to tweak a recipe. Maybe it's because of where I grew up that I can pick up some of that stuff. It's where the art and science sort of merge.

"We tweak the recipes regularly, but only marginally. 'How do you get the last out of that dry hop?' We've tried a few different things. The other margin might not make much difference, but I think we've got our dry-hopping process to a point that we extract quite a lot from what we put in. We put in a ton."

"Do you have a favorite style?" I prod.

"It's always the latest we've brewed," he replies. "I like changing it up all the time—different days, different beers. Right now, Citra Crush is a Northeast-style IPA, a hazier IPA. Big dry hop. A specific yeast that adds a lot of fruity esters, adds haze, and you balance out the bitterness with oats and wheat. Crikey IPA is effectively our flagship. You have to try that."

I recognize the word from an Austin Powers movie. "Crikey is a British term that means what?"

"Damn!" he responds.

This American India Pale Ale is pretty damn good if I don't say so myself. Crikey hits the sweet spot at 6.8% ABV and 53 IBUs, giving you your money's worth without blowing out your palate. There is a veritable citrus orchard of fruit flavors here—grapefruit, apricot, orange, and tangerine—exploding from its Amarillo, Citra, and Simcoe hops, the latter of which adds the light piney note that I taste.

I wonder what Robbings thinks of all the ingredients people are putting in beer nowadays, fully expecting his answer to be at least somewhat reserved: "What happened to the days of malt, hops, yeast, and water?" I ask. "People are trying crazy ideas like adding peanut butter and jelly beans—all kinds of crazy shit, pardon my French. Is that something you would do?"

"The way I think about it is not what it is—peanut butter—but it's a flavor profile," he semi-shocks me. "It works in a food like peanut butter and jelly, so who's not to say that it couldn't work in a beverage?

"Have you ever had Branston Pickle? It's a chutney in the UK, like spicy and dark. We named our dog Branston, for the record." Several of Adam's friends and beers seem to be named after one another. I wouldn't be surprised to see Thor on tap very soon, or perhaps a Robbings family cat named Crikey.

"I think a big nut brown with an additional spice layer that is similar to Branston works. Or we could spice our Roasted Rye IPA and run it through a jockey box with one of those temperature controllers to bring the temperature to like 120 degrees and add spices to make a mulled beer, just like a mulled wine. It could be fun to do on certain days."

The more I listen, the more I realize that my witty host isn't quite the buttoned-up conservative brewer that I had expected. Like his growing talent for combining complementary ingredients, he has gradually blended in with the inventive melting pot of people around him. He has become a bit of a risk taker, as evidenced by his example of an interesting beer-food pairing recently hosted at Reuben's.

"We did a coffee, beer, and donuts pairing," says Robbings, who informs me that his choices are limited because he is a vegetarian. "We worked with a local donut shop and paired different beers. We paired a barrel-aged stout with a chocolate donut, and those complementary profiles make sense. There was a raspberry-glaze doughnut that we paired with Crikey. That worked out nicely. The fruitiness of the donut melded with the hop profile that we had." It's possible for me to get my mind around a drinking an aromatic coffee stout with sugary pastry at an early afternoon brunch, but I have to admit, any IPA (breakfasty grapefruit and orange flavors notwithstanding) with a jelly-filled doughnut makes me cringe. To each his or her own, I guess.

"You switched from a career in finance to brewing," I observe, as we wind down our discussion. "Back in the UK, what do Mum and Dad think about all this?

"I've got three degrees, so for me to give up that and start with beer, they weren't happy," he sighs, then carries on. "Now they realize it's the right thing. They do come over a bit." The Robbings are fortunate to have such a talented entrepreneur for a son, a guy who focuses on serving a perfectly executed pint instead of concentrating solely on sales. I take a final parting taste of Reuben's out-of-this-world Life on Mars IPA. At 8.2% ABV, drink too much of the hopped up American amber ale, and you won't make it back to the hotel, let alone the roughly thirty-four million miles to the red planet. I pause after another taste of the reddish-brown beer and thank my lucky stars that Adam chose crushing hops over crunching numbers. Crikey, this is good stuff!

Adam Unfiltered

On the Reuben's Brand Name

Adam and Grace named the brewery after their son Reuben, who is now a precocious eight-year-old. He celebrated his third birthday by riding bikes and trikes with friends round and round the cement floor at the brewery's first location. I ask Adam, "What does your son think of having a brewery named after him?"

He laughs "There's another brewery and creamery in Phinney Ridge, a mile or two away from us. We went there when he was four-and-a-half, and he saw the tanks. Reuben said to the server, 'You're a brewery, aren't you?' And the guy said, 'How do you know?' And he answered, 'Because I'm Reuben from Reuben's Brews.' So that's what we have created!"

IPA haven CLOUDBURST BREWING in downtown Seattle. Photo courtesy of Catchlight Photography

CHAPTER 6

CAUGHT IN A DOWNPOUR OF IPAS

Cloudburst Brewing—Seattle, WA

PIKE PLACE MARKET in downtown Seattle is packed on Memorial Day weekend as I maneuver through throngs of tourists and head down Western Avenue. I'm not here braving the holiday crowd to buy tonight's salmon dinner from one of the famous market's fishmongers. Instead I'm on a mission to visit Cloudburst, a tiny brewery that some of my IPA-crazy friends have been raving about lately. Luckily, I'm dodging people not raindrops on my way to meet proprietor Steve Luke.

Dry as the desert and beginning to hallucinate, I arrive at a rolling garage door opening in an old red brick building with a Cloudburst logo emblazoned above and to the left. Patrons are lounging at tables or standing, from the entrance back to the bar, merrily drinking various hues of liquid, from hazy yellow to coffee brown. The paint-chipped walls and wood beams that rib the ceiling inside give the place a weather-worn charm and authentic old-city feel. I wonder if I've somehow stumbled into the Seattle underground (some parts of the city were built on top of the original structures, creating an eerie catacomb-like tourist attraction).

I order a glass of the Amusement Technology IPA, listed at 6.4% ABV and 65 IBUs on the handwritten paper menu behind the bar, then plop down on a chair where I can people watch and keep a look out for Luke.

The hazy Citra-hopped beer on the table garners the other half of my attention. Amusement Technology has a little alpha-acidy bite to it, but it's refreshingly juicy on this warm afternoon in the Emerald City. It's a fermented version of what you might get tossing not-quite-ripe oranges, grapefruit and tart berries into your blender, adding a slice of mango, and flipping the start switch. The consistency is not quite thick enough to call this India Pale Ale an adult smoothie, but it's the perfect sustenance for a writer thirsty for more than a good story.

As I amuse myself with a low-tech look, smell, feel, and taste-test sequence, a lanky thirty-something guy with a bushy red beard and matching shoulder-length hair under a Seattle Mariners baseball cap strides in from the sidewalk. He is in jeans and a white t-shirt with a YCH hop farms logo. This dude has brewer written all over him, and I bet my photographer that this is our guy.

Sure enough it is none other than the talented brewmaster himself. Luke greets us and leads us along the facing wall to a side door that opens into the brewery's storage room. Inside, he clears space from the clutter and turns a chair into a make-shift table so we can park our pints and get down to business. Luke loves this 112-year-old place. Among other businesses over the years, it was most recently a bike shop ideally classified for light manufacturing. "You're drinking in our load zone right now," he informs me. "It's not the finest tasting room by any means, but it's got soul." That it does.

I can tell that Luke has spirit too. He is genuinely passionate about the craft that he fell for while making money to help pay for school. His beer journey started out as a twenty-one-year-old at the Allagash Brewing Company in Portland, Maine. "I was in college, sweeping floors and putting bottles in boxes," he remembers. "They were so awesome that I thought, 'This is an industry that I could hang out in for a while.'" He enjoyed the people so much that he came back for a second stint with the increasingly popular East Coast brewery, this time to do more brewing than keg cleaning.

Eventually Luke ended up "hanging out" at Seattle-based Elysian Brewing for four years, codeveloping and refining recipes with co-founder, mentor, and friend Dick Cantwell. They brewed everything from big bold

IPAS to spicy pumpkin stouts for one of the Northwest's hottest spots for craft beer. While he and the team created smash-hit beers like Space Dust IPA and Punkuccino, Luke thought about what he might like to do next in life. Then, a few months before beer behemoth Anheuser-Busch InBev swooped in and ponied up big money to buy his employer in early 2015, he began putting the pieces in place for his biggest career move yet: opening his own brewery.

By March, Luke had lined up eighteen investor/partners who believed in the project, and he worked his ass off at spinning their gold into a silver lining of his own. He added a $350,000 SBA loan to the $250,000 that he had already raised, secured the commercial space we are sitting in now, and started filling the back half of the building with mostly used equipment, like an old dairy tank that he would later repurpose into a hot liquor tank.

In July, Luke left Elysian with more than moral support from his wife/dentist Holly. "Even though I had no savings to open a brewery, I had someone who was paying our bills," he says. "So I had some comfort with taking the risk."

He and a small crew of former Elysian coworkers opened Cloudburst's tasting room in January 2016. "For everything that happened with our build-out, we still got into the space and making beer within six months," he recalls. It didn't take long for Seattle's craft beer fanatics to find his special hole in the wall.

By 2017, Cloudburst was producing 1,800 barrels of beer and only distributing in the city of Seattle. Luke doesn't envision ever expanding the local niche brewery into a mammoth operation. "The goal is to never really do more than 3,000 barrels," he points out. "With our space right now, we could probably do about 2,500. I've brewed at other large facilities in the past. I like production brewing, and I think there's something to be said for consistency, but with this project here, it's kind of the opposite. We don't really ever brew anything twice. Sometimes we'll bring something back on a whim—we usually just brew two double batches of an IPA recipe. Then we'll start from scratch again. It's ever-changing. People are always asking at bars, 'What's new on tap?' and our thinking was, 'If you're buying our IPA, it's always new. So you keep the handle, and we'll rotate it for you.'"

The one thing that Cloudburst does brew on a regular basis is its Happy Little Clouds, which Luke calls a "bastardized German pilsner." "While using traditional German Pilsner malt and German lager yeast, we use a blend of noble German hops (Saaz), new German hops (Mandarina, Huell Melon) and American hops (Mosaic)," he explains. A yellow-gold pint of beer bubbles below a nice thick head of cloud-cover foam. Happy Little Clouds is a dry-hopped, 33-IBU pilsner that, at a relatively tame 5.3% ABV, makes having a third and maybe fourth beer today a real possibility. It's crisp, clean, and so simply good that it's easy to see why Luke keeps making batch after batch.

"It's the beer that we get to tweak, and we try to make it better every time," he adds. "To brew a flawless pilsner is one of the biggest challenges in brewing that we are constantly striving to make."

But Luke confesses that IPAs are an obsession, and there is always a downpour of them on tap roughly forty feet from where they are brewed. "IPAs are probably 70 percent of our production," he reports. "It's my own personal favorite for sure. It's what I'm drinking at other breweries and bars." He prefers IPAs in the 50-60 IBU range. "Bitterness is present but not dominant, certainly a fruit-forward hop profile that finishes dry and crisp," he adds. "Those are IPAs that I can personally drink more than one of. Anything bigger than that, if it's a New England style IPA or an imperial IPA, I'm happy with six to twelve ounces, but I'm not drinking that back to back to back.

"At this point, people know what a Cloudburst IPA smells and tastes like because we keep a consistent profile throughout. When designing an IPA, we put our hop varieties into four quadrants as far as flavors go. Since we're doing new recipes every few weeks, we go to different quadrants so that they don't run together. We don't come out with two tropical in a row; we take it more savory or more citrusy. That's how we're building our IPA recipes."

Citra usually tops Luke's hop shopping list. "There are very few hops that you can build an IPA around, but that also play well with other varieties," he explains. "You can make a citrus single hop IPA, and it's still interesting. It can be your second or third most used hop, and it's adding something positive to the equation." Getting those combinations right is becoming increasingly important.

"Five to six years ago, the general masses couldn't pick out hop varieties or know what their favorite was," according to Luke. "When I was brewing in New England, I'd make a new IPA, and no one would say, 'Oh, I taste the Mosaic in that.' Now almost every drinker in here knows what Citra tastes like, and it's often their favorite hop. When you give someone something that they aren't familiar with, they're like, 'Am I supposed to like this or not? It tastes like lime and cedar. I can't identify it, so I'm not sure.' As long as you can translate the brewer's enthusiasm for those new flavors over to the customer, you're good. You just think outside of the box a little bit: 'We all like Citra and Mosaic, but maybe you'll like this too.' It's the same with brewers as it is with drinkers—keeping an open mind. That's what's so cool about where hop varieties are going and where beer drinkers are going."

He and fellow brewer Zach Kornfield have made hundreds of IPAS to date. The list of recipes is so long that they probably can't remember all of them.

"How do you come up with a new name every two weeks?" I wonder. "Do you guys just drink a lot and make shit up?"

Luke laughs like maybe that has been the case more than a few times. "It's always a challenge," he admits. "We have a big name board in the office and everyone is encouraged to put an idea up there. So you never know what name is going to be get picked. You don't know who wrote the name or what the reference was sometimes. Everyone here has pretty much named a beer at this point."

Branding the brewery wasn't quite as easy. "I was working on the business plan off and on for a couple of years, and you're always tinkering with it until you're like, 'Alright, I have to get this done!'" he says. "When we were getting this off the ground, I was thinking about names, and *burst* is a fun word to say, phonetically. Hop bursting is kind of *the* technique. Then *Cloudburst* was a word that I thought resonated with the beers that

I wanted to end up making. We wanted them to come off as unexpected and a rush of flavor. A cloudburst is a rush of rainfall. We're also in Seattle, and it rains all the time here. It's just like naming kids: two-thirds of the people think it's great and the other third think it's dumb. But it becomes familiar and stops feeling weird to other people."

Speaking of weird: "What shouldn't have worked out in one of your beer recipes that turned out great?" I prod.

"Our dark beers will have coffee or chocolate, and sometimes we get creative and push boundaries," he says, setting the stage. "So we did a coffee beer that was based on Turkish coffee, and we added a bunch of cardamom that we picked up at the market and crushed it. That's a spice that can get really weird really fast. We didn't know if people were going to like smelling cardamom with their coffee—that's a little out there. And it was probably the best coffee beer we've made here. It was well-received and moved pretty quickly. It is always surprising to me when people end up liking something that you don't think they'll like. But my favorite beer isn't necessarily someone else's favorite beer."

He brings up a good point. I mention that not everyone is going to care for any type of ale, let alone punchy hop-laden IPAs. "It's always going to be hard when someone doesn't like your beer to not take it personally," Luke shares. "I think we make ninety-nine people happy out of a hundred. Trying to not let that one negative person bug you and not dwell on it . . . that's hard."

Earning industry accolades helps him know that he and Kornfield are on the right track. In 2018, Cloudburst won its first World Beer Cup medal, a bronze in the Fresh or Wet Hop Ale category for its Simcoe- and Citra-hopped Fresh Frozen. Other ales have advanced through the rounds, only to fall a little short.

Just participating in some of the bigger beer competitions can be motivating. "You get out of the first round, that means you made a great beer, then it becomes more subjective as those rounds go on," notes Luke, who has judged at the Great American Beer Festival and the World Beer Cup as well. "There were plenty of rounds where I was judging and thought a beer should have gotten a silver or bronze, and I was outnumbered that day. Those beers and brewers will never know they were only one person away from getting a medal."

There isn't a dark cloud in sight when it comes to Luke's outlook on the little brewery's future prospects. He vows to never sell out. "There's nothing else that I'd rather do," emphasizes Luke. "At this size (four full-time employees) and where we landed, that's great as long as our bills are paid and everyone's happy. I still could be making every batch of beer here in ten to twenty years. By our design, that's what I want. I'm also our bookkeeper (his undergrad degree was in Economics, but that doesn't mean he likes balancing the books), and I help out with lots of other things. Everybody else wears lots of different hats too, most notably our Director of Sales, Noah Schellhammer. But the passion is making the beer!" That is good news.

Fortunately for Seattle, the long-term forecast calls for a whole new line-up of hop-bursting IPAS here at Cloudburst. It's as dependable as the rain!

Steve Unfiltered

On Paying Attention to the Details

Luke and Kornfield, who both completed UC Davis's highly respected Master Brewers Program, had the opportunity to study under beer guru Charles Bamforth. Some of the important principles that the renowned professor taught them have ended up paying off for the brewery in strange ways.

According to Luke, Bamforth had ways of making his key points, like the importance of immaculate housekeeping, memorable. "He once asked, 'What if Ken Grossman (founder of Sierra Nevada Brewing Co. and industry icon) walks into your own brewery? Keep your brewery as clean as if Ken Grossman walked in, and you're not going to be embarrassed by how it looks.'

"Most brewers tend to have some OCD tendencies because you have to be paying attention to specific details, and the more you can control those, the better you sleep at night. There are many right ways to do things and even more wrong ways to do things. You should be neat and tidy to begin with, and those were words that resonated with me." It's a good thing he took the professor's message to heart.

"When Sierra Nevada was in town for beer camp last summer, a representative for Sierra Nevada had reached out to us about a pre-festival event," recollects Luke. "They said they were going to stop by, and I was like, 'Oh shit, now he really is coming in!' We cleaned all day long. We didn't know if he actually wanted to walk around the brewery. 'He's probably seen thousands of breweries. What's going to excite him about another brewery?' So we thought we would just get to meet him, but he pulled me aside and asked for a tour. All that cleaning was for a reason!"

CHAPTER 7

CATCH OF THE DAY

Fish Brewing Company— Olympia, WA

TROLLING THE CROWDED TENT STALLS at the Tumwater Brewfest, just beyond reach of the eerie shadows stretching from Olympia Brewing's shuttered factory, my long checklist of craft beers to sample was dwindling when I flipped one last wooden token toward the server at the Fish Brewing booth. As luck would have it, I was about to reel in the "catch of the day" with the last of my bait.

Bone-warming August afternoons in the Pacific Northwest make visitors and especially sun-starved locals extra cheerful, so my host must have been in high spirits as he poured me a generous cup of beige-froth-capped dunkel. Deftly manning a few tap handles while glancing sideways to answer my stream of questions, he soon suggested a trip to the source of the malty brown ration that I gulped down like a man stranded at sea. I cherished the final, sweet drops of the 4.7% ABV liquid pastry as if they might be my last, silently swearing I would return to Fish again someday.

It's nearly a year later, and I'm back in town to find out if all of the brewery's beers are as good as this castaway's imaginings. Fish Brewing is less than a mile from I-5 as the seagull flies, in the heart of Washington's state capitol. Cool waves of ocean breeze from Budd Inlet are keeping things comfortable on what might otherwise be a sticky, hot summer evening.

Although word of Fish Brewing's ales has spread well beyond beer festival crowds, the brewery makes an effort to toot its own horn every day. In fact, it acquired the old steam whistles from the abandoned Olympia site and hooked them up to its own boiler. At 5 o'clock, their deep, throaty *wooooo* punctuates the end of another hard day's work and announces that it's time to relax and drink good craft beer. Now this siren's song is beckoning me from several blocks away.

When I arrive at The Fish Tale Pub ten minutes later, it's time to experiment, so the Organic India Pale Ale is the first item on the menu to catch my attention. All of the ingredients in the popular IPA are grown without pesticides, contain no genetically modified plants, and haven't even been touched by fertilizer (at least purposefully). Maybe it's knowing the backstory that makes this award-winning English-style IPA taste especially pure. Or maybe it's because it's not much of a jump for me to imagine the brewery squeezing its citrusy flavor right out of a whole orange, peel and all. The pale, copper-colored 6.7% ABV ale is made with citrusy New Zealand-grown Pacific Gem hops. At 42 IBUS, it has an addictive mildly bitter flavor, with a hint of black pepper that is like irresistible chum to an IPA land shark like me.

Crafting beer, like Organic India Pale Ale, created from ingredients grown by Mother Nature is serious business. Fish needs to be sure that it covers all of the angles to meet strict government criteria. The USDA and Washington State Department of Agriculture audit the brewery to ensure it maintains its organic practices. That means not comingling products as well as purging and sanitizing equipment after brewing each batch of non-organic beer.

Head Brewer Shawn Vail, who completed Siebel's International Diploma course after earning a degree in engineering, points out that everything beer touches has to be cleaned before coming in contact with it. "One thing my first boss said to me in my interview was that brewers are just glorified janitors, and in a certain sense that is true," he muses. "But I love it, and I can't imagine doing anything else. Craft brewing is an amazing and fun industry, filled with awesome people that support one another, even though they're in competition with each other. And even though it's hard work, I get to work with my hands, and I have a physical product to show for it at the end of the day."

Over the years, the Fish has netted its fair share of accolades. In 2000, *The Malt Advocate* named Poseidon, the brewery's barrel-aged imperial stout, Domestic Beer of the Year. Dozens of other awards followed, driving demand for its broad range of beer styles, encompassing everything from funky organic IPAS to its Leavenworth Biers brand of German-style lagers and weizens. Today, the brewery's two operations pump out more than 15,000 barrels of beer per year just to keep pace.

It's the perfect place for the well-traveled Vail, who started homebrewing back in 2007 and later worked at San Diego-based Stone Brewing, among others. Prior to joining Fish, he took a dream sabbatical in Denmark refining his craft at Ebeltoft Brewing. The open-minded brewer has the versatile beer palate required by a brewery taking on so many different styles but admits that he does have his favorites. "I tend to gravitate towards hoppy and sour/wild as my top two categories I drink most often," shares Vail. "Out of those broad categories, I would say that I tend to go for IPAS and spontaneously fermented beers. I love hops. The aromas and flavors that they add to beer are fantastic. With spontaneous beers, they're so unique and nuanced. I love the sense of terroir that you get from them."

The head brewer has always enjoyed pushing the limits and experimenting with novel beers. "We have our Reel Ale series, which is a new beer every release, so we have plenty of opportunity to make and release new beers," he says. Those include buckle-your-seat-belt strong Ten Squared Barley Wine Ale (100 IBUS and 10% ABV), Hodgon's Double India Pale Ale (89 IBUS and 9.9% ABV), and Swordfish Double Cascadian Dark Ale (65 IBUS and 7.5% ABV) amongst other rotating options. "The newest iteration of this series is a Belgian dark strong fermented with black currants," he adds, as if we weren't already tempted. So little time, and so many possibilities.

As the evening winds down, I've covered enough territory on the menu that I've concluded that my first, favorable impression of Fish Brewing wasn't merely a mirage. A fly on the barstool, I watch ultra busy server Geneva as she stretches to close out a tab with one hand and skillfully fills a precious pint with the other, not spilling a drop. At this point in the research process, I doubt that I could pour a pint with two hands, let alone multitask. She wisely suggests Fish's chocolatey Mudshark Porter for my grand finale. This creamy, dark beer doesn't require a fork, but it's just thick enough that it leaves a slice of bitter cocoa on the palate, imprinting another lasting impression that's sure to lure me back.

All too soon, it's time to head out the door and hike back up the hill to the Governor Hotel. First, I pause just across the street from the circa 1894 brick building that was once one of the manufacturing centers for Boeing's airplane wings and now produces high-flying craft beers. The words above the blue and salmon-colored fish mural on the Jefferson Street side of the downtown facility speak volumes. It reads, "Brewery of the Year, 2015 Washington Beer Awards." And if the fading laughter escaping the patron-packed brew pub is any indication, I'm not the only one who's hooked.

Shawn Unfiltered

On the Importance of Scale Testing and Timing

Things don't always go exactly as planned in craft brewing, but that doesn't stop bold brewers like Vail from experimenting. Earlier in his career, he recalls working on a recipe for a Baltic porter that was refermented with cherries and incorporated a rum-barrel element, among other twists. "Since the timeline for this beer wouldn't allow barrel aging, we decided to soak the oak chips in rum for the flavor," Vail remembers. "Whenever I am making something new and/or using ingredients I haven't used before, I always like to do a small-scale test to get an idea of how it's going to taste and whether I want to make any changes. So after testing the barrel alternatives, we had the beer sit on the rum-soaked oak chips for three days.

"Another nice thing about doing the small-scale test is that a lot of ingredients scale up proportionally. Once you've found an amount you're happy with in five to ten gallons of beer, it's usually pretty close when you add the equivalent amount in 120 barrels (3,720 gallons) of beer." As it turns out, the young brewer discovered that oak chips are not an ingredient that scales up proportionally.

"Luckily, I tasted the beer after twelve hours on the oak chips, and it was ready to be moved off of the oak," he explains. For his fellow savvy brewers, the creative but fundamentally sound Vail wants to be clear that he didn't add an ounce of rum to the beer. "Just the oak chips," he says. "The beer ended up tasting great, but it only took twelve hours versus the three days I was anticipating." Call it intuition or the good fortune of "tight lines," but nothing tastes better than a beer rescued from the brink.

CHAPTER 8

HEADING INTO THE HEART OF HOPS COUNTRY

Bale Breaker Brewing Company—Yakima, WA

IF I HAD A DIME FOR EVERY TIME I heard a brewer mention Yakima, Washington, I'd be able to buy a round of IPAs for all of the happy souls downstairs in the tasting room at Bale Breaker Brewing. Or maybe the proceeds would have paid for the thirteen gallons of gas my Jeep burned making the five-hour trek north, then east, then north again from Albany, Oregon. Truth be told, every drop of fuel was worth the long trip to visit the Pacific Northwest's beloved hop country. Now I am finally here, in a unique place cleared out from fields of humulus lupulus, filling my own tank with Top Cutter, a citrusy, 6.8% ABV IPA powered by Simcoe, Citra, Loral, and Mosaic hops. The farm-fresh floral notes couldn't be more appropriate for this rural agricultural setting.

Sitting at the table with me and an assortment of ales, are Kevin (aka Quinn) and Meghann Quinn, and Kevin Smith (aka Smitty), partners in the brewery that I've been hearing about from highly respected industry peers like Tyler Brown (Barley Brown's). Meghann and her younger brother Smitty grew up running around the hop fields that surround us. Their father Mike and brother Pat still farm the land, supplying hops to some of North America's biggest names in brewing. The three owners convinced dad that it would be a good idea to carve out one corner of the family farm and build a brewery on it. That wasn't easy.

But willingness to work for a dream runs deep in this family. The Smiths' great-grandma, Leota Mae, started planting hops here during the Great Depression. "Our great-grandparents started farming hops just down the road from here in 1932, the year before Prohibition ended," begins Meghann. "There were some rumors and rumblings that Prohibition was going to end, and they had been farming different things like potatoes. They decided to grow hops for when Prohibition was lifted. They planted five acres, just down the road from here.

"Our great-grandparents farmed that land until the mid-1970s. They only had one daughter, our grandma, who became a teacher. My dad was the oldest grandchild, and he would come back and work on the farm with his grandparents every summer. His grandfather passed away when my dad was nineteen. He ended up coming back to help his grandma on the farm, and he never left. Our dad has been running it continuously since then. We grew up on the farm with our older brother. This was our life."

Until, as young adults, Meghann and Kevin decided it was time for a change of place. At the time, hops were not the hot commodity they are now. "My dad would talk with purchasing guys, and they would hammer him down on price," she continues. "It was tough, but that's what we grew up with."

When they graduated from high school, the Smiths all decided to leave the farm behind and head to the University of Washington. "We all wanted to go to the city, never go back to that town," recalls Meghann. But Pat, who had become an investment banker in Seattle, said he was done with the lifestyle of crazy hours. "He moved back to Yakima and became the fourth generation of our family doing the farming," she says. "This was as the craft-beer industry and homebrewing grew. We would all talk at family functions and say, 'Wouldn't it be cool to start a brewery at the hop farm?' And my dad would be like, 'That's the worst idea ever!'"

Pat, who was pursuing a graduate degree in business in addition to farming, didn't agree. He ended up writing a business plan for a brewery on the hop farm as part of his studies. "We figured this was an opportunity to do this really intense analysis," points out Meghann. "It really made us see things."

"We thought it was a thing that would not only be fun to do but it was a good time for the industry. We felt that there was a need for a strong brewery east of the Cascades. There was really nothing going on out here."

"We would all come back during harvest," adds Quinn, who met Meghann in college. "It was over those four or five weekends when you could meet all of the breweries. The craft brew industry was really changing then. We started meeting these people, and they were so great. We ended up going to a few Craft Brewers Conferences before we really decided that we'd open the brewery. We thought, 'Dude, this is the coolest industry, we have to be a part of it!'"

Meanwhile, Pat bought a pilot-scale system to test hops grown on the family farm. He turned the farm's original milkhouse into a small-scale licensed brewery that actually sold kegs at one point. "I remember that the first couple years that Pat had it, we would come and brew beer a month before harvest," shares Meghann. "The beer would be ready during harvest. Mike would pour our beer to whoever happened to be around. One time, Mike called us and said, 'Jamie Floyd (Ninkasi Brewing) tried it, and I said it was my kid's homebrew, and he could be critical. Jamie said it was commercial-quality beer coming off of a homebrew setup.' And we were going, 'Holy shit!'"

Eventually, Mike couldn't resist the strong, logical case that his children had built for a brewery. "He was stubborn for about a year, then he got into it," remembers Smitty. "At that time, I don't know if Dad was worried if we would be competing with his customers or something. I think that was his initial fear. Then once he realized how fraternal the industry is—that it's very collaborative, not cutthroat—then he thought it would be a really cool idea."

With the project green-lighted by their father, work began on the brewery site, as five acres were cleared from thirty-seven acres of prime farmland. "This was an entire Cascade hop field, all the way out to the corner," Meghann says, pointing through the southeast wall. "A lot of our marketing has to do with the number 41 because it's where we're from." The brewery, tasting room, patio, and parking lot sit atop what used to be Field 41. That is my cue to take a taste of the former field's namesake pale ale.

This 4.5% ABV, transparent golden ale has been dry hopped with prodigious amounts of Cascade and Simcoe. It has that bitter first bite, but goes down nice and smooth, delivering the trademark citrus flavors of its fresh-squeezed hops. "Back when we came out with it in 2013, people would taste it and ask if there was grapefruit in it, and I'm like, 'No, it's all hops,'" says Quinn. It is so smooth that I might not get around to any of the other beers tonight.

When Bale Breaker opened for business, ramping up the operation and making it successful wasn't an easy task. But failure wasn't an option. According to Quinn, he and Meghann gave up successful careers and put everything on the line to start the new venture. They and brother Smitty had to make a living at it, and that was going to require volume. "We weren't going to be able to start with one barrel," he quips.

Nothing was a given, including the ingredients that surrounded them. "We kept the hop farm and Bale Breaker very separate companies," reports Meghann. "We don't get hops for free. We buy them and have contracts just like every other brewery. We are brewing our family's hops, but we are still buying them through the proper channels. It was very important that neither business would benefit or suffer because of the other business."

The brewery opened for business on April 13, 2013 and sputtered a bit, as start-ups often do. "When we opened, our canning line was a little delayed, so we were draft-only for two weeks," sighs Meghann. "Then our distributor was like, 'We'll take thirty-six cases, eighteen of each style.' Their projected monthly total sales was eighteen cases of each per month. We were like, 'This is a disaster. Why did we do this?' One palette of cans is 330 cases.

"So the distributor picked up the first order, and we ran more than they ordered because you just have to run it. Then they called us two days later, and they were like, 'We need more. We'll take anything you have.' They ended up selling 500 cases in the first week! They completely undershot it. But we had all this beer in kegs because they didn't order it in cans. They were like, 'We need cans now.' We had no beer available in the cans, only in kegs. We only had three fermenters. We only had four employees. One day we stayed here until three in the morning, moving beers out of kegs into the brite tank . . . one by one."

"We pushed sixty-four barrels back into the tank," grumbles Quinn. "Then it lost carbonation, so we had to carbonate it again just to re-can it. I'm not a physics major, but a three-sixteenths inner diameter hose pushing thirty-two barrels into a brite tank took us like, nine hours." In retrospect, they made the best of a bad situation.

"We were back there smoking cigars," laughs Meghann. "We didn't all need to be there, but it was more for moral support. We were all in this together." They made enough to cover the initial spike in demand and haven't looked back since. Today, the brewery produces about 30,000 barrels of beer per year, and it sticks to the signature style that has helped Bale Breaker make a name for itself in Craft Beer Country.

Smitty says that the brewery initially opened with two hop-forward beers, a pale ale and a dry-hopped IPA. He looks back, "We knew it would make our story authentic. Being on a hop farm and making hefeweizens doesn't make any sense. The reason we all got into it is because we all enjoy hoppy beer."

These three also have the advantage of knowing the main ingredient in their product like few others. The farm gives them access to hop breeders, who are literally experts in the field. "Actually knowing and getting into their heads to understand a little more than other people do, the actual stats of the hop, the actual makeup of the hop and how that affects its flavor and specialty is helpful," notes Quinn. "We spend a lot of time creating these recipes to have all this flavor and aroma."

The partners decided that being a hop-forward brewery didn't have to all be about making the bitterest beer in the land. "We really focused teaching people that hoppy doesn't have to mean bitter," says Meghann. "A lot of people come into the taproom, and they say that they don't like hoppy beer or IPA, and we're like, 'Just try it.' The hops that we use to bitter are hops that intentionally don't have that lingering bitterness."

"So I hear there are over two hundred varieties of hops," I interject. "If you guys want a new flavor, do you have the capability to go out there and tell someone to develop a new hop for you? If so, how do they do that?"

"There's a male and female plant," explains Smitty. "You have to pollinate the female plant. Let's say you have a Simcoe male and a Citra female plant, and you cross them. Every seed that comes out of there is genetically unique. It's like humans. Your parents can have five kids, and they're all genetically different. Some of them (we shift back to hops now) yield terribly, some of them have amazing aromas. They have to cycle through and try to find the ones that work."

The growing variety of hops is the spice of this brewer's life. "I remember ten years ago, people were making single-hop beers," he says. "But it's like, 'I don't make food with only coriander.' It wouldn't be very good. It's really fun to mix and match. Just like you would when you're cooking—citrus from here, pine from there. That's the brewer's challenge with the hops and IPAS. How are you going to make it stand out?"

At this point, everyone is getting along so well that I decide to see if I can disrupt the beer-induced state of harmony. "I'm going to throw a nasty question out there," I try to prepare them. "Some people say that making hoppy beers is easy because you can easily cover up your mistakes. What do you guys have to say about that?" I don't have long to wait for the fireworks.

"I think it's bullshit," protests Smitty, not mincing any words. "You can take a lazy approach to a hoppy beer and make a terrible beer. It's kind of like anything. If you put the right amount of time and effort into it, you'll put something out that's really good. Our beers are so dry, there's so little malt, it's really all about the hops. If you have any little fermentation defect, it's going to glare through. We're banking on the hops. The malt, to us, is really an avenue to deliver hop flavor to your mouth."

"Like the tortilla chip to the salsa," observes Meghann.

"You can definitely screw it up," Quinn chimes in. "A hoppy beer shouldn't be all about the hops. If you aren't extremely careful, you're going to detract from your goal and take away from what the beer is about." They are a savvy trio, and I'm not about to step in it again.

It's time for an air-clearing break and taste of the beer I've been anticipating all night: the Leota Mae. The 6.2% ABV IPA doesn't disappoint. Although there are bitter notes in the golden ale, tropical-fruit flavors shine through. But I know it's the hops and not mango and pineapple tossed into Smitty's industrial scale "blender" that are responsible for the roadside fruit stand of flavors in my glass. For me, it's as remarkable as the woman that it's named after. "There is a faint sweetness to it," I observe.

"That's what we're really trying to do," confirms Meghann. "It's the hops we choose. The hops impart the sweetness. They're so fruity and punchy. They have so much character that they almost make it taste like a juice."

I'm sure that Leota Mae could be sweet too, but by now, I'm getting the sense that she was one tough lady. The farmhouse where she was matriarch, the same place Meghann grew up (the family moved and turned it into an office not long after Smitty was born), is just about a mile and a half from the brewery. Her strong influence on everything here, from her great-granddaughter to the down-to-earth artwork on the cans stacked in the brewery cooler, is palpable.

"A lot of people love our beer and buy it in the grocery store," relays Meghann. But it's difficult to share the whole story on the face of a can or side of a cardboard box. "It's really hard to be able to tell them the sacrifices my great-grandma made to make this all possible. Leota spent 100 percent of her time here on the farm. She would wake up and do all the typical farm wife things, like cook breakfast and do laundry, and then she'd go out and run the farm. She would work harder than any guy on the farm, and she was like sixty." Although Leota Mae lived to the ripe old age of ninety-nine, she wasn't around to see her great-grandchildren turn her treasured hops into gold. "The reason we named the beer after her is a nod to her and because it's where we all stand," concludes Meghann.

It just feels like this brewery was meant to be, fated to spring up from the ground here in the heart of hop country. Anything that first took root in the Depression and made it through the next eighty or so years while continuing to bear fruit is perennial. Looking around the room at Meghann, Quinn, and Smitty, I see that same drive to thrive here at the table, and that is reflected in the meticulously crafted beer we are drinking.

"Why did you name the brewery Bale Breaker?" asks my photographer, pausing between pictures. She saved the best question for last.

For Meghann, picking the prefect name for the brewery was one of the hardest parts of the process. "We went through so many different iterations." She thinks all the way back to when their dream crossed over to reality. "We settled on Bale Breaker because the hops are packaged in bales as they leave the farm. They get sent to breweries around the world. We thought it was fitting because our family had been packaging bales of hops and sending them out to other breweries, and we were going to start breaking the bales ourselves. Finally, it was our turn."

The Partners Unfiltered
Farm to Kettle to Can to Mouth

Bale Breaker may be the only craft brewery on a commercial craft farm that brews with 100 percent of its own hops. If that's not the case, they are certainly one of very few.

"This is a different model," I suggest. "The hops are right here. They don't have far to travel."

"During fresh hop beer season, they come off of the vine, and we can get it into the kettle in four minutes," smiles Smitty.

"We've timed it, actually," notes Quinn.

"I remember my dad was driving the hops from the farm, and he got stuck behind a school bus," laughs Smitty. Otherwise, it wouldn't have taken so long.

Freshness is important, from farm to kettle to can. "We are about 70 percent cans and 30 percent draft," points out Meghann. "We have to be super conscious about shelf life and make it taste good after three months, through the cycling of hot and cold. This is a lot of what we spend our time on. Will Top Cutter taste good in six weeks when most people are going to drink it? We have to care about how well it can and will age."

I take that as an invitation to test Bale Breaker's 100-IBU Bottom Cutter Imperial IPA to see if it makes the cut. "It's a little lower on the booze scale for an imperial," Quinn assures me. Bottom Cutter is a mere 8.2% ABV. It's the perfect terroir-kissed choice to wind down the evening here at Bale Breaker. The unfiltered, double-dry-hopped ale, infused with indigenous Citras, Simcoes, and Ekuanots, tastes so fresh that it has me wondering if Mike passed the school bus on the way from the field to the brewery. I can't help but think that Leota Mae would have loved this homegrown IPA too.

CHAPTER 9

BRINGING IT ALL TOGETHER IN BOISE

Boise Brewing Company—Boise, ID

"CRAFT BEER BRINGS PEOPLE TOGETHER." Since beginning my journey researching some of North America's best breweries, I've probably heard and made that claim hundreds of times, backed by just as many examples. The ethos of collaboration between breweries is so deeply imbedded in this industry's culture that it is difficult to find a brewery that isn't working with its "friendly" competitors in some fashion or another. So when I roll into Boise, Idaho on a bone-chilling winter's day, I'm not surprised to find a brewery that has taken the idea of partnership to a whole new level.

My destination is Boise Brewing, the only community-supported brewery on my radar in the Pacific Northwest. That means that the brewery doesn't have one owner who poured his or her heart and life savings into what is literally a pipe dream. In this case, four hundred people have a small piece of the action, shareholders in the maze of piping that transports golden liquid between the stainless-steel vessels on its way to thirsty customers. Their personalized beer mugs hang from pegs on adjoining walls, greeting me as I enter the brewery from Broad Street.

I cozy up to the bar and order a beer befitting the weather outside; my lips are soon thawing on a welcoming pint of 6% ABV Dark Daisy Chocolate Milk Stout as I wait for the guy who probably created it. My host's name is Lance Chavez, and his role at the co-op is a skosh more important than most of his partners'. He is Head Brewer here (his preferred title . . . if I have to use one). I know him immediately when he approaches me at the u-shaped metallic bar, my back to his shiny brew kettles in the open floor plan. The stocky, black-bearded Chavez fits the stereotype of a Northwest Brewmaster so well, he could play the leading man if Hollywood ever decides to make a Craft Beer Country movie. Fortunately for Boise, he isn't an actor and is dead serious about his role here at the brewery.

Before he ever set foot in this building, Chavez had brewed more than a thousand batches of craft beer at Sockeye Brewing on the other side of town. That is where he learned the ropes, as an assistant brewer and later as a salesman.

A lot has happened since he left one of B-town's other favorite breweries to help his partner Collin Rudeen turn his vision into a start-up. But before we delve into that story and other tales, the parched brewer suggests a round of refreshments from the eight taps under the chalkboard menu.

Sufficiently provisioned for the time being, we head up a flight of stairs to a loft above the bar and settle down at a table with two pints of Syringa Pale Ale. The honey-hued 5.5% ABV ale is the brewery's regional spin on classic pale ale, featuring Bravo, Simcoe, and locally grown Idaho 7 hops. With nearby hop farms in every direction except atop the northern mountain range shadowing Boise's foothills, the juicy green aromas emanating from my glass reinforce the sense of place. At 55 IBUS, it's a relatively mellow way to ease into our conversation.

Chavez tells me that before Rudeen ever approached him with the idea of starting a brewery, his business partner-to-be thought about creating a community-supported garden. Simply put, he envisioned a model where everybody would contribute money and labor, and share in the bounty of its harvests. When the vegetable co-op died on the vine, he began talking with Chavez, a softball buddy of his wife's, about a more exciting alternative. Ultimately, the two decided to take advantage of a little-known program through an Idaho Finance Department called SCOR that allowed them to sell stock in a company. After their first push to raise the capital necessary to get the brewery started, the duo had more than two hundred investors. They later doubled that number.

Now all they had to do was create beer recipes and build a brewery. Easier said than done. "I was doing recipes out in Collin's front yard, trying to nail down some standards for IPA, pale ale, blonde ale, and porter," laughs Chavez. "I had many professional batches under my belt, so I knew what I was doing, but it was just about formulating the recipes with Collin's homebrewing system." Whether those kinds of experiments are conducted in a garage or on fescue, creating flavors good enough to sell cases and kegs, win lofty awards, and garner the attention of curious beer writers is no easy task.

Still, selecting the right ingredients and establishing the processes to brew consistent recipes with repeatable flavors didn't turn out to be the partners' biggest challenge. "We started as Bogus Brewing," says Chavez. Bogus (Basin) also happened to be the name of a nearby ski run in the area, and they weren't keen to share the brand with an upstart brewery. "We were a month out—had ordered our glasses, t-shirts—and that's when we got the letter," he continues. "That threw a wrench in the works. We came into an amicable decision with those guys without having to bring in lawyers. We'd change our name, and they'd help us recoup our costs for glasses, et cetera." As an added gesture of good will, the ski outfits also promoted Boise Brewing with an email blast. In the end, Chavez feels like the brewery came out on top. "Bogus is a great name, but Boise is better for us because it's pretty lofty to rep your town," he contends.

Chavez is outwardly proud of the place. He looks around the room, happy to have moved operations from his partner's yard to their current digs, just north of the Boise Zoo. All the entertainment one needs in a day is within easy walking distance. "This used to be a music venue called The Venue, an all-ages place," he reminisces. "We had to rip the stage out and redesign this whole place. Colin and I started this. We even picked the colors on the wall." Recipes locked in, brand name changed, and paint dry, Boise Brewing's doors opened in June 2014.

These days, the brewery is rolling out about two thousand barrels of beer per year. A miniscule portion of the annual production run has shown up at our table nestled in a taster tray. We decide to take a short breather and compare notes, exchanging impressions of two-time GABF silver medal-winning Black Cliffs Stout (it has since won gold at the 2018 World Beer Cup). Color true to its name, it's a dark, seductive, 65-IBU beer with a definite edge. "I am a big hops guy, and I love IPAs, but I also am a big stout fan," notes Chavez. "I really wanted to combine that hoppy–stout flavor together." So he mixed a little leftover Snowboarder Porter with Hip Check IPA to create this irresistibly warm, 7% ABV stout. "Hip Check is heavy on Amarillo hops, and combining that flavor with the chocolate malt was like, 'It's got to happen!'" his eyes light up. Chavez's not-so-secret ingredients turn out to be an Amarillo-Centennial hops combo, along with "just the right amount" of chocolate malt. "We also use a bit of the deep, debittered black malt, which helps cut down on the astringency," he adds. "I like to use that because it gives you a nice, dark, deep color and a bit of roast."

"It's smooth, very delicious," I say, picking through the complex farm full of flavors. The slight tartness on the back end reminds me a little of the gentle bite delivered after a swig of Italian Roast coffee; then again, maybe it's more like the tang of the wild blackberries invading my back yard. Nevertheless, this double-dry-hopped hybrid (it runs on hops and malt) is plenty good enough that I would gladly have a second cup.

In fact, there isn't anything here that I've tasted by now that I wouldn't like to try again. But I'm sure that the accomplished brewer has made his mistakes along the way. "I've screwed stuff up," he confesses. He remembers inadvertently leaving one of the valves on a tank open at just the wrong time. "I was just coated in yeast from head to toe," he laughs. "It took me a second to figure out what the hell was going on, and it was still blasting out until I figured out that I needed to shut the valve. Almost on cue, my boss came in, and the yeast is dripping from the ceiling, and all I said was, 'I got pitched!'

"I think screwing up every once in a while is necessary. It keeps you on your toes in the brewery. A mistake wakes everybody back up. I've got two assistants here, and they're going to screw up. That's how they're going to learn and get things right. When I screw up, they're like, 'Whoa! We're okay.' Nobody's perfect."

That said, the Hip Check beer we are tasting is pretty damn close. In hockey, a hip check is a defensive maneuver aimed at knocking an opponent off balance (and maybe out of his or her skates). At the brewery, it's a dry-hopped, 7.6% American IPA with enough Northwest hop character that you definitely feel its impact. The high alpha-acid hops in this 100-IBU ale deliver a crisp, clean, bitter flavor, without the sharp citrus acidity that I've encountered with some other big IPAs. I wonder if Chavez's green-gardening partner Rudeen secretly dumped a fresh box of earthy Brussels sprouts in the wort when he wasn't looking.

My self-confessed hop-head host is in his element. "We get our hops from several different providers—YCH (Yakima Chief–Hopunion) in Washington, Crosby Farms in Oregon, and we contract locally. When we make our fresh hop beers, we drive out to the fields, pile up hops into our car and bring it back and brew with it. We thought, 'Why don't we do a fresh-hop fest to celebrate how close we are, drive up there, and fill up a bunch of bags?'"

So they created a Hoptober Freshtival that is held every year at the end of October. "We wanted to do something local that speaks to Boise," he tells me. "I appreciate all beers out there—the Germans do what they do awesome—but I'm proud of my American brewing heritage. We do hops pretty good here in the Northwest. We take everything and soup it up—you get a bigger, badder aroma. I'm proud of that."

Chavez winces when I ask him, "What is the baddest of the bad?" He squirms, uncomfortable being forced to pick. "I was always a big fan of Simcoes, but Mosaics are just a little bit better. I think Mosaics are a bit juicier of a hop, but they're the same type of aroma and flavor—a little fruity, juicy, and citrusy. I've kind of had a crush on Mosaics lately, throwing those suckers in everything," he continues before unleashing a hop farm's worth of personal favorites. "I like Chinooks and their big-time grapefruit hops. I like the Amarillos because of their earthy pungency. I like Cascades as a classic flavor, and Centennials are good for a good all-around hop to use. I don't know, I like them all for different reasons."

It's like a kid in a candy store with just a dollar to spend. Delightful and painful to watch all at once. "It's been great being able to experiment with them," Chavez says, slipping back into hop hypnosis. "The Idaho 7 has kind of a tropical aroma—mango and pineapple. They are harsh on the flavor, but aroma-wise they're outstanding." It's time to bring him back from his alpha acid-induced trance.

As we finish our beer, the crowd downstairs is raising the volume, but without drowning us out. I recognize that there is one more thing that is different about this place. It's relatively easy to engage in good old-fashioned conversation with the guy across the table from me. "We don't have TVs on the wall because we want people to talk to each other, and we encourage that," shares Chavez. "We have a thing on Mondays that if you give us your cell phone, we put it in an envelope, and you drink twenty-two-ounce pints for the cost of a regular pint. That gives people the incentive to just talk. Brewers don't get paid that much, but you do get satisfaction when you sit in here and people are loud and raucous. You feel like you had something to do with that—people having a good time." It's those moments, kicking back and watching everything and everyone coming together, that make the hard, day-to-day work of running a brewery worth the blood, sweat, and tears.

Like everyone else, Chavez has his good days and his bad days, but thinks he has found his true calling. "I don't have plans to do anything else," he says as we polish off our beer. "I really enjoy the brewing part. I still have goals. One is to hopefully win Brewery of the Year at GABF. Whether that's attainable or not, who knows? They keep giving me medals, so they're encouraging me." That motivation to be creative works out well for at least four hundred local fans (the investors get a free growler fill per month, so what is not to like?) and the many others Chavez and his partners have brought together in the name of good beer. After a last-call pint with my host, it's time to pour myself out of my barstool and head for my hotel. Boise Brewing and its warm cast of characters are hard to part with, especially on a cold winter's eve.

Chavez Unfiltered

On Recipes Gone Awry

"When it comes to craft beer recipes, are there any where you'd never go there again?" I ask.

"Absolutely," Chavez says without hesitation. "I once made a Belgian strong dark. I have no business making Belgian beers. I had cinnamon, some cloves, some dark candi sugar, and I can't remember the yeast, but it stalled out. I kept giving it time, but it didn't work out. It was flipping disgusting," he grimaces.

"It was one of our beers of the month, and that was a fail. We sent a bunch out to distributors, and they were like, 'We can't sell this shit.' We were like, 'Well, bring it back.' My assistant is also a distiller, and we gave him nine kegs, and he turned it into whiskey." Waste not, want not!

CHAPTER 10

BEER AND THE LOST ART OF CONVERSATION

Barley Brown's—Baker City, OR

TYLER BROWN, FOUNDER of Barley Brown's Beer, is one of those guys that you just warm up to immediately, even if it's over the phone. Try as we might, we couldn't seem to arrange a meeting at his remote craft beer outpost in Baker City, Oregon due to the ice storms, forest fires, solar eclipses and other acts of nature that continuously unraveled our best-laid plans.

With no luck up to this point, I decide to roll the dice during another road trip and just drop in at the brewery unannounced. Whether my big-time bet pays off or not, the drive east on I-84 through the Columbia River Gorge is worth the gamble. There are times on that route where the rolling hills, pine-lined plateaus, and colorful cliffs trick the eyes into thinking they are viewing a painting. The reddish-brown to forest-green vistas, divided by the deep blue waters of the twisty Columbia River, are so surreal that most of the five-hour drive passes in a flash.

When I finally arrive at the brewery in the historic, old west town near Hells Canyon, the apologetic bartender informs me that Brown is out of town on personal business. I uncross my fingers and text Tyler to let him know that we've missed each other yet again. He sends me a quick reply to stay put. He has just returned from Idaho and can be at the brewery inside of an hour. Miracles do happen, though I am concerned that a meteor might crash into the brewery and spoil our serendipitous rendezvous.

Thanks to social media, I recognize the stout, salt-and-pepper-bearded brewer as he wanders in, catching up with staff behind the window that separates the tasting room from the brew tanks and other equipment. In his jeans, jacket, and baseball cap, he looks like your typical middle-aged northwest rancher, made sturdy by season after season of hard work. His handshake clamps down like a vise-grip. When he sits down next to me at the bar, I ask him if he grew up on one of the countless farms out this way, planting and harvesting any of the ingredients that he would later use to make award-winning beer.

As it turns out, Brown was raised in the food business, with a baker for a father. So I was in the ballpark or at least outside the concession stands. Turning raw grain into irresistible consumable products and making enough money to support a family was in his blood from an early age. So was dirt bike racing, which may explain his throttling handshake.

A red Honda CR250R motorcycle hangs high on the wall behind us. "I grew up racing dirt bikes, worked my way up to expert/pro class, but never made any real money at it," recalls Brown. "I typically had to work two jobs just to pay for the racing expenses." He went to school at the American Motorcycle Institute (Daytona Beach, Florida) to become a certified motorcycle mechanic but couldn't land a sustainable gig. Truth is, he spent more time homebrewing than turning wrenches, so he moved back home to work in the family restaurant business. Around the same time, brewing shifted from a hobby into an obsession.

In 1998, the self-taught brewer opened Barley Brown's. Branding the new business was easy. "My wife Corrina and my dad Bill came up with the name," he explains. "Barley is the foundation of great beers, and Brown is our last name. And yes, some of the local farmers grow malting barley in Eastern Oregon. Baker City also has a malting facility named Gold Rush Malt that purchases local barley and makes local malt."

I'm thrilled that Brown chose brewing delicious beer over opening a repair shop or brushing past tumbleweeds on his 1986 Honda. Barley Brown's is well-known for its highly decorated Pallet Jack IPA. The combination of Amarillo, Citra, Columbus, and Simcoe hops have helped make this powerful, 7% ABV ale a GABF gold- and silver-medal winner. Brown adds that IPA is his favorite style. "I love hops!" he says. Now he is able to carve out time for yearly trips to Yakima to crush, smell, and purchase his favorite ingredient in person.

Today, business is good and life ain't bad either, but there were lessons to be learned along the way. When I ask Brown what mistakes he'd made, he looks up toward the ceiling. I'm guessing his answer has nothing to do with a leaky roof overhead in this relatively dry corner of Oregon. "Early on, I made the mistake of trying to do everything myself—brewing, cooking, repairing, dishwashing, et cetera," he remembers. Brown learned that he could do a lot of things, but it was hard to excel at everything. So he hired great people and grew to trust them.

"Our Barley Brown's brewing team of Eli Dickison, Addison Collard, Trevor Davis, and myself, all graduated from Baker High School and have never worked at any other breweries," notes Brown. "Eli and Addison both worked in the kitchen at the brewpub with me when they were younger." That continuity and teamwork have undoubtedly helped Barley Brown's earn twenty-four Great American Beer Festival medals as well as Brewery and Brewmaster of the Year trophies.

One of Brown's ales that has won multiple medals at contests far and wide is Turmoil. It just happens to be one of my favorite styles, Black IPA. Weighing in at 7.8% ABV, Turmoil is as good as it looks, hops shining through the deceiving 40+-SRM/Lovibond midnight hue. Color plays tricks on the mind, so I imagine a hint of licorice where there isn't one. Close your eyes, and after a few blind taste tests of the 90-IBU ale, you might recognize the fruit orchard and forest pine flavors of the Yakima, Washington-grown Simcoe and Cascade hops.

Tyler, who strikes me as a humble guy for someone who has been so successful, claims to be one of the originators of the style. It's easy to take him at his word. "This beer was conceived in Moxee, Washington," he shares with me. He came up with the idea after wandering around the verdant Yakima County fields on a hop tour with local grower Mike Smith. "This was the early 2000s," he guesses.

"You still had a mohawk way back then?" I tease him.

"No, a mullet," he shares with an amused look that makes me wonder what the truth really is.

About the same time, Brown ran into a fellow brewer from northern Washington, who told him how he was staining the mash in milling a dark malt. "They layered it over the top of the mash," he explains. "The sparge water runs through the top layer of dark malt and uses the lighter mash below to soften the dark-malt character and reduce the harsh bitterness associated with dark-roasted barley.

"I came back to Baker City, and we were drinking a Rogue dark, hoppy beer," he recalls. "I said, 'We've got to turn our IPA black,' so I said, 'Let's just do it!'" A few days later, around Christmastime 2001, the brewery had its first experimental batch.

"The beer comes out, and it's black, and it's awesome!" recalls Brown. "It doesn't have a big malty character to it. We were trying to come up with a name for it. What we were going for was that if you look at the beer, it's black, but it smells hoppy like an IPA." He and his crew deliberated over what to call the new creation. "The name Turmoil came up because I said, 'It's going to create a lot of turmoil with servers trying to explain this beer.'" The name stuck to the ale that is disguised as a stout.

The Brewer's Association eventually recognized Black IPA as a style and developed a guideline. "Turmoil won the very first gold medal in the category at the GABF," he adds, clearly proud of the accomplishment. The medal still hangs at Brown's restaurant across the street in the brewery's original location, where Turmoil is a great partner with the Snake River Kobe Beef burger.

Despite gold, silver, and bronze medals at the GABF, a couple of gold medals at the World Beer Cup, and other accolades, the friendly debate over who was really first to brew Black IPA continues. "People claim that Shed in Vermont brewed a dark, hoppy beer," points out Brown. "Brewers are creative people. There is probably some guy in his garage who was doing it twenty-five years ago and said, 'What if we dry hopped this?' There are probably a lot of people that did that. I think the cool thing with ours is that we brewed it a long time ago, and we're still brewing today."

Barley Brown's took its Black IPA a step further when it started brewing an imperial version, Chaos, in 2006. "We originally called it Moxee-style black ale," he informs me. "We didn't want to use the word Indian because it's so overused. I've never been to India, and I've never had beer from India, that I know of. So we're not big on throwing that name on there."

The latest vintage is working its way through the fermentation process in the big silver tanks behind the brewpub glass. "We brew it once per year and hold back enough kegs to serve it until the fresh batch comes on," he reports. "It transitions from being a big, aggressive, highly hopped beer to mellowing out and becoming balanced. It goes through these different stages through the year, becoming almost like a black barley wine. We'll keep bottles for four to five years as it continues the transformation with oxidization. The hops change. It's a fun beer." It's good to see palpable passion come out in someone who has been at it for so long.

"You love beer, maybe even more than motorcycles!" I observe.

"Yeah, probably more beer nowadays," he admits, though I sense that he sure wouldn't mind taking down the old dirt bike, firing it up, and going for a ride.

Nowadays he's usually going a hundred miles an hour just to keep up with the business at hand. "When we opened, the goal was to do five thousand barrels on our fifth year," according to Brown. "We hit that goal at about two-and-a-half years. We kept growing, and we hit this point where we were like, 'This isn't part of the plan. We didn't plan to be big. Our plan was to be good, controllable. Everybody does every job. We've always wanted to focus on making quality draft beer."

"You don't want to sell out to the big guys, do you?" I ask.

"Oh, no!" he insists. "The unfortunate thing is that true small brewers have to compete against that big machine. They're big, and they have resources that aren't available to us."

Brown is sticking to his game plan, and so far it's working out. In 2017, Barley Brown's produced just under six thousand barrels. "The cool thing about it is that we brew social beer," he says. "We brew beer that you have to go to a bar or restaurant to drink. You don't get to buy a six pack, sit at home and watch the *Walking Dead* while drinking our beer." That said, you can fill a growler and take it home, as long as you promise not to disrespect his beer by consuming it in a trance while watching zombies devour humans on TV.

"It's a competitive market for draft, but the fun thing for me is to go into a cool restaurant, and they only have a few taps," Brown continues. "If you put a beer on tap, you don't have to worry about someone saying, 'Oh, that's on sale for $6.99 at the grocery store right now.' We don't have that option. It's only going to be available right here and at your neighborhood bars and restaurants. It kind of keeps us unique." It also creates a supply and demand situation that drives scarcity and a mad (as in not having all of his mental faculties) beer writer 372 miles to the middle of nowhere in hopes of finding the man behind some of some of his favorite beers.

"We want to see the American bar come back," concludes Brown. "We want that to exist again. We want that to unite people!" Sometimes getting folks together takes a little good luck. Despite all the scuttled plans, we are finally sitting side-by-side on barstools today, sharing good old-fashioned conversation over craft beer worth talking about.

Brown Unfiltered

On Uniting Beer and Food

"I'd be hard pressed to find a common food that doesn't pair with a beer," shares Brown. "Our brewers brew a few beers using jalapeños. We brew a beer named 'Hot Blonde,' which is a golden ale brewed with a dose of Citra hops, a little lemongrass, and fresh jalapeños. That beer pairs great with our salmon salad. The dressing we make for this dish is a tequila honey lime vinaigrette, and I find that the jalapeño beer brightens a mild dish, such as this one." You had us at Hot Blonde, Tyler.

CHAPTER 11

ADVENTURES IN BEER TASTING

pFriem Family Brewers— Hood River, OR

HOOD RIVER, OREGON, A SMALL PORT nestled thirty miles north of snow-capped Mt. Hood in the picturesque Columbia River Gorge, is known for its watersports. Although the region is famous for its windsurfing and other H_2O activities, another form of liquid-based entertainment is driving thirsty visitors an hour east from Portland.

Only the desperate souls trying to make it home, thrill seekers out for a little fun, and frozen fools like me, looking for a warm pub with plentiful beer taps, attempt to brave the icy I-84 corridor in the midst of the worst storm of the winter. Cars are abandoned alongside the slick highway, covered in snow. Even four-wheel-drive vehicles are having trouble negotiating the treacherous road, often fighting for traction on patches of black ice.

The defroster in my jeep is set to max to thaw my eyeballs and help the franticly waving windshield wipers give me a reasonable shot at seeing the hazards that lie ahead. Giant white flakes are falling so furiously that it feels like I'm trying to navigate through a snow globe shaken by an excited child. The lengths that one goes to for beer. It had better be worth it!

Late that December afternoon, having survived the harrowing journey, I step inside packed pFriem Family Brewers. No one is wind or ice surfing the mighty Columbia across the street. Patrons at tables and the bustling bar are enjoying pints and taster trays of beer of all hues on the SRM color wheel, from nearly transparent golden to opaque black. Brewers are at work in the background, moving around the shiny stainless-steel tanks, trying to keep pace with the crowd consuming last week's work.

Josh Pfriem, co-founder and brewmaster, catches me in fly-on-the-wall mode, startling me out of my people-watching trance with a tap on the shoulder. The fit snowboarder/brewer is wearing a long-sleeve, blue and brown plaid shirt, with no hint of a beer belly underneath. He gives me a warm smile beneath a bushy beard and his eyes light up behind old-school glasses. It's one of those times when you feel like you have known someone for years, and everyone is immediately at ease.

He orders a pint of Pilsner, a 2015 GABF Silver Medalist, and a flight of tasters for me to sample. "Pick out your favorites, and I'll try those," I request. Pfriem smiles and puts together a thirst-quenching list for Restaurant Manager Jakob Lillvik that includes the Pilsner, Wit, Mosaic Single Hop Pale, Blonde IPA, Belgian Strong Dark, and Bourbon Barrel Aged Imperial Stout.

We head for his office upstairs, where we don't have to contend with the noisy crowd. A royal-blue stone on his clutter-free desk reads "You R A Rock Star Dad," and his daughters' pictures and artwork are taped on the walls above trash and recycle baskets. A zip-locked sample bag of Simpson's Malt sits atop of stack of beer books next to an old wooden cigar box on a malty-brown carpet.

One taste of the pFriem Pilsner confirms the paper weight is correct: Josh is indeed a "rock star," one of my idols when it comes jamming out beer that excites the taste buds. The slightly hoppy pils, a 4.9% ABV, 38 IBU lager, is not your average lawnmower beer. With a rebel blend of Perle, Saphir, Tettnang, and Spalt Select hops, pFriem's interpretation is more like sitting on freshly cut open amphitheater grass and taking in an outdoor concert of slightly floral and crisp citrusy notes. This sunshine in a glass with a slightly cloudy aromatic head makes me long for summer.

As I gush on and on about his liquid work of art, Pfriem just smiles and nods his head. He can relate. As a business marketing student at

Western Washington University, he fell hard for craft beer. "I was really struck by the flavors, nuances, and community that it brought together," he recalls. "Right away, I was attracted to it at a very high level, and I started homebrewing almost immediately. And when I brewed that first batch of beer, I knew one day I was going to be a brewmaster and open my own brewery."

That long journey included several stops with breweries that shaped him into the brewer he is today. "I landed my first brewing job at Utah Brewers Cooperative down in Salt Lake City," he says. "That was a really cool opportunity—a really great group of guys and really high quality brewery."

While the quality was high, the alcohol content wasn't; ABV is limited by Utah laws. "We were only able to brew 4% beer," he explains. Undeterred, the rebellious home brewer began concocting his own higher ABV ales behind closed doors. "I'd keep taps in my garage and have people over after biking and skiing," he laughs. "I'd have great 4% beers on tap too."

When an opportunity to return to the Pacific Northwest knocked, Pfriem jumped on it. After working as Head Brewer at Chuckanut Brewery in Bellingham, Pfriem's career path led him to Hood River, where he went to work for Full Sail Brewing. There, he wore many hats, handling everything from training the brew crew to working with a lab and wastewater treatment. "Those were a great couple of years, but all the while, I was waiting for the right opportunity to open up," he shares.

Josh's dream finally became a reality in 2012, when he took the plunge and opened his own artisanal brewery with friends Ken Whiteman and Rudy Kellner. The three agreed to use the Pfriem family name as their new craft brewery's brand. "At the time we opened the brewery, there was plenty of beer out there—plenty of brands, lots of noise," points out Pfriem.

"One thing that Annie and I have always been really attracted to is the European culture and tradition. There are lots of great American breweries and lots of cool things happening in America, but there has always has been a lot of cool things going on in Europe that weren't interrupted by Prohibition and are centuries old. When you look at history, most times it was a brewer's family that started a brewery and put their last name on it as a commitment to quality and stamp of approval." He liked the idea of personally endorsing his beers. "Seeing that this is my family's name, I'm going to show them my dedication to it.

"We take a very high level here to every beer we put out. Max Kravitz's sole job is to make sure we're not missing anything and that the quality is top notch and that we're pushing the envelope." Testing those limits sometimes leads to good surprises . . . and sometimes to unpleasant outcomes.

"Things have gone wrong, and it is really critical to learn from those mistakes. One of the most humbling moments in my career was when we started brewing pilsner here. Those first couple of months of brewing, it just wasn't what we wanted it to be. We had precursors and things that were not coming together that you need to have all come together in a lager brewery. I thought, 'This is not good.' We had a great reputation for quality at the time. I had waited until we were about nine or ten months in before we started brewing lagers, and it was just nowhere near where I wanted it to be. I was pulling on my hair and banging my head into walls. But instead of just bagging it and calling it quits, we fought it vigorously and relentlessly. I called up everyone I knew in the industry to round up ideas.

"Then we got it. It wasn't one thing; it was ten small things. We learned a lot about our process through that; we became incredibly better brewers, and this brewery prevailed!"

Now the Pilsner is pFriem's flagship beer, outselling every other style that the rapidly growing brewery produces. "It's won more awards than any of our other beers," according to Pfriem. One of those victories defied the odds against considerable competition. At the 2016 European Beer Star competition in Nuremberg, Germany, pFriem's prized Pilsner took a bronze. "Obviously, the Germans crush it with pilsner and a lot of lager beers, especially because it's judged on their soil," he points out proudly. "The only other breweries that have medaled with German pilsner since the beginning of the competition are a couple breweries out of Austria and that's been it. That is until we won bronze this year in German pilsner. We were able to medal alongside of the Germans, which was pretty crazy!"

"Isn't that a little like a team from Munich medaling in brisket at a

Texas pitmasters championship?" I ask. "What does it take to brew beer of that quality?"

"You have to love beer," he answers without pause. "Everything else comes after that. When we make beer, we're making it for ourselves, we're making it for our families, we're making it for our friends, and we're making it for our fans. Every time we make a beer, it's got to hold up to everybody's expectations because if you love something and it lets you down, that brings disappointment. That edge keeps you going day to day. You're not producing or manufacturing. If you get that mentality, you lose quality and things will diminish over time."

"Does that love ever dip or wane at all?" I ask. "Or is it a continuous passion for beer?"

"You're married, right?" responds Pfriem. "I love my wife. We have a wonderful marriage and a great relationship, but it's work, man. Any person that says their relationship is not a lot of work, I'd say that they are a liar. Our relationship with beer is the same way. There are sometimes you're on cloud nine, and it's tons of fun, and other times you're having issues, and the only thing that's keeping you going when you're in the trenches is that you love it. That's enough to weather through to another day. And then you get there, and you're so glad you didn't give up and that you kept on loving it and kept on making things happen."

Sometimes Pfriem and his team are inspired by others in the industry. "There is collaboration just within the spirit of being connected with people in the industry that you really respect and have similar minds," he explains. "That's another form of collaboration that's not as marketed, but I think it's really sustainable and ongoing. At the heart of all those collaborations, you learn a lot from each other. We're trying to solve the same problems and creating some of the same solutions but coming from it in entirely different ways. You want people to break your bubble and bring in new thoughts that will challenge your ideas."

That said, don't expect to find a gumdrop ale on one of pFriem's tap handles anytime soon. "We're pretty conservative," he admits. "We do a lot of things the pFriem way, but we also have a more traditional approach. We want to make beer that people are going to drink. To me, I feel like we've failed if someone only wants a sip or two or a small glass of something. That's not how you drink beer! That's how you eat candy.

"Our goal is if you get down to the bottom of the glass—that last sip is so good that you want to have another one, no matter what is was. Granted, there's going to be a little bit of diversity there between Pilsner and a big, boozy, barrel-aged beer, but I think the consumer will eventually get a little bit fatigued."

That doesn't mean that Pfriem never experiments. "Most nights, if I'm going to have four beers, they're going to be four different beers," he shares. "I'm going to build my palate up, and it's going to have a gentle beginning, a big point, and a climax, depending what day of the week it is. I think that's the fun side about craft beer that has a long future. People's palates get bored if you're just always leaning towards the same thing."

My own palate has been exposed to so many beer styles from so many great breweries that it will probably always be distracted by the next new thing. Tonight, I've managed to sample the majority of the tasters, picking a few favorites in the process, including the Wit. "It's one of our original year-round core beers," points out Pfriem, waxing poetically: "It's creamy, yet dry, effervescent, yet fruity. An earthy, lovely wit is a thing of beauty!" His musings, mixed with my favorable impression of the mellow, 18 IBU Wit, have me imagining an afternoon bike-ride break in the Belgian countryside. Stopping at a crossroads café, I'm able to relax with a glass of this slightly floral, 5.1% ABV beer, before pedaling back to reality and completing our interview.

With a touch of sadness, I eventually work my way to the end of the line. There stands the Bourbon Barrel-aged Imperial Stout, decadent and dangerously smooth for an 11.5% ABV beer. "It's been aged in bourbon barrels," volunteers Pfriem. "It's a symphony!" Indeed, several flavors are in harmony—chocolate, cherry, and a shaving of coconut among them. The big imperial stout's six-malts-strong backbone is balanced with Warrior and Chinook hops, making this 70 IBU marvel walk the tightrope between bitter and sweet.

In a state of beervana, I float a final challenge Pfriem's way. "Out of all these great beers that you serve, do you have a personal favorite?"

"It's like your children," he grins. "You love them all, but there's a time and place for each one of them. That's exactly how I feel about our beers. We're not going to make a beer if we don't love it. But, there are some beers that we make that I'll have once a year. There are other ones, like the Pilsner, that I'll drink by the gallon. Not all beers are created equal."

Yet every beer that I've tried today has been delicious, and that is impressive, since we've covered old and new-world styles, a bouquet of flavors from bitter to sour to sweet. "I'm really proud of the diversity that we give," Pfriem concludes, taking another taste of his Pilsner and reflecting: "What I think is unique about us is that we are a brewery for the people. We are here to not capitalize on anything but to offer something. That is at the heart of our mission, and it's a great ride. The beer business is going through an interesting stage right now, and anything that goes through puberty is awkward, but then it finds itself. I think the US beer scene will find itself and have a nice home. What I hope is that pFriem is part of many that are really passion-driven people that really care about their craft and want to make something and get it out to people who are really excited about it. We're really proud of that."

Josh Unfiltered

Seafood and Beer Bliss

As the chilly afternoon slips away into a frigid evening, visions of a big, juicy pub burger joined by an elegant Belgian Strong Blonde dance in my head. What a nice way to settle down in preparation for a long winter's nap in snowy Hood River. But before I plop down on one of pFriem Family Brewers' barstools for supper, I ask my host to provide me with one of his favorite beer/food pairings.

"I always try to let the chef drive what they can do with the beer," he tries to wriggle free; but I persist. "I grew up in Seattle, so I love seafood," Pfriem finally gives in. "As a pup, my dad would feed me steamed vanilla clams as a snack, so I'm just a sucker for fresh oysters in half shells paired with a Wit or Pilsner. Steamer clams paired with really complicated lower alcohol beers, I absolutely love that!

"My favorite high-level food pairings are all very delicate, and they're paired with delicate beers. Where you screw that up is if you try to pair it with a clumsy beer. Oysters on the half shell with barley wine is an example—sick!" For Pfriem, there's nothing like experiencing a little seafood and beer bliss to cap off another busy day at the brewery.

CHAPTER 12

NERDING OUT ON CRAFT BEER IN P-TOWN

Breakside Brewery— Portland, OR

MY BEER ODYSSEY HAS TAKEN ME WEST, chasing the setting sun to a South Pacific island 2,513 miles from home, east to the never-ending adult carnival that is Las Vegas, north of the border to picturesque Vancouver, Canada, and south to sun-baked San Diego. Yet I haven't managed to visit a single brewery in craft-beer-obsessed P-town, a mere sixty miles from my doorstep. That was the case until a friendly group of guys sampling ales at an Albany taphouse came to the aid a fellow beer nerd in need. "With so many great choices, what brewery should I feature in Portland?" I put them on the spot. They threw out a number of tempting options, then seemed to reach a consensus on Breakside Brewery. After making waves at the recent Great American Beer Festival in Denver with four bronze medals in 2017, Breakside was already on my radar. So this little straw poll just helped me settle the indecision rattling around in my head. I thanked the ad hoc selection committee and made a mental note to investigate the increasingly popular Northwest brewery.

When my ever-dependable photographer and I arrive at Breakside's inconspicuous southeast Milwaukie brewery, I wonder if we have ended up at a secret warehouse location for a fight club or a rave. But the light industrial building turns out to be one of three Breakside brewpubs in greater Portland. The seventy-four medals hanging on the wall behind a long row of taps confirm that we're at the right place.

The pub is packed tight this rainy Saturday afternoon. I slip through the happy crowd to the bar and ask for Ben Edmunds, Breakside's Head Brewmaster. A few minutes later, our host joins us, and we quickly realize it is futile to try to talk over the buzz emanating from the crowd. We grab two paddles loaded with tasters and head through a side door for a quiet conference room with plenty of table space for beer.

Once there, it doesn't take long to find out just how much Edmunds is immersed in his craft. "I love beer," he says, which is not much of revelation. "I think about it an unhealthy amount. I think about it obsessively. I don't dream about beer, but I dream about work sometimes," he confesses. I share that I sometimes have nightmares about work that force me to pubs for therapy sessions. He smiles and moves on.

Edmunds' infatuation with beer started sometime around 2001. "I was living with friends on the east coast at the time, and we were all interested in farm-to-table, seasonal, and slow foods," he remembers. "When we'd go on hiking trips, we sought out restaurants that we thought would be more home cooking, authentic, representative of the place. We found ourselves being drawn to brewpubs, which were bastions of place. They weren't about seasonal food, but it was the beer that was brewed on site— something handcrafted there. I really started enjoying the wide range of styles, seeking out more beer, and from there, got into home brewing. That is where I went from enjoying beer to nerding out on it!"

In fact, Edmunds dove deep into beer, studying the science of brewing at the renowned Siebel Institute in Chicago, then got his first gig at Upright Brewing in Portland. When opportunity knocked a second time, it was just too good for the young brewer to pass up. With founders Scott Lawrence and Tony Petraglia, Edmunds helped launch Breakside's original Deacon Pub. He has been with the brewery ever since. "They offered me a position as a pub brewer, on a three-barrel system," he recalls. That was seven years ago. "We still brew on that," he continues. "The beers you have in front of you are brewed on that system. I'd argue that it's one of the most award-winning breweries in the world, square foot per square foot, because it's where our most well-regarded and medaled recipes come from." It's a credit to Edmunds and his brew crew that Breakside is getting that kind of recognition.

"With so many great beers in the craft beer world, what does it take to medal nowadays?" I ask the expert.

"It's crazy," admits Edmunds. "Year after year, there's so much good beer out there and great breweries who walk home empty-handed. I judge GABF, and there are always good beers on the table that just don't win. The competition is just that stiff. I think this year, ninety-seven out of every hundred beers that were entered lost. It's easier to get into Harvard!" He is right. By comparison, a whopping 5.2% of the prestigious university's applicants were accepted for the class of 2021.

"To be honest, I feel fortunate," says Edmunds. "I don't know that there's any secret to our success. One thing we do is that we enter lots of competitions and try to get lots of feedback. At GABF, you only get four entries per brewery, and it's $180 per entry. I'm going to put my best foot forward. It's not the ones that I enter that I'd like to win or that I want to win. The ones that we enter are the ones that we think have the best shot—based on feedback from smaller competitions, where you're only paying thirty dollars. Can you imagine going into another type of competition, like an athletic event, without having practiced, and try to do well? You do your spring training in order to get ready for the big dance."

"How subjective is it?" I wonder out loud.

"It's like a jury, like a consensus base," he replies. "At the end of the day, to be successful in that setting, you can't just please one beer nerd. It's the beers that hit the most people's sweet spots. It's six or seven judges in the medal rounds. The beers that push through are pleasing the most people."

One of Edmunds' favorites is the brewery's pilsner, a 5.2%-ABV, 28-IBU blonde, brewed with two malts and Hallertau, Liberty, and Mittelfruh hops. "In some smaller competitions, this beer has done pretty well over the years," he reports. Breakside Pilsner has won at the Oregon Beer Awards, North American Beer Awards and Best of Craft Beer Awards. "Because it's done well, we've entered it at World Beer Cup and GABF," he adds. "It's never won at either of those competitions. It's probably our biggest loser. It's our number-three seller, but it's not landing. That's a great example of how what we want doesn't align with what is most likely to happen."

That is certainly not the case for me tonight, since what I want most is neatly aligned and within easy reach. Miniglasses of Breakside's highly decorated beers stand at ease on the table, awaiting my command. Lunchbreak ISA (India Session Ale) has won medals at the World Beer Cup, Great American Beer Festival, North American Beer Awards, Oregon Beer Awards and Best of Craft Beer Awards. This fruity IPA registers in at a mellow 4.7% ABV and 31 IBUS. Its five hops, including Amarillo, Cascade, Galaxy, Rakau, and Simcoe give it an orchard's worth of flavor. If it weren't 40°F and drizzly outside, I'd be tempted to take a growler to the park, flip open a beach chair, and enjoy sixty-four ounces of this golden, white-capped Northwest pale ale. It's a great start to our tasting session, and I briefly consider just ordering a pint and calling it good.

Instead, I ask the thirty-six-year-old northwesterner how Breakside is able to sustain momentum in such a saturated market. At last count, Portland had close to one hundred craft breweries. It's not easy, according to Edmunds. "It's not really a demand problem," he believes. "The market itself is strong, but you just have a flood of competitors. You have more people, who are expanding at a rapid rate. The pie just isn't big enough for everyone to grow at the rate which they want to."

Survival of the fittest has come into play. I mention that nineteen breweries closed in Oregon last year alone. Edmunds is not surprised. Even companies that brew award-winning beer are susceptible to failure. "To make even average commercial beer, if you follow industry practices with a modest budget and you're not hamstrung by equipment or lack of capital, that is not that difficult," he points out. "Making excellent beer is very difficult. I think that if you aspire to that, you have to accept that you don't always make excellent beer. You're constantly on a tightrope or razor's edge between average and world-class beer. It's the daily practices of your staff and your systems that keep yourself on the side of the world-class line. It's a thin line."

Ales like Wanderlust, which has medaled at the GABF, North American Beer Festival, Oregon Beer Awards and Best of Craft Beer Awards, help keep the brewery on top. The 6.2% ABV IPA includes five fresh northwest hops. The Amarillo, Cascade, and Summit provide strong grapefruit and orange-peel flavors in this hazy golden beer, while Mosaic and Simcoe add a second layer of citrus and earthy notes. At 64 IBUS, Wanderlust travels just far enough that I'm able to explore the nice blend of hop juice, without taking it over the bitter edge to alpha-acid heartburn. "So far, so good," I tell Edmunds.

"We have some customers come because they want a wide range, but I think most people aren't drinking to find innovation," he says. "They're drinking to find what they like. They come back to a similar thing again and again. Creatures of habit, in the best of ways, you know?

"I think that there is such a thing as innovation in brewing. But I think a lot of breweries, from a marketing point of view, use words like innovation for things that are not pedestrian but not fundamentally new either. In terms of developing new processes, equipment, and cultures for fermentation, things that are truly unique in brewing, I don't think that many breweries can be described that way. That doesn't mean that there's not a lot of room for opportunity to be creative and tinker around. It doesn't have to be something new under the sun. If we happen to be innovative, it's in the quest to do something that's kind of interesting. But you can't set that as part of your goal. It needs to be a practice."

They say that practice makes perfect, and there is no better example here than the brewery's number-one seller, Breakside IPA. That level of success could be attributable, at least in part, to the fact that it's Breakside's most award-winning beer, taking home GABF Gold in 2014 and Bronze in 2017 for the American IPA category and medaling at several other North American contests. Breweries don't repeatedly earn glowing reviews and the glimmering accolades hanging in the pub by churning out under-whelming products. Edmunds and his crew brew the copper-colored India Pale Ale with Chinook, Citra, Columbus, and Falconer's Flight hops. The latter is powerful enough in the hazy, 6.2% ABV beer that a falcon adorns the label on Breakside's IPA bomber bottles. Falconer's Flight is actually a blend of Northwest hops (Simcoe, Citra, and Sorachi Ace) that imparts tropical fruit flavors, like the mango that I'm tasting now, followed by a pinch of pine. Subtle fruit flavors, like tangerine and light grapefruit, keep the bitterness in check in this 73-IBU ale.

Although Edmunds isn't shy about trying experimental hops and blends in his recipes, he doesn't stray much when it comes to ingredients anymore. "Early on, I was interested in creating beers with non-traditional things and not brewing classic styles—brewing beers with culinary ingredients that were savory or were more cocktailesque," he recalls. "I'm thinking of fenugreek, St. John's Wort, pepper, and roasted duck." But the more Edmunds tinkered with ingredients, the more he came to appreciate "self-realized beer" and decided to avoid trying to turn sour ales into wine or oatmeal stout into an entrée. "Being a brewer is like trying to be a genre writer, like a mystery novelist," he suggests. "You don't need to define mystery novels and upend all the conventions of it, you just need to realize the best within that genre. That's how I think of brewing—realizing the ultimate *beerness* of beer. It's something you have to be able to put into a pint because it's not a cocktail. It's not a four-ounce pour. You need to think beer and drinkability. It's meant to be consumed in quantities." Having overindulged on higher alcohol beers over the holidays, I start to protest.

However, Edmunds is trying to make a point. He believes that it's best to embrace beer for what it is and resist turning it into something that it's not. "There's this creative impulse in young and ambitious brewers, and being comfortable in your own skin—as a brewer—means realizing that you don't need to push boundaries for what beer tastes like," he contends. "We started in the experimental and kind of boundary-pushing side, and frankly, the beers were fun experiments, but not great beers."

Nowadays, the brewer's refined process leads to outstanding beers like Breakside's India Golden Ale. This American double/imperial IPA is a big, 8.2%, 80 IBU beer, generously packed with Chinook, El Dorado, and Mosaic hops. All three varieties are noted for their tropical notes and combine here to create a bright fruit basket of flavors that pauses on the palate between tastes. The retronasal orange-peel aroma and soft piney finish on this mildly bitter beer make additional pints all too tempting for those with nowhere to drive tonight. India Golden Ale, which was introduced as a seasonal in 2015, hasn't earned the same level of recognition as some of Breakside's other beers, but it's another example of an ale that has really built fanfare in the region.

"We've had a really great run," reflects Edmunds. "It's beyond our wildest dreams of what we could have achieved as a small, scrappy startup brewery."

"Then why not just reap the rewards of your hard labor and retire now?" I offer, only half joking. Alas, despite his many accomplishments, Edmunds is still only thirty-seven.

"For me, there's a few things that keep me going," he shares. "I do believe we can always get better. Every time we make one of these beers, it's how do we make it 1 percent better? How do you constantly seek that 1 percent? You have to have patience for that. It's the one difference between being a brewer and a chef. If you're cooking, you screw up a dish, and you can fix it in eight minutes. In brewing, you live with your mistakes. Dumping a batch isn't an easy thing to do."

Fortunately, that isn't something Edmunds has to do on a regular basis. "There's not a single beer that we make that I don't love," he says with a smile, and then adds a caveat: "It is the Northwest, and I think we've made our reputation on American hoppy beers." Sticking with what they do best has made Breakside a popular choice, even at the epicenter of the persnickety Portland beer community. Edmunds, who mentions that he doesn't ever want to see production grow beyond 75,000 barrels per year, thinks that the brewery could eclipse 30,000 barrels in 2018. "It would make us about the ninth or tenth largest brewery in Oregon, or one of the 120 largest breweries in the country," he estimates. But getting too big too fast could ultimately kill the creative culture he has helped foster here.

That would be a sad day at Breakside, one I don't foresee in this brewery's future. Having worked my way through all of the samples and my list of questions, it's time to call it a night. But first, I ask Edmunds what food and beer pairing he would order if it were his last meal on earth. He takes a deep breath. I'm not prepared for his clever reply. "I was coming back from Siebel Institute (World Brewing Academy) in the Munich airport, and they have a Hangman's Meal," he says with a poker face. "I think it's literally like a cigarette, a glass of water, and a raw or hard-boiled egg. If that's the fate I'm going to face, I don't think what beer I have will be the last thing on my mind. But one of the reasons I'm a brewer is that there are so many great beers in the world, some of which we brew ourselves and most of which are not brewed by us. One of the reasons that I'm a brewer is that I don't have to choose," he concludes.

"I can relate," I chuckle after finishing off the last of the Wanderlust. Only a craft-beer writer has it better.

Ben Unfiltered

On Finding the Perfect Ingredients, Whether Near or Far

Many of the hops that Breakside buys for its beers are northwest grown. "We have good relationships with those farmers, personal ones," emphasizes Edmunds. "We source their fresh/pelletized hops every year. We contract with them and support their family farms. We seek to use the best local ingredients. We love to partner with local suppliers, even for caramel, salt, Woodblock chocolate, coffee, and all top artisan products."

But the brewery isn't afraid to look outside the region for worthy suppliers. "We're also committed to high quality ingredients from elsewhere in the world, like 100 percent German-grown malted pilsner," he adds. "We do pull from the wide range of international ingredients that we think are world class," from Slovenia and Germany to Australia and New Zealand.

For a brewery best known for its flavorful IPAS, it's best to keep a variety of options on the table, from classic and groundbreaking hops harvested overseas to the fresh regional ingredients mixing in brew kettles behind Breakside's bar. And there is no better place on the planet to share that good work than craft-beer-crazy P-town.

CHAPTER 13

FROM START-UP BLUES TO WORLD CUP GOLD

Public Coast Brewing—Cannon Beach, OR

THE FIRST TIME THAT I VISITED Public Coast Brewing in Cannon Beach, Oregon, was its grand opening in May 2016. While I was in the stunningly beautiful coastal hamlet to interview a restaurant chef, I took the opportunity to top off a great day with a stop at the brand spankin' new brewery for a brief tour and a few beers. Apparently sensing the big moment, the pub's computer system decided that it would be a fine night to crash, creating a bit of mayhem in the process. Despite it all, harried staff kept the taps flowing and my pint glass full of a variety of quaffable IPAS. After draining the last remnants from a third or fourth glass (but who's counting?), I made my way out the door into the cool ocean air. "Typical start-up blues," I thought. "This place just needs a little aging."

Fast forward two years, and beautiful Haystack Rock, the 235-ft. monolith that rises out of the nearby surf sand is still standing guard over the artsy town. Seagulls flock around the rock this afternoon, though legend has it they were once driven away when the town's early business leaders decided to adorn the towering perch with bright lights to draw visitors with fat wallets. Thankfully, those days are long past. All is as it should be here in "utopia" as I make my way back down North Hemlock Street in search of my own pot of gold.

‹ PUBLIC COAST BREWING in stunning Cannon Beach, Oregon, home of Haystack Rock. Photo courtesy of Catchlight Photography

There is no end of the rainbow when I arrive at 264 Third Street. In fact it is a beautiful, sunny day in the beach town, clouds held at bay far off the shoreline. I wouldn't miss the opportunity to lounge in the sand soaking in such perfection for anything less than the perfect beer. So here I am, twenty-four months to the day that Public Coast stumbled out of the gate, sampling the brewery's '67 Blonde Ale, a 2018 World Beer Cup Gold Medal winner.

Inside, I waste no time ordering a pint. Friendly bartender/Restaurant Manager Mike brings me a sunny yellow glass with a nice thin band of white bubbly foam ready for a whiff. Like a savory soufflé or maybe a simple fried egg, I crack through the creamy white outer layer to get to the liquid prize. What I find inside is a nice crisp ale with a noticeable bite. Despite being doused with noble hops, the 5% ABV, 19 IBU gateway ale is made for this seaside setting. What better way to start the afternoon than with this approachable, lager-like beer named after the 1967 Beach Bill, which established the public ownership of land along the Oregon Coast from the water to sixteen vertical feet above the low tide mark?

About the time that I finish off the last of the '67, restaurateur, hotelier, and brewery founder Ryan Snyder shows up. I am not sure that there is anything in the hospitality business that Snyder hasn't done. But turning this place that was once an eatery into a brewpub was probably as fun as any project he has ever taken on. Now he and Head Brewer Will Leroux, whom we join under the brites on the brewhouse floor, are brewing beer that is getting noticed on the biggest competition stages.

Ironically, one of the first brews that Public Coast made for public consumption was the earliest version of its award-winning blonde ale. "Crazy story about that beer," begins the clean-cut Snyder, who is so lithe and fit that his metabolism must be on overdrive. "I had gone to the Craft Brewer's Conference right after we brewed it." Meanwhile, Leroux stayed back to keep a watch on things, hoping there would be something good to share with the boss when he returned.

"I came back, right before we're going to open," recalls Snyder. "The big fermenter had the blonde in it, and I couldn't wait to do a tasting. I looked at the gauge in the back room, and the temperature had started to rise. It was calling for glycol, and the chiller wasn't working. So I got on the phone and told Will there's a problem. By the time we got it fixed, it has been a handful of hours and the fermentation was almost up to ninety degrees. You're pretty much done at ninety."

"We were wondering, 'Is this first batch going to be the worst batch in the world?'" adds Leroux, a stocky brewer with a long greying beard (probably from worry) that juts out under round spectacles.

"Sure enough, a couple of days later, we came back in here, and the tank temperature was dropping," continues Snyder. "Now the temperature was below where it's supposed to be. The solenoid had gotten stuck open with particulate from all the piping. Everything was brand new. So the glycol was chilling when the beer didn't need to be chilled anymore. So now we were going the opposite way. We're like, 'Oh crap, we don't know if we are going to have to put this down the drain.'"

The new brewers wracked their brains for a less wasteful, more tasteful solution. That was no easy task. "It's a very clean style of beer," notes Will. "Blondes are almost harder to make than IPAs because you can't hide anything. You have to be careful." They had to find a tasteful way to cover up the early equipment hiccups and resulting processing glitches.

"So we asked, 'What can do that's a little different than this?'" remembers Snyder. "I like aromatics, so I wanted to dry-hop. Will told me it was going to add three to four days to the process." They agreed that delaying availability sounded much better than the alternative.

Their instincts turned out to be right. "That ended up becoming a staple of the beer," shares Snyder. "We dry hop that to this day with Saaz."

"What's interesting about ours is that it's dry hopped just like a pilsner or lager, so it has a lot of lager characteristics to it," adds Leroux. He says that although the basics for brewing the '67 Blonde Ale remain the same, the process and the recipe have been tweaked in the interim. They made the wise decision to stick with dry hopping the beer, and the fix that they engineered back in the beginning paid big dividends.

So has the advice of consultant Fred Bowman, a local brewing legend from nearby Portland. When Snyder learned that Bowman developed the recipe for one of his all-time favorite beers, Uncle Otto, during his storied stint brewing at the Portland Brewing Company, he had to have him on his team. "When they sold that company, they shut down arguably the best beer in Oregon, which was a German wheat," laments Snyder. "We had Fred up here after we stabilized, and he brewed a wheat recipe with Will."

Since that particular brewing process didn't require a lot of fermentation, Public Coast planned to have its Uncle Fred weizenbier ready for the hot summer holidays in 2016. "It's one of those beers that you overcarbonate, so it wasn't quite there for the Fourth of July," remembers Snyder. "We had to release it the Monday after. I came in here, and I'm like, 'That's good enough.' I had one of those 128-ounce growlers, and when you pour off of it with the carbonation (straight from the tank), it's like pure foam. So you have to do a trickle to get beer out of it without it being pure foam. It took like an hour! I think I had three pints of another beer while I was waiting for it," he laughs.

I'm not near as patient as Snyder. It's time to try a taste of the legendary Uncle Fred, foam be damned. This time, a thin layer of foam rings the top over the hazy, deep-gold-colored beer. The classic banana flavor indicative of the style jumps out and pretty much dominates my palate. At 5.6% ABV, this old German classic, with its wheaty backbone, is a little stronger than your standard lawnmower lager; but I know I can get away with drinking more of them than dirty banana cocktails. "I would wait an hour for a growler of this beer, and might even be able to do it without a crutch," I tell Ryan.

Delayed delivery of some of the beers here at Public Coast is actually planned. The brewery's barrel-aged, Belgian-style beers take their sweet time before they are ready to be introduced to the public. "Now you even have a barrel room," I glance through the glass doors toward the front of the brewery.

"In the winter when things slow down, the barrel program ends up being this great culinary avenue," says Snyder. He points to Leroux. "It's his baby, he gets to do what he wants. We've had sea-salt barrels, tequila barrels, whisky barrels, and wine barrels. It's carte blanche for him to take the flavors from those barrels and implement them into different beer styles and cross the flavors up. I love that piece. He can create something that is really more culinary-based than traditionally beer-based."

"That's right, Will was a chef once upon a time," I say, connecting the dots. A few years back, the irresistibly persuasive Snyder talked his friend Leroux into ditching the stovetop and oven in favor of king-sized appliances like mash tuns, brew kettles, and brites.

"What barrels do you like best?" I ask the former cook.

"I think every one of them adds a different dimension," he says. "We just released a tequila barrel with mole in it. The tequila and mole are both really mild, but you definitely get the aspects of both, and it plays nice with the brown ale that we're doing with it. I'm finding that whiskey barrels are really potent. It's like rosemary, you don't need very much."

Leroux's thirty years in the kitchen give him some advantages here in the brewery. "It helped me to understand flavor," he explains. "Beer is grains, yeast, water, time, temperature, patience, and understanding what the humidity is going to do to a certain yeast strain at a certain time. Beer and baking are so similar. I'm able to understand the flavors and how it interacts on your tongue—maybe a little bit more hop. Hops are the salt and pepper or the spices in a spaghetti sauce. That's how I approach it. A little bit more of this hop this time is like a little more oregano in a tomato sauce. It's how you manipulate all of those ingredients. Salt, pepper, acid, all of those things work together well. That's the advantage I have, even though I've only been brewing for three years, because I've been living food for thirty-plus years."

"Watching Will as a chef for all those years, the one thing I can tell you that he did differently than everyone else I've ever worked with, is that he lived in that space," observes Snyder. "He is a forager and has his bees and all these things that made him this unique bundle of a human being. He would come to work and say, 'This is how I implement this in the gap.' That greatness is coming through. I knew he would brew good beer, I knew it!"

"I think it's important to bring up the fact that quality has always been number one for us," notes Leroux. "Each one of these beers is like my kid. I'd rather take an extra five days and dry hop it and make sure it tastes amazing instead of being average."

As you might imagine from a chef and a restaurateur, harvesting fresh, regional ingredients for their ales is a top priority. Although the coast isn't noted as a hops-growing mecca, they've found a reliable source not far from Cannon Beach who supplies some of the "spice" for their IPAS. "Will works with a local farmer," says Snyder. "The guy agrees to plant however many hop plants for us. They call us when the hops are ready. Neither one of us had ever picked a hop before we met them. They showed us how to pick them. We brought them back, loaded them up, came in here and dry hopped. We did our first fresh hop beer that afternoon."

Although I don't have the opportunity to taste that homegrown recipe, I do get to try the Oswald IPA. This is a surprisingly laid back, easy drinking, 76 IBU ale with strong grapefruit notes and a touch of pine. The mischievous Snyder named the Citra, Chinook, Simcoe, and Mosaic-dry-hopped IPA after former Oregon Governor Oswald West, a champion of the Oregon coastline back in 1913, but probably not much of a beer fan. As it turns out, Governor West was a teetotaler, so the 7.6% ABV beer certainly would have been hands-off.

For the hands-on Snyder, getting into the craft-beer business has been a dream come true. While living in Las Vegas in the mid-1990s, he was running taps at Holy Cow Brewery for restaurateur/brewer Tom Weisner, who later launched Big Dog's (see Chapter 30). The hop aromas and sound of equipment in the small brewery made such a strong impression on him that he never gave up on the idea of someday opening his own place.

Now that Public Coast has a World Beer Cup award hanging on the wall, Snyder hasn't let it go to his head. "We never approached this as we have all the answers," he says. "We don't approach it that we're doing something brilliant because we won that medal. We're making great beer, but there's a whole lot of great beer out there. We don't know what tomorrow holds. I know we don't have all the answers, but we're having a hell of a good time."

Today the little brewery that sputtered at the start is humming along like a well-hop-oiled machine. "Sometimes we're at capacity, and that's why we've doubled ours in the past year," reports Snyder. "Now we have seventy barrels of fermentation at all times. We hit just under 1,000 barrels last year, and this year, we'll do more than that. Frankly, I think in 2019, we'll be well over 2,000."

That draws Leroux's attention. "Oh really?" he laughs, eyebrows raised in amazement . . . or quite possibly terror.

At this point, nothing that Snyder comes up with surprises me. After all, in about the same time that it will take Public Coast's Pinot Noir Golden Ale to ferment in a wine barrel, his little brewery turned a beer on the brink of going under (as in down the drain) into a solid gold international hit. I can hardly wait to check back with these guys in another two years to see what he and his "chef" have cooking in the big bright kettles.

Ryan and Will Unfiltered

On their Favorite Food and Beer Pairings

"Alright, what are your favorite food/beer pairings?" I ask the chef and the restaurateur. Who better to answer that question than these two guys, right? So Leroux jumps right in and throws me a curve ball.

"I think there's time for everything—a blonde ale and a hot dog, or an eighteen-month-old, barrel-aged, whiskey, candy-cap stout with the best ice cream you could ever find. People ask me all the time, 'What's your favorite beer?' and I'm like, 'The one that's in my hand at the time.'"

I want something better than a hot dog. "Assuming it's your last meal and beer, what are you having?" I ask the chef, because I can't imagine it will be another "death rocket."

"I'm having one of our hamburgers and a blonde ale," he replies. "Ask me again in twenty minutes, and it may be different."

"For me, this is an easy one," volunteers Snyder. "I'm taking a strawberry and citrus spinach salad with a little gorgonzola with the Valencia Orange Hazy IPA. That is a killer pairing. The orange juice that's in the citrus, when I make it with fresh-squeezed oranges, and if I can get Valencias? That's how I'm making it, and the strawberries just sweeten it up."

That hits Leroux above the belt, and I can see that the chef squirm as he gets ready to exit his brew-kitchen and head to dinner. But first he asks, "Can I change my answer? Has it been twenty minutes yet?"

CHAPTER 14

FROM BLACK BUTTE TO DEEP DARK ABYSS

Deschutes Brewing—Bend, OR

BLACK BUTTE IS AN EXTINCT, 3,076-ft. stratovolcano that towers over US Highway 20 about five-and-a-half miles west of Sisters, Oregon, in the Deschutes National Forest. It also happens to be the name of the dark, chocolatey porter rising eighteen inches from the table to my mouth at the Deschutes Brewery Bend Public House, roughly thirty-seven miles to the southeast in downtown Bend. In fact, it might be argued that the ubiquitous Black Butte Porter, invented by owner Gary Fish in 1988, is more widely known than the basaltic andesite mound that it's named after, despite the volcanic rock's 1.43-million-year head start.

Fish approaches my table, shakes my hand, and joins me as I savor the last precious drops of his rich, 5.2% ABV dark beer with its creamy mouth feel. In this case, many years of practice made perfection. After growing up in the restaurant business and helping a friend open a brewery in Northern California, Fish decided to try his own hand at the brewpub business.

The young entrepreneur couldn't have picked a more challenging yet promising place for his start-up. Though Central Oregon hadn't even begun to blossom into the destination it is today, it was a hidden high-desert treasure. Lava tubes and other geologic wonders blanket the region with rolling black and tan basins that are broken by forests of fir, ponderosa, and lodgepole pine. Snowmelt fills the area's glacial blue mountain lakes and frothing whitewater-braided rivers.

In the early 1800s, French Canadian fur trappers working for the Hudson Bay Company unwittingly paid it forward, helping Fish with his future branding efforts by naming one of the area's ruggedly gorgeous rivers the Riviere des Chutes (River of the Falls), or the Deschutes.

Two centuries later, Fish found his sweet spot in the sleepy little town of Bend. "We had no idea what we were doing or what we had gotten into really, because this was a very blue-collar kind of Bud Light town and was very depressed," he recalls. "Half the storefronts were boarded up downtown. There were only about 15,000 people in Bend at the time, and when it was time to start hiring, I got to the end of the first week and only had fifteen applicants. I figured those fifteen people applied with me because they'd pretty much worked everywhere else in town," chuckles Fish.

Deschutes faced an uphill battle, just like many of the other craft beer pioneers. "There were a lot of late night discussions about what the hell have I done?" he recalls. "It was anything but easy. Then again, I've always believed perseverance counts for a lot, and we needed a lot of it. Things did get better, and our ability to deliver to customers improved, the food improved, the beer improved. We were a small, growing business. Some tavern owners in Portland had come through Bend on holiday and tried the beer. At the time, it was just really starting to catch on in Portland. There were only a small handful of breweries there, and people wanted to pour our beer. We got a call from a wholesaler saying, 'Hey, guys up here are asking for your beer. Can you send us a few kegs?' So we scrounged up some beat-up, old, dented Golden Gate kegs, and we were in the manufacturing business. We were selling beer, we were paying off debt, we were adding tanks, we were starting to grow out the back of this building. It was really something!

"Eventually we added on to the building here and filled all the space up with tanks. We were renting the building across the street behind us as our warehouse and running a forklift between the two buildings with chains on it in the winter. You'd go down that little slope in the parking lot behind us, and you'd know you're alive," he laughs.

The brewery's first three beers were Cascade Golden Ale, Bachelor Bitter, and Black Butte Porter. "A light, medium, and dark," remembers Fish. Back then, he was just trying to keep things simple. That was a reasonable strategy for a start-up, but as Deschutes beer became more popular, it was stifling growth. "I was in denial of our growth for most of the time—we were never going to get that big," he recalls thinking. "We were pushing this kind of new age thing: we're in it for the beer, we're not in it for the money, which is all complete crap. This is a business, and if you're not in the business, you're a homebrewer. It needed to grow, we needed to pay people better, we needed better benefits, we needed to get better equipment, we needed a better lab, we needed all these things that require business to generate profits. I was in denial of that for a long time, and I built a culture that quite frankly became pretty toxic for a time. The correction to that took a long time to figure out." He finally did, and today Deschutes is thriving.

Nowadays, there are so many options on tap at the Bend Public House that one needs a map just to navigate a taster tray. In fact, Deschutes bottles twenty-one beers in its Year Round, Seasonals, Reserve, and Bond Street Series, plus a variety of Limited Release Pub-only Specialties. Craving comfort on this chilly fall day, I reach for the 2012 Abyss and take a sip of the bottomless-pit-dark imperial stout. "It's become very much a cult classic," notes Fish. Having had several years to mellow, the 2012 still provides the coffee-bean flavor characteristic of the newer vintages, with molasses and licorice flavors lurking in the background along with a hint of chocolate.

The 2015 Abyss is next in line. Indistinguishable in color from its older vintage/predecessor, the 50 percent barrel-aged imperial stout is a little like a cool, sugar-free version of creamy Irish coffee. As the rich, dark-roast beer trickles down my own abyss on the way to warm my cavernous belly, it leaves an aromatic hint of whiskey during its descent. "You know, we never designed those beers to taste like bourbon, but we wanted that flavor integrated into the beer itself, so they are bourbon barrels," reveals Fish. "We've always built beers to be complex and drinkable. Anybody can dump whiskey into beer and make it taste like that. We just never felt like that was the best way to make a really flavorful complex beer. We always have really pushed ourselves to not pander, but to really try and build a better beer."

"If I were to really twist on your arm hard and force you into yelling out your favorite beer, what would come out, Gary?" There is nothing worse than asking a brewer to pick his favorite creation. "It's a little like trying to select a favorite child, isn't it?" Fish faces the paradox of choice, but refuses to be cornered.

"I literally don't have one," he answers, locking eyes with me to re-inforce his sincerity. "You can ask the bartenders here. I drink in small, half-pint glasses, and I rarely ever have the same two beers in a row. I love what's new, what's seasonal. I will say that my go-to beer of one of the beers we have on regularly is the Bachelor Bitter. I love IPAs, but I'm not a huge fan of the incredibly bitter."

Even with the wide range of palate-pleasing flavors out there, Fish thinks that there is still room for new beers that will excite the senses. "We've only just scratched the surface," he believes. "They say a wine-maker can make bad wine out of good grapes, but he cannot make good wine out of bad grapes. That's the only ingredient a winemaker has—it's grapes. We have an unlimited spectrum of ingredients. Not just in malt, hops, and yeast. I mean, the Abyss has vanilla bean, cherry bark, and blackstrap molasses."

Deschutes has garnered accolades for more than its brewery's intricate flavor combinations. Fish cut his teeth in the wine industry, then the restaurant business. He has decades of experience pairing food with adult beverages. "I tend to look at beer and food that kind of supplement each other, rather than complement one another," explains the restaurateur. "If you drink the Abyss, it's got a lot of chocolate and coffee notes, and you'd think, 'Oh, that would go great with chocolate!' To me, that is redundant and kind of boring. It doesn't mean it wouldn't go great with chocolate, but I think it would go much better with tart berries or something that plays against the chocolate. When you're pairing food with beer, there are gaps in each flavor profile. I think you want to try and fill those gaps to have the most complete experience that you can.

"What's really good with that Obsidian Stout is a scoop of vanilla ice cream. Kind of a stout float. I think that Black Butte Porter with that red sauce, shrimp cocktail would be good. Not only the acidity of the tomato but the sharpness of the horseradish, and to go along with a beer that's got a fairly round, smooth character to it. Lots of flavor, lots of complexity, but nothing sharp or tart. Kind of rounded with sharp edges."

Edginess continues to attract new customers to bold breweries like Deschutes. "The allure of craft is independence," according to Fish. "It's the rebellious nature of a lot of these companies that has attracted so many of the younger generation. They say, 'I'll give you all kinds of chances. This batch wasn't very good, but I'll come back and try the next batch because I think you're getting it together. I mean, I like you, and I can come down and talk to you.' I get it. 'But when you sell out, you've lost my loyalty. Once that's gone, and there's another guy down the street, I'll find out what he's about.'" Fish knows that he can't afford to coast to the finish line.

Although he has been at it for thirty years, Fish has no immediate plans to exit the business he loves. "It's something I'm not in a hurry to do, but I'm not gonna live forever," he recognizes his limits. "I've turned over most of the operating responsibilities to others now, who are far better at it than I ever was. We'll continue to try to do the right thing, and you know, when the opportunity comes up, and it's the right time and the right place, you never know; but we're not for sale! I think I can keep doing this for a long time. I could sit and talk about beer forever!" But, of course, all good things must come to an end.

Gary Unfiltered
On the Meaning of Craft Beer

I touch a nerve when I ask Fish for the definition of a craft brewery. "I think a lot of people make a big deal out the words *craft beer*," he says. "Is craft relevant any more with the big breweries buying all the little breweries? Do we care? I maintain that absolutely we care, clearly we care.

"Look at all the different places where you see the word *craft* used now. Ten years ago, you would have never seen that. I was at a trade show in Germany in November and craft was everywhere. Clearly people care."

Fish argues that when companies are bought out by the behemoths, they change, even if their beer doesn't. "Clearly, they have unlimited access to resources, and not just money, but technology, expertise, engineering, all that kind of stuff," he contends. "They have unlimited access to distribution—they can sell their beer all over. It doesn't mean that their beer is not ever as good as it was before. It doesn't mean the people are bad.

"But to me, the word craft connotes something much different than that. I think people care, and not just in the beer industry. Look who else is using the word craft. Every consumer goods industry out there is using the word. Do you know where it started? It started with beer."

To Fish and many others in the industry, the term craft is much more than a clever trade-show marketing tool. It's a badge of honor identifying a brewery as fiercely independent, artisan, and willing to collaborate with others in the industry for the betterment of beer . . . even if the bottom line suffers a bit.

CHAPTER 15

THE BEER-BREWING LAWMAN IN LEDERHOSEN

3 Sheets Brewery—Albany, OR

THE LAST TIME I WAS in Munich was in 2004, on the last night of Oktoberfest. The sliding glass door in my hotel room opened to a back porch that overlooked the fairgrounds, lit up like the grandest holiday celebration, filled with thousands of revelers singing and drinking themselves silly. Since I was one of the last guys to the party that night, traveling sober and solo without anyone to toast *"Prost!"* it was a bittersweet evening indeed. But I comforted myself knowing that there would be many more chances to celebrate the autumn harvest of beer and bratwurst.

Little did I know that opportunity would wait a dozen long years before it came knocking, far from beer halls of Bavaria. Sergeant Klint Sheets and his wife Beth, owner-operators of 3 Sheets Brewery, kindly invited me to celebrate Oktoberfest with family and friends at their Albany, Oregon home. How could I resist? Ringing the doorbell, I imagined drinking golden lager from a *Maß* (a one-liter beer stein), locking arms with a crowd of fellow merrymakers, and singing *Ein Prosit* under a pennant-festooned tent.

Although my vision deviated from reality, the spirit of the Volksfest was alive and well at the Sheets house. Food covered every square inch of the dining room table, where we loaded up on appetizers before making our way outside to search for the star of the show. I found our multitasking host, who also happened to be celebrating his forty-fourth birthday, racing around his backyard in lederhosen and a feathered alpine hat. Klint was busy flipping brats on the grill and occasionally darting over to an impressive lineup of kegs to pour guests Black IPA, Huckleberry Cream Ale, as well as his own frothy rendition of an Oktoberfest lager.

Always willing to help a friend in need, I strategically positioned myself within easy reach of the ten taps and volunteered to play Quality Assurance Director for the evening. Upon assigning myself that crucial role, I started comparing notes with fellow beer enthusiast Joe Gutierrez, who, like his barbecuing buddy Sheets, was also decked out in festive black shorts and striped suspenders. I had met Gutierrez and his wife Stephanie once before, during an informal tasting panel session to evaluate one of 3 Sheets' new ales.

"What do you like about the Black IPA?" he asked me. That's a bit of a problem question, since I had recently devoured a plate full of white and golden corn chips smothered with spicy artichoke-jalapeno dip. I wanted to sound like a real beer connoisseur, but I honestly couldn't taste a damn thing. So I roll my eyes skyward, and traveled back to the time I tasted Sheets' first test batch and cleverly offered, "Well, the aftertaste is a little like cold cola."

Joe winced, and his body language said, "Are you out of your mind?"

"I thought you said it tasted a little like 'a bursting bubble of black licorice?'" chimed in his eavesdropping wife Stephanie. Her memory proved much better than mine, recalling my very descriptive burp-influenced review of the ale word-for-word, despite the fact that it was nearly six months ago.

"You're right," I agreed. I managed to dodge further questions by taking a prolonged second swig, hoping that would also fan out the hot pepper flames still burning in my mouth and leave a nice cool slick of *that* unmistakable licorice flavor on my tongue.

Instead, the gustatory cortex in my brain registers something different: "Italian-roast coffee!" I blurted out. Joe nodded his head in approval. "That's what I get too," he concurred. Maybe it's time to call it a night while I'm back ahead," I thought. Then I came to my senses and dutifully manned my foamy station until my wife finally dragged me out the door in the wee hours.

The first time that I met Sheets in person, he was not sporting his colorful Bavarian costume. It was a rare rain-free day in Albany, and he greeted me in jeans and a t-shirt emblazoned "I'M A RUGGED MANIAC" as the garage-door entrance to his home brewery rolled open. It was quickly apparent that the former bodybuilder is one "RUGGED" dude—I'd hate to be on the wrong side of the law with this badass patrolling town. He politely welcomed me into his little hops laboratory, and a whiff confirmed that I'd found the right street address.

There was something exciting about visiting the smallest craft beer maker on my radar. Of course, many of the big brewers that I'd met in my quest for the best in the west started in their garages too. None of them had forgotten where it all began and what they went through in the process of making it big.

At that moment, whether Sheets ever achieved their level of success or contentedly continued concocting ales out of his garage indefinitely really didn't matter to me. It was fascinating to unearth a hidden gem, a working nanobrewery that had been bootstrapped to life by a passionate hobbyist in the process of morphing into an entrepreneur.

We toured the garage-based production facility, which didn't take quite as long as my field trips through much bigger craft breweries like Maui Brewing, 21st Amendment, or Alaskan. This short excursion pretty much required standing in place and pivoting to look around the production facility every thirty seconds or so. "I like to describe this as my tweaker construction," chuckled Klint. "Everything you see here was either done by me or my friends, including the concreate floor."

We took a few steps and entered his walk-in refrigerator, made with two-by-fours, lots of foam for insulation, and sporting a state-of-the-art CoolBot controller. It might have been the highest tech piece of equipment in the garage, helping Sheets control the temperature and energy costs. "Hey, I'm the one paying the power bill around here," he pointed out. "My wife Beth won't come in the walk-in because it's too cold. It's got to be twenty before I even put a jacket on." As my teeth began to chatter, Klint took the hint, and we exited the ice box before a rescue party was required.

Even back then, the hardest part of Sheets' job was ensuring his beers were consistent. "When I went from my five-gallon homebrew batches to sixty-gallon batches, the hop utilization is a little bit different," he noted. "You have to adjust things to get that same bitterness that you're going for in the IBUs for the IPAs. I didn't want to have a good batch of beer, then a weak beer the next time out."

All that shoptalk made me a little thirsty, so we wandered from the garage into the backyard and visited two old household refrigerators retrofitted with tap handles. Sheets claimed that his most popular and strongest beer was the Green Beret IPA, named after his father-in-law, Command Sergeant Major Richard "Dirty Dick" Noble, who spent thirty years serving his country. The late Sergeant Major never got the chance to sample the ale that honors his memory, but he would probably have approved.

Klint poured me a cup to see if I agreed. Like Dirty Dick, Green Beret is a no-nonsense, in-your-face IPA. I took a sip, and the bitterness brought me to full attention, like I was on drill duty. "Well son, DO YOU LIKE IT?" I imagined the Sergeant Major barking at me, nose-to-nose.

True to its namesake, the 7.5% ABV Green Beret IPA is definitely not for the mild of heart. I took one more pull and let the blend of Cascade, Chinook, and Citra hops explode in my mouth. "Man, this had to turn out right for you to name it after your Sergeant Major and father-in-law," I observed.

There was a time when Sheets couldn't imagine making a 65-IBUs-bitter beer like Green Beret. "I swore up and down that I wasn't going to even do an IPA," he admitted. On a trip to Germany, he and Beth experienced local craft beers that had been produced for generations, and they fell for the much gentler lagers.

"When we came back, there was nothing that tasted like the German beers from over there," recollected Sheets. "So we spent hundreds of hours researching and experimenting. That's when it all started."

The amateur brewer eventually got good enough at the craft that his beer was worthy of a handle at a local taphouse called the Growler Garage.

That's where I discovered 3 Sheets' banana bread-flavored Betty's Bavarian Hefeweizen, which ultimately led to the garage brewery tour and tasting, which landed me the coveted invitation to the Oktoberfest party, which brings us forward to today.

It's funny how journeys sometimes end up at an intersection, where we find avenues that lead off different directions to places that we have only dreamed of. When a new opportunity suddenly appeared on the horizon, the hardworking part-time brewer stopped to consider the possibilities, adjusted course, and went for it. Just a few days before their annual Oktoberfest bash in 2016, the Sheets signed a lease for their very own pub in downtown Albany.

It took another year to renovate their new place and get the necessary city permits, but they persevered and finally opened their doors in October 2017. "This is my hobby that turned to something I can't keep up with," muses Klint. "On my days off, I'm brewing." That is good news for those who crave his craft beer.

Now local favorites, like the refreshing, 6% ABV Strawberry Blonde and the crisp, 6.1% ABV Raspberry Summer Sour as well as a rotating selection of other handcrafted ales, lagers, and stouts, are available somewhere other than the Sheets' backyard fridge. Oh, and if you are really lucky, you'll find the *braumeister* has made a batch of his German Chocolate Cake. This isn't the traditional frosted variety, but Klint's chocolatey-stout rendition that incorporates a hint of coconut-pecan and a pinch of salt. It's definitely a rare treat well worth the hundreds of calories packed in each ten-ounce pour.

Although this cozy pub isn't much bigger than the Sheets' little brewhouse back home, it's on First Street downtown, where anyone over 21 can wander in the front door without the aid of a garage-door opener. If a fraction of those folks join the growing fan base of 3 Sheets faithful, the craft beer-brewing lawman in lederhosen may need to move his Oktoberfest celebration to the local fairgrounds. There I can imagine the throngs chanting, "*Zicke zacke, zicke zacke, hoi, hoi, hoi*," then raising beer mugs full of lager in unison and toasting one of the best little breweries in the west.

Klint Unfiltered

On Man's Best Friend and a Beer to Remember

Sheets has always been a big fan of dark beers, especially when the north-western weather turns dark and cold. One of the taps on the kegerator out back is labeled Old Ace Porter and includes a rough sketch of a dog. Klint branded the beer after Ace, his beloved 130-pound black lab that thought he was a lap dog, a sidekick "with a heart of gold" that he lost a few years back. Maybe he named the beer after Old Ace because it's consistent, dependable, and a good friend on chilly Oregon evenings.

The down-to-earth brewer likes pairing Old Ace with a nice T-bone (the dog probably liked that combination as well). "Beth just cooks that with a little salt and pepper," he shakes his head. "For me, it's that combination you get with a little bit of the chocolate plus the savory flavor from the steak." Old Ace offers hints of coco and coffee bean, without any one flavor dominating the palate. Even though nothing replaces the warmth of man's best friend, a nice toasty porter is pretty darn comfortable when the sun sets on another craft beer-tasting adventure.

CHAPTER 16

STUMBLING ON OLD CRUSTY IN ROGUE NATION

Rogue Ales—Newport, OR

THE YAQUINA BAY BRIDGE STRETCHES across a deep-blue ocean inlet that laps at a stubby seawall supporting the shops and seafood restaurants lining the bayfront in Newport, Oregon. A stone's skip from the north end of the 3,223-foot arch, the historic Yaquina Bay lighthouse beacon pierces the coastal fog on many days. But as lady luck would have it, the skies are relatively clear and the sun is peeking through hazy cloud cover just off the coast this December afternoon. I'm on a mission to visit one of the area's other major bucket-list destinations, Rogue Ales, on the south side of the span.

The enormous gunmetal-gray, ribbed-metal facility stretches about the length of a football field just east and in the afternoon shadow of the bridge.

Growler in hand, lady luck strikes again as I enter through the repurposed old red grain silo that welcomes all visitors to the heart of the Rogue Nation. Inside the stronghold, I wind through the production area, then the gift shop, and up a flight of stairs to the bar. As good fortune would have it, I'm standing next to one of the Nation's pioneering members, author Greg Starypan. Starypan just happens to be on-hand drinking his favorite beer, Old Crusty Barleywine. When I ask how long the local mystery writer has been coming here, he tells me 1989 and points to a glass-worn plaque imbedded in the bar next to his pint. It reads "Crusty Greg." So when Starypan and his buddy suggest that I try his namesake 10.7% ABV, 101 IBU beer, of course I must oblige . . . albeit reluctantly.

The bartender pours me a one-ounce taster, and I like it, despite the odds. Full confession: barleywine is not my favorite style, but this oh-so-smooth rusty-brown ale, with a hint of butter toffee, is worth filling a crowler (the canned-beer version of a growler). The bartender warns me that this is potent stuff and puts it in a brown paper bag. I promise him I won't open it until I reach the parking lot. Crusty Greg gets a kick out of that, and we say our goodbyes.

The words "Dare, Risk, Dream" are highlighted in a red band that encircles the top of the thirty-two-ounce can. That same message was on Brett Joyce's beanie the first time I met Rogue's ruler at the brewery months earlier. Brett says his father Jack, who cofounded Rogue in the mid '80s, impressed those and other lessons on his son from an early age. "It's so easy to play it safe," he observes. "Dare means you have to have the courage to try something different. Risk means you have to put things on the line. You have to take some chances with that beer. And maybe it all starts with a dream. If you don't dream, you probably can't begin to dare. As a company, we are always so much better off when we do things that start with a dream."

Jack and a group of colleagues from shoe giants Nike and rival Adidas used that very formula to create Rogue. They were rebels by nature, according to Brett. "As the story goes, somebody walked by them in the lunch room and said, 'Now there's a bunch of rogues if ever I saw some.' He kind of meant it as an insult, but they remembered that and kind of liked it." "We are a bunch of rogues," they agreed. So when the rebellious bunch decided to launch a brewery, they had the perfect brand.

The elder Joyce ended up leaving Nike in 1988 and went to work on his tiny craft-beer business at the brewery's birthplace in downtown Ashland, Oregon. "We opened in '88 and made the classic mistakes," remembers Brett. "You couldn't put it in a worse place. We were totally landlocked and at basement level. They had nowhere to grow."

Despite or perhaps because of those challenges, the partners opened another location in sleepy little Newport in 1989. "Based on consumer feedback, they kind of intuitively knew that the timing was right," recalls Brett. "Remember, there was really no craft-beer industry in 1989, yet they doubled down and opened a second brewery." You have to have balls to do that—maybe even be a bit of a "rogue" running through your veins.

The craft-brewing business steadily grew and so did the brand's admirers, to the point where the marketing-minded Jack and his team dreamt up another great idea: a nation of beer-guzzling fanatics. "It started as the IAR—the International Association of Rogues," points out Brett. "It was a card that we issued at our pubs. It gave you a discount on merchandise and a discount on your pints of beer, and it was kind of a fun thing that people liked."

In 1998, the IAR morphed into something a little catchier that appealed to its feisty fans. "The Rogue Nation was born as a way for all of our hardcore fans to be part of our movement, our mission, our brand, our fun and our humor," he shares. "It was just a way to get together and enjoy each other.

"We never envisioned it was going to be so big. We have a quarter of a million people in the Rogue Nation. We would have been happy if we had gotten a thousand, probably. But if you have fun with stuff, you never know how you're going to end up."

It's a formula that has worked for the Joyces for decades, and I wonder if it is sustainable forever. "How do you remain true to your name and continue to be rogue with hundreds of other craft brewers in an industry inventing new beers daily?" I interrupt.

"Frankly, I love the creativity," he says. "So if other craft brewers are doing out-there stuff, I applaud that. That is part of the fun of the job— the creativity. Every brewer has to make their own decision for what they want to do. There is never going to be a point where people run out of ideas. You can always find another fun idea."

Like Rogue's Beard Beer, which boldly goes where no beer has gone before—at least that I know of. "We were trying to get an airborne yeast from our farms or the brewery," explains Brett when I ask him about the quirky project. "There was not much we could find just floating around. On a lark, we just took some trimmings off of John's beard (John Maier, Rogue's longtime brewmaster) and that was the only yeast we got to work. People ask, 'Well, what does it taste like?' and I always say, 'Well it doesn't taste like beard.' You just never know how or where the creativity is going to come from."

Joyce orders a taster to the table. I'm a bit squeamish. Apparently John has been growing the same beard since 1978, but I doubt that I would feel any more comfortable if the yeast was harvested from his five o'clock shadow. Some brewers I've met refer to yeast as "critters" and this only acts to heighten my trepidation. But Beard Beer turns out to be good, just like everything else I have tasted at Rogue. This Belgian-style ale has a ripe citrusy flavor. I wonder if the hazy orange color of this sweetish, saison-like beer has me imagining orange peel, pear, and other orchard fruit, or whether I'm actually detecting those flavors. Regardless, the wild yeast is certainly doing its job.

Rogue Farms in Oregon's Willamette Valley (near Independence) provides more-conventional natural ingredients for this brewer's beers that won't mess with my mind. "We grow our own hazelnuts, honey, pumpkins, marionberries, and jalapeños," notes Joyce. I am happy to switch my focus from yeast to anything else. The Hazelnut Brown Nectar has always been a favorite of mine. It's an earthy American brown ale with a light hazelnut aroma. Among the fourteen ingredients are Rogue Farms' "Dare" and "Risk" malts. Rogue's own "Revolution" and "Independent" hops are bit players in this production. The homegrown hazelnuts and local malts take center stage in an award-winning beer that is comforting, whether it's the hottest summer afternoon or the coldest winter evening. An argument could be made that this seductive brown might even find partners at brunch, pairing with a few slices of sourdough french toast and a salty helping of crisp local bacon. I store it to memory, and we move on.

Farm-to-table is a big deal in Oregon, and that concept takes on new meaning at Rogue Farms' 1,200-acre spread. Row after row of hops, fifty-two acres in all, climb up to eighteen feet on more than 78,000 coirs (braided coconut husk, used to train hops). Most of the brewery's hops, the Revolution and Independent included, come from fields that surround the rural taphouse/shack and gift shop. When autumn rolls around, and it's finally time for harvesting and brewing fresh hop beer, the humulone- and lupulone-laden cones are shipped seventy-seven miles west to the coast, where they are transformed into a delicious liquid form.

It's appropriate that Brett and I close our visit on a bittersweet note. Truth be told, I could listen to his stories all day, but he has to get back to the work at hand. The bartender pours me samples of Rogue's 4 Hop, 6 Hop, and 8 Hop IPAS. "This has four hop varieties in it, and it's 4.4% alcohol," points out Joyce. "The 6 Hop uses six varieties and is 6.6% alcohol, and the 8 Hop is, of course, 8.8%. These are all brothers." We start with the least complex of the siblings, the quaffable 4 Hop. "We were excited to have something lower on the ABV scale. Sometimes the lower alcohol beers have less flavor. We put a big hop nose on this. You could drink three or four of them pretty easily." When we finally find our way to the 8 Hop, I'm surprised. It tastes slightly sweet. "That's because with the higher ABV, you have to have more malt background in there," explains my host. Indeed, there are six malts blended in with the Rogue Farms Liberty, Newport, Revolution, Independent, Freedom, Rebel, Yaquina, and Alluvial hops, balancing out the 80 IBUS. This is a lesson that you cannot rely on IBUS alone to express the bitterness of a beer if that is what you are searching for . . . or avoiding.

"Beer is so versatile," continues Joyce. "There is the old adage, 'Wine is complicated. Beer is complex.'" There is so much going on with beer— the diversity of styles, the hop and malt and carbonation kind of change your palate. You can cook with it, you can grill with it, you can marinate with it, and you can put it with your ice cream, so there is so much you can do with beer!"

Sometimes that is as simple as finding something irresistible to eat with it. Joyce says when it comes to his own favorites, he is definitely old school. "For me, a wood-fired pizza and a great IPA—and forget about it! Pizza and beer is nothing new, but a great IPA and a pizza with pepperoni, prosciutto, and arugula, and that's it for me. Just take me away now!" He adds that he drinks according to his mood or the occasion. "It just kind of depends on the time and place. That's the great thing about beer: there is no wrong answer. However you feel, you can drink to that!"

"Is this better than being in the shoe business?" I ask, already knowing the answer, as I finish the last remnants of the fragrant 8 Hop that is so fresh that it actually makes me believe you can taste the color green.

"Absolutely," he laughs. "You can't drink a shoe." Apparently, the ancient Greek goddess of victory doesn't stand a chance when her foe is the Sumerian goddess of beer.

Brett Unfiltered
Craft Beer's Potential in America

"I still think we are in the third or fourth inning," Joyce says of the potential market for craft beer in America. "The whole country doesn't look like Oregon. There are parts of the country where craft beer still has small market share. Oregon is an outlier. Oregon is an example of where the future is going to be. It's going to take time for every state to get to where we are as a craft-beer state, but I think it's just a matter of time. There is nothing but opportunity. I can't wait to see what it looks like in five or ten more years."

Brewer Jamie Floyd with the NSP rocket that took NINKASI's yeast into space and back to earth (hanging in the background)

CHAPTER 17

TAKING CRAFT BEER TO NEW HEIGHTS

Ninkasi Brewing—Eugene, OR

EUGENE, OREGON IS FORTY-FIVE MILES from my writing den in Corvallis, but it might as well be on another planet. It's home to the University of Oregon, which regularly churns out many of the creative thinkers that help give the state's second-largest city its innovative edge. Nearly every experience I've had in Eugene has been a food and beverage odyssey of some sort, so why should today be any different? I'm orbiting downtown, looking for my landing spot for the afternoon, Ninkasi Brewing. Once there, my mission is to meet with co-founder and out-of-this-world craft brewer Jamie Floyd.

Having touched down in the brewery parking lot, I make my way into an expansive lobby that includes rock-climbing handholds running up one wall. Directly opposite, a red-nosed rocket hangs high above the twelve taps of a contemporary metallic bar that will serve as the launch pad for this afternoon's interview.

Floyd bounds down the stairs from the loft above to greet me. Even though he has been at this for a while and had to bear the growing pains associated with starting a brewery, he has weathered it well. I can spot a few lines on the boyish face under the Ninkasi ball cap, but that's just a sign of hard-earned wisdom. Floyd asks me if I need a beer to relax and loosen up my vocal cords for the interview. I accept his gracious offer, and he pours me a pint of his popular Helles Belles. The 5.3% ABV Munich-style lager, made with four malts and three varieties of Hallertauer hops, has that classic bready flavor that makes it such a great comfort beer.

When we head back upstairs and settle in at a conference table, refreshments in hand, I ask Floyd how on earth he ended up launching a brewery. As it turns out, he was a Northern California, Bay Area kid who grew up surfing and dreamed about cruising around the solar system. "I convinced myself at a young age that I was going to be an astronaut," he says. "Then things changed."

Floyd moved to Eugene and enrolled at the University of Oregon. When he wasn't busy studying, he spent the scant spare time he had on a new hobby: hombrewing. Brewing was a natural fit for the ever-curious student, since he had been interested in the process and the science behind fermentation from an early age. "I started fermenting things at fifteen," he confesses.

When he wasn't experimenting with beer recipes, he was immersed in school, where he majored in Sociology and double-minored in Environmental Studies and Women's Studies. "Since beer brings people together is social settings, maybe getting a degree in Sociology is a good way to prepare for a career in brewing," I suggest, trying hard to connect the dots.

"The original brewers are some of the first sociologists," Floyd kindly pitches in. "You have all these people living together who didn't speak the same language. The breweries were the hubs that were the social fabric— there to educate and nourish. Beer is important to humanity. When beer is doing its job is when it's comfortable in your hand and you're talking with the friends that are around you."

After graduation, the pseudo social scientist traveled a bit, then returned to Eugene and took a job as kitchen manager at Steelhead Brew Pub in 1994. After all, what better place than a pub to be a fly on the wall and observe people as they interact? Oh yeah, and he also continued to flirt with his growing passion for beer. "I worked there for about a year before I was offered a job as an assistant brewer," he recalls. "My general manager wouldn't let me quit my cooking job, so for about a year and a half, I had two full-time jobs. He probably liked my work ethic more than he liked my beer," he chuckles.

Lack of fanfare didn't cause Floyd's interest to waiver. In fact, he became obsessed. "When I first got into professional brewing, it clicked that I was meant to do this, and it's where I would put most of my energy for the future," he remembers. "I fell in love with everything from recipe development to historical perspectives in beer." Floyd immersed himself in the business of brewing for the next decade, honing his skills to the point that he began teaching it to others.

About that time he began to realize it was time to take his passion for the craft to new heights. "After eleven years at Steelhead, there wasn't much else for me to learn there," he notes. "I wasn't getting any younger." He finally worked up the courage to start his own brewery with a local acquaintance. "Nikos Ridge, my business partner, grew up in Eugene, but went to college in New York," he says. "He spent his summers working the stock exchange floor and got an economics degree with a math minor at NYU, so you can see where we'd fit together." While Ridge had no brewing experience, he brought to the table the business and financial acumen that Floyd lacked.

The aspiring craft beer entrepreneurs spent their spare hours looking for a good opportunity. Nearly a year later, one finally knocked. They found tanks, a mash tun, and most of the other equipment they needed to get started at a shuttered brewpub that had been sitting idle for five years. The family that owned the place was no longer interested in operating a brewery and decided to lease it to the partners. "We put that brewery completely back together and started brewing in June 2006," recalls Floyd.

They named their new venture Ninkasi, after the Sumerian goddess of fermentation. "I thought that beer is so overmasculine, it would be nice to bring some feminine energy in," he continues. The Ninkasi logo incorporates Floyd's favorite colors, light blue and black. "The initial design was based on an Egyptian Revival mirror," he points out. "I wanted something that looked modern but felt timeless." Maybe the logo's ornate, ancient style would win the eager-to-please goddess's favor as well. It sure couldn't hurt.

In fact, Ninkasi has combined good fortune with hard work to become one of the Northwest's beloved brands. Through a little luck and a lot of effort, the brewery has been successful to the point that it produces just under 100,000 barrels of beer per year.

Floyd has put his heart, mind, and back into making Ninkasi what it is today. He seems to be part artist, part scientist, part mystery. The enigmatic brewer strikes me as an old spirit, with thoughts and ideas running deeper than the Nile, or at least the nearby Willamette River. Perhaps he is the reincarnation of an ancient Sumerian astronomer. Maybe this restless soul has too many interests to be pinned down and classified.

Whatever the case, Floyd will always be a dreamer. The boy in the brewer never let go of his fascination with the final frontier. "On a personal level, I'm still super nerdy about space," he confesses. "Nikos is probably the much more quieted version of the space nerd."

Ninkasi's founders found a way to make all of the stars align and weave their common interest into the business. "We were offered the opportunity to be a sponsor of an amateur rocket launch into space," reports Floyd. "So we got invested in it. We could have just had our logo on the side of the rocket, but we decided that we wanted to be closer to the projects. We came up with the idea of defying all odds and getting yeast up into space and back and making beer with it."

So the brewery developed its very own Ninkasi Space Program (NSP). "You can see it right there," says Floyd, pointing through the open-office floor plan to the twenty-foot-long rocket that I spotted earlier. "At least the first 40 percent of that has been in space seven times," he explains, gesturing toward the tip. "The bottom portion was made at the metal shop that we have on site. We do some weird stuff here." No shit! I've seen similar exhibits in air museums, but never mounted to the ceiling of a brewery.

Like most space programs, NSP has had its ups and downs. The brewery's initial attempt at creating the world's first yeastronauts took place near Black Rock City, Nevada in July 2014. The launch site also happens to be in the immediate vicinity of Burning Man, the annual, anything-goes festival that heats up the already red-hot desert each summer. The yeast was carefully packed and refrigerated in the tightly sealed capsule. All systems were go. "Then a train came through, and we had to stop the countdown," reports Floyd. They tried again: ten, nine, eight, seven, when a new obstacle rolled up to the launch pad. "Some random hippies came by in a Jeep, and it took a few minutes to get them out," he sighs. I can imagine the roving free spirits now, barely visible through a cloud of reefer haze as they skid to a stop: "Dude . . . what is that? Can we climb on it?"

"It *is* the Burning Man area," Floyd reminds me, with a wry smile.

The two untimely delays threw the carefully planned mission's coordinates just far enough off kilter that when it did finally get off the ground, it was headed for trouble. But first, the rocket took Ninkasi's yeast to new heights, across the Karman line (sixty-two miles), where it spent six minutes in outer space. Topping out at seventy-three miles above sea level, "yeast altitude record" presumably secure, the space ship arced downward and began its short voyage back to Mother Earth. The only problem was that the ground crew couldn't locate their spacecraft and its fragile crew . . . for twenty-eight days! "We built a system that would keep the yeast alive for twelve hours," he informs me, shrugging his shoulders.

As it turns out, the capsule was baking on the desert floor about eight miles away from the launch pad and two miles outside the team's search perimeter. Fortunately, there were no burning men or a charred Jeep in the vicinity. Unfortunately, millions of innocent yeast cells lost their lives.

That hurts, so with a somewhat straight face, I manage to choke out, "What was the point of this?"

"Yeast has never been in space," Floyd vollies. "Let's be real. Nothing lives in space. Yeast didn't show up on the planet on the back of some asteroid. Not on the outside of it, certainly!" he contends, proving beyond a doubt that he is indeed a space nerd.

"That's the thing, I am close enough to the space program to know how hard it actually is," he continues. "The reality is the G-force leaving the planet, the infinite cold of space, radiation, all these things destroy yeast in a second. We had to develop a system that would keep it alive the whole way. Everybody else wants to know what we were trying to do with it, but we just wanted to get it back and brew with it. That's a pretty long way for the yeast to travel." Or humans, for that matter. The great majority of *us* have never been more than 45,000 feet above terra firma, let alone airborne microscopic fungus.

But Floyd doesn't give up easily. He also learns from mishaps. So in October 2014, NSP sent another batch of brewer's yeast heavenward from Spaceport America in New Mexico's Jornada del Muerto (near White Sands). On the second try, three strains of space-bound Saccharomyces road along with a payload of scientific equipment, reaching 77.3 miles in altitude before making their way back to the desert floor. There, the elated crew recovered six vials of healthy but famished yeast, ready to settle down and soak in nice warm tank full of wort. The happy critters were cold-transported back to Ninkasi's lab in Eugene, where they were propagated and tested before being used to ferment its first cosmically tasty batch of Ground Control.

"It's a barrel-aged imperial stout, with hazelnuts and cocoa nibs," shares Floyd. The dark-chocolate brown beer greets me with a whiff of cocoa. There are no signs of extraterrestrial life tagging along with the astroyeast. Just a nice star-anise-spiked imperial stout, with currents of bourbon, Oregon hazelnut, and coco nibs flowing under the creamy-brown micro-bubble head. My primary gustatory cortex (the part of your brain that perceives flavors) confirms that this beer is more than a clever gimmick. Although the well-traveled yeast fuel this high-powered 10% ABV stout, Ground Control doesn't need Houston or any other help to support its rich, boozy-smooth flavor.

Few people in the galaxy have a better grip on what excites our taste buds than Floyd. Over the years, he has become an expert at detecting desirable and undesirable flavors in beer. Back in the 1990s, prior to opening Ninkasi, Floyd joined the Oregon Brewer's Guild. "There were so many people starting breweries—they didn't have the experience, and the consumers didn't have the knowledge to tell them that the beer was bad," he explains. "There was an effort to work on quality standards for Oregon beer that attracted me. I was also engaged in sensory thought." Floyd became so immersed that he ultimately ended up being elected to the Board of Directors, then eventually president—the first who wasn't an owner of a brewery.

It's heady stuff, but the longtime expert preaches a little humility when experiencing or—taking it a step further—analyzing craft beer. "What you have to first do is separate your ego from the beer," he suggests. "We teach the sensory technique for evaluating beer. It is the neurological and biological study of the most efficient way to go about it. You take a look at the beer, and you examine it for its color, carbonation, clarity, head space. This is all sending messages to your brain about what it might be.

"The next thing that you're going to do is take a quick sniff, awakening your olfactory senses, which makes up about 80 to 85 percent of what you experience as aroma and flavor. Then you go back and you do small sniffs and one long sniff."

Now that your sense of smell is wide awake, Floyd suggests taking a taste, followed by another sip. "Let it sit on your taste buds for a few seconds, and then swallow it." He explains that the process activates the trigeminal topiary expression (the trigeminal nerve enables us to recognize hot, cold, creamy, bubbly, and other mouthfeel sensations before we swallow), followed by the gustation phase, where we experience sweet, sour, bitter, umami, and fat flavors.

"The final part is what we call retronasal, which sounds super fancy, but what you're basically doing is exhaling through your olfactory system. I call that fine tuning. All of those things create the experience of flavor."

Floyd recommends delving into the craft-beer scene with a sense of adventure. "You can't really develop a good understanding of flavor if you don't experience the negative sides of it too," he argues. "If you only drink Bud Light your whole life, that's what you're going to get! If you're not experiencing outside of those parameters, you don't know what else there is to have. You have to temper what you love with your curiosity. This is where people find new things. You have to explore!"

"There are over two hundred-plus hops to explore, and those numbers are climbing," I blurt out. "How do you even begin to dissect the flavors? Can anybody really be accurate?"

Apparently so. "I've been a part of many harvests," replies Floyd. "I get to examine and smell hops in raw form. My understanding of these hops is at a different level. Not many people read hop-oil reports, but you can start to see patterns. I've got some Type A tendencies, so my mind organizes and develops these things. There are hops that I haven't had a ton of experience with, but I've been able to see most hops at one time or another. We've done collaborations with other breweries, so I'm not having to learn two hundred hops."

Floyd adds that it's a field that is evolving at a rapid pace. It can be a challenge just keeping up with the latest developments. "All the raw ingredients change over time," he points out. "That could also have a lot to do with the water chemistry and the malts and yeast that they're using with it. The neat thing about beer is that when you adjust a part of it, you see a whole different side of it. There's so many variances. In the early part, you're throwing stuff in to see what happens. On the other side, as you get further into it, you're relating that information to new information."

The hop talk hypnotizes me and forces my hand to reach for a glass of Total Domination on the table top. "It's the very first beer we brewed," he says, as we pause for a taste. "It's still the number-one-selling IPA in Oregon."

I'm expecting a palate dominator, but it's pretty smooth for a beer measuring in at 81 IBUS. "It leaves a nice bitter taste on the palate that sticks around for a few seconds, then fades to the background; however, it's not overbearing or overly acidic," I observe. The unmistakably citrusy 6.7% ABV beer is brewed with Summit, Amarillo, and Crystal hops.

"I love hop flavor and aroma, and I like bitterness perception, but this beer is indicative of a lot of the beer styles I made early on in the '90s," says Floyd. "There's no dextrose or hop extracts in this beer—just the four ingredients (malt, yeast, hops, and water). A lot of the IPAs that developed later on use the dextrose and stuff that really sharpen the flavors and change the experience. We use an English-style yeast that promotes ester production that carries a lot of flavor between hop flavor and malt flavor. You have a continuous flavor that is balanced. It's citrus, floral, some stone fruit."

Fine-tuning beer to create the perfect balance in a production run is one thing, but replicating flavors over a longer span can be nearly impossible, according to Floyd. "Some breweries make their IPAS with a target flavor that they try to meet all the time," he says. "That will be an interesting dynamic to watch, as time goes on. I think that generation has passed where they want a beer to be exactly as they remember it. It's just like music: everything has already been played, yet everything is new."

As I finish off the last of my beer and listen to this modern-day philosopher's insights on everything from early human society to tomorrow's space-faring beer consumer, I glance over his shoulder at the pride of the Ninkasi Space Program hanging in the background. "It's hard to say what's going to be important to people in the future, but I think there's a lot that could happen that could change all that," he hypothesizes. "We went from Prohibition to having a bloom of breweries to having twenty in the '80s, and now we're back to 6,000 breweries. Will people get sick of it all and just want to drink lager again? Probably not. People will go through processes where they want the kitchen sink in every beer because it's new and cool. Then there are people who just want to drink beer. The more people think about beer, the more that they have an expectation around the beer. Human curiosity around that kind of stuff has just been unleashed. In a way, it was hamstrung for half a century."

As we make our way out into the night, I think that the future looks as bright as a full moon for Ninkasi. "It's a big gamble that worked," Floyd says of the brewery. Those who aim high sometimes miss the mark (and lose yeast in the process). But those who never try will never have the pleasure of watching a fellow beer geek's face light up as he drinks the last precious drops of his ingeniously conceived stellar stout.

Jamie Unfiltered
Opening Up to Creativity, While Respecting Tradition
Floyd sometimes gravitates toward the staunchly old-fashioned stuff when it comes to beer recipes. "The German part of me loves Reinheitsgebot (the German beer purity law regulating ingredients), but 12 percent isn't that strong," he quips of his Germanic heritage. "When I make Helles, I make Helles (a traditional German pale lager). I wouldn't make a banana

Helles. I try to be respectful of other people's cultures. It's hard to make lagers taste like other things and make them taste well."

Yet, as happens with flavors in barrel-aged beers, time matures brewers' minds, often adding new twists to their repertoires. Although Floyd still sticks to tradition in some classic styles, he has become much more relaxed and open in his approach. He is perfectionist when it comes to what kinds of hops he includes in his ales, but is frequently willing to experiment. "We have always been known as a hoppy brewery, and that is not going away," he says. To widen its horizons, Ninkasi recently hired Dr. Daniel Sharp, a leading expert in all things Humulus Lupulus (the field of hops science).

"But I'm not stuck in that world," insists Floyd, true to form. "Some of the styles that we produce now weren't even around twelve years ago. We are in the innovative cycle, and our brewers are going to keep experimenting with and making other beers." That is promising news for the brewery's more adventurous fans. Who knows what exotic, alien flavors might flow from the Ninkasi beer tap of tomorrow?

CHAPTER 18

CHILLING OUT AT AN AUSSIE'S BEER OASIS

Walkabout Brewing—Medford, OR

THERE ARE MANY CHARACTERS in Craft Beer Country, but none more memorable than Ross Litton, Founder of Walkabout Brewing. It took months for us to coordinate calendars for a visit to his little southern Oregon Brewery, and it turned out to be worth the wait. True to the brewery's name, Ross is a bit of an adventurer, seemingly walking about in another time zone every time I'm passing through Jackson County.

Litton is about as far from his home in Western Australia as one could get. His wasn't a little jaunt into the Outback, the arid Australian interior, to wind down from another busy week at work. In 1990, Litton's own walkabout took him 9,187 miles to Medford, Oregon. He has called the area home ever since.

Ross remembers how he cut his teeth in the craft-beer industry working for Jack Joyce, the former Nike exec who cofounded Rogue Ales. "Jack was a total character because he used to take me around and say, 'This is Ross from England, one of our brewers,'" recalls Litton. "And I'd go, 'No, I'm not. I'm fucking from Australia!' And he goes, 'Ross, Ross, don't say anything. English brewer sounds much better than any Australian brewer. They don't know if you're from England or Australia.' I'd go, 'Yeah, but fuck you! I'm from Australia.'"

Like many in the industry, Litton learned from his experience working at someone else's brewery, turning the knowledge he picked up at Rogue into his own opportunity. By 1997, the ornery Aussie was brewing out of his own garage for local taverns and his own consumption with an ever-growing cadre of friends.

On the memorably warm winter day that I finally catch him at home in Medford, we find most of the original equipment still in place, albeit a little dusty. Ross generously shares from his personal stash of ale as he takes me on a brief tour of the remnants of his mothballed start-up. Although he still stores enough beer at the modest ranch-style house to satisfy a doomsday prepper, demand for his ales started to exceed what the meager operation could supply, so the restless Aussie stepped up his game and moved the microbrewery out of the neighborhood.

These days, Ross and son Cameron operate their little craft-beer oasis about fifteen minutes away in an industrial section of Medford, across the street from a—gasp!—Budweiser distributor that could probably fit the entire Walkabout Brewery in its cooler. But this isn't a pissing contest between the David and Goliath of beer. In fact, the Littons claim to be on such good terms with the distributor that they borrow a forklift from time to time. Relations are friendly enough that Walkabout even features a Budweiser tap in its lineup. "It's always good to get along with your neighbor," smiles Ross.

Folks come from far, wide, and across the street to hang out and drink well-made ales in the brewery's shady patio area and fenced-in backyard. Visitors park on picnic benches and wander the well-manicured lawn, where rainbirds like me can escape to enjoy a drizzle-free afternoon in February, a rarity back home in Benton County.

Walkabout is worth the short detour west from the I-5 corridor, the western artery that runs into the California border about sixty miles south. Cameron poured me a nice cold flight of craft beers, and we sat on the patio and joked with Ross. Our casual conversation was fueled by the brewery's noteworthy Worker's Pale Ale and my favorite in the tap lineup: Jabberwocky, an English strong ale checking in at a healthy (depending on how you look at it) 7.0% ABV. Asked why he named it Jabberwocky,

Ross says with a wry grin, "Because if you drink too much of it, you start to jabber." Beer Advocate rates the ale a solid 82 (the last time I checked), but the more I drink, the higher my own taste buds score it. Down under the bubbly head, this bittersweet, copper-colored ale, loaded with Cascade, Perle, Willamette, and Chinook hops, pleases the palate, beckoning you back for another satisfying taste.

Pressed for his own favorite, Ross settles on Worker's Pale Ale. "I kind of look at it as just a bigger session beer," he shares. "Worker's Pale Ale was a beer I brewed way back before I had a brewery. One of my friends said when I start a brewery someday, I should call it Worker Man because that's what everyone likes to drink after work. I explained to him there's a lot of women that like to drink beer after work as well, so we've got to call it Worker's."

Paying attention to details like that have certainly helped business. It doesn't hurt that road warrior Ross is always out making new friends. "That's really why we're successful—it's him going around and being an actual person that people are associating with beer," states Cameron. "He still goes out and buys a beer for people. They love that." I'm pretty sure that, like me, they love the banter, too.

"He's a likable guy," I observe, to which modest Ross replies, "Oh, don't give me that!" But the salty brewer wouldn't be as much fun to chill out with if he were an arrogant old bastard who wore that considerable Aussie charm on a shirt sleeve.

The Littons are the kind of people that you root for in the industry. You yearn to see their beers win their way into patron-flooded taprooms and neighbors' refrigerators. Ross found a way to build his successful business from the garage floor up, so there is no reason to think that the father/son team won't continue to succeed, despite mounting competition.

"When I go to another region, I want to drink their beers or what they make there," shares Ross. "We're in a boutique-kind of industry, and I consider ourselves a boutique brewery. Eighty-five percent of our sales are in Jackson County. We're out there in other places like Portland, but our sales aren't there." So for the time being, he and Cameron are perfectly content to sell the majority of their artisan-made ales in and around the valleys of Southern Oregon.

If there is a fork in the road ahead, Ross will weigh the options and decide the best way forward, just as he always has. "I was brewing at the house for fourteen years, and I didn't plan to leave," he points out. Then demand outgrew the capacity of his little homebrewing operation.

Cameron wasn't a key cog in the business back then, but he remembers realizing that his dad's beer had really made it to the big time. "I'm like, oh my God, here's a beer from our garage at the store!" he laughs. "It was very cool!" That's the nature of a Walkabout. You can never be sure what you are going to discover around the next bend, and that makes life just a bit more exciting.

Ross Unfiltered

A Dangerous Proposition

Ross was pretty much unfiltered throughout our visit, so pulling out all of the stops is a dangerous proposition. When he invites me over to his house for a beer in the back yard, it turns into yet another adventure. We play fetch with his dog Ollie between drinking our pints of Red Back IPA. Being the free spirit he is, Ross offers me a bag of hops' home-grown plant-family cousin. "Would you like a bag for the road?" he generously offers.

"Can I homebrew with this stuff?" I mess with him. That draws an impish smile.

When that hazy conversation clears, we bring the focus back to the copper-colored substance in our sixteen-ounce glasses. "Red Back is my English-style ale," he says. Not likely to be confused with a lawnmower beer, Red Back is a 7.4% ABV, 64 IBU afternoon thirst quencher. "There are a lot of IPAs out there, so it's going to go back to a seasonal kind of a thing," notes my host. "We're going to just do it around Halloween time . . . or whenever." This is how Ross rolls, ever adjusting his plans. After all, life is supposed to be an enjoyable journey, not a hassle, and this brewer is truly living the dream.

Beer pairs with nearly every food imaginable, but
maybe none better than a good old fashioned burger,
like this juicy rendition with a MCMENAMINS' IPA.
Photo credit: Kat Nyberg, McMenamins

The search for the best breweries from the South Pacific to the Pacific Coast began in Maui, Hawaii

The father-son team of Ross and Cameron Litton walk the brewery floor at WALKABOUT BREWING in Medford, Oregon

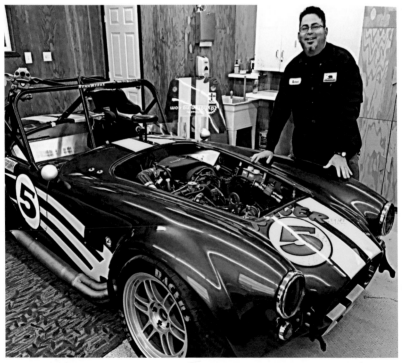

Ricardo Norgrove, brewer, race car driver, and COO at BEAR REPUBLIC BREWING (Healdsburg, California), maker of Racer 5 IPA and other ales, with his Factory 5 Cobra

Adam Robbings (right) with the author in the tasting room at REUBEN'S BREWS in Seattle, Washington

Brett Joyce, President of ROGUE ALES AND SPIRITS, outside the company's brewery in Newport, Oregon

Ben Edmunds, Head Brewmaster at BREAKSIDE, talks about the brewery's beers during a tasting session at the company's Milwaukie, Oregon facility

BIG DOG'S Brewmaster David Pascual pours a glass of his 9.5% ABV, date-infused Belgian Quad in the Las Vegas brew house

Hanging out with hop-loving brewer Steve Luke, founder of CLOUDBURST BREWING, just down the street from the Pike Place Market in Seattle, Washington. Photo credit: Catchlight Photography

CHUCKANUT BREWERY owners Will and Mari Kemper taste the fruits of their labor at the brewery's Bellingham, Washington location. The couple also operates the South Nut brewery and tap room in nearby Burlington. Photo credit: Chuckanut

Craft beer hounds Joby, Ryker, and Tallula (left to right) explore a hop farm. Photo courtesy of Alise Long, Jeff VanDomelen, and Catchlight Photography

Drinking Coal Porter with brewer Ian Croxall (background) at SANTIAM BREWING in Salem, Oregon. Photo credit: Catchlight Photography

21ST AMENDMENT founders Shaun O'Sullivan (left) and Nico Freccia (right) take a break at the San Leandro, California brewery. Photo courtesy of 21st Amendment

Inside the brewery and event hall at FACTION BREWING in Alameda, California

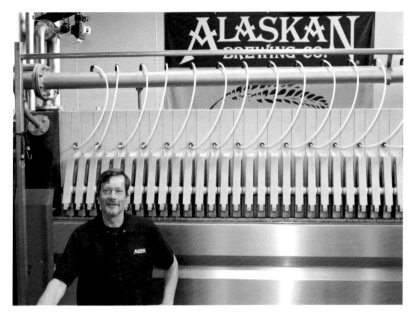

Geoff Larson, Co-founder of ALASKAN BREWING COMPANY, with his mash filter press that helps turn spent grain into fuel. Photo credit: Catchlight Photography

Gary Fish, founder of DESCHUTES BREWERY, displays one of his IPA's primary ingredients at the company's brewpub in Bend, Oregon

In the tasting room with Barkley the Beer (part bear, part deer) at ANDERSON VALLEY BREWING COMPANY in Boonville, California

Klint and Beth Sheets, Owner-operators of 3 SHEETS BREWERY, in their Oktoberfest gear at the Albany, Oregon taproom. Photo credit: Catchlight Photography

The author with PFRIEM FAMILY BREWERS founder Josh Pfriem (right) in the Hood River, Oregon brewery's barrel room

Lance Chavez, Head Brewer at BOISE BREWING, tests the gravity of its popular Hip Check IPA

Matt Brynildson (aka Merlin) testing his Nitro Merlin Milk Stout in the taproom at FIRESTONE WALKER BREWING in Paso Robles, California

Conducting a beer tasting exercise with Paul Wright, owner of ISLAND BREWING COMPANY in Carpinteria, California

The taster tray of my dreams and a couch to crash on afterward at PROPOLIS BREWING in Port Townsend, Washington. Photo credit: Propolis

KARL STRAUSS BREWING Mosaic IPA. Photo courtesy of Karl Strauss Brewing Company

Relaxing with PUBLIC COAST's '67 Blonde Ale, winner of a World Beer Cup gold, overlooking Haystack Rock in Cannon Beach, Oregon

Patrick Rue, Founder of THE BRUERY (Placentia, California), tastes a barrel-aged Strong Ale. Photo courtesy of The Bruery®

Tomme Arthur, Owner of THE LOST ABBEY in San Marcos, California, sampling hops. Photo credit: The Lost Abbey

BALE BREAKER BREWING founders (left to right) Kevin Quinn, Meghann Quinn, and Kevin Smith at the Yakima brewery in the heart of hops country. Photo credit: Catchlight Photography

Jamie Floyd, co-owner of NINKASI BREWING, displays his love for hops. Photo credit: Catchlight Photography

Peter Zien, CEO at ALESMITH, on the brewery floor in San Diego, California

Piper Corbett, who helped open PROPOLIS in 2012, destems Washington-grown cherries that are brewed into Cherry Damaina—a fruit beer. Photo credit: Propolis

Newlyweds JJ and Amy Sellner enjoy a few pints of craft beer at the STONE BREWING WORLD BISTRO AND GARDENS in Escondido, California

Pairing food and a selection of ales at GREAT NOTION BREWING in Portland

Robert Horner, who forages for some of his beers' ingredients in local forests, enjoys a glass of PROPOLIS's Spruce, a 7.5% ABV Golden Saison. Photo credit: Propolis

STRANGE FELLOWS founder, brewer, and Belgian-style beers fan Iain Hill makes exquisite sours and other beer styles in the East Vancouver, B.C. brewery. Photo credit: Olga Zwart

The patio at ANDERSON VALLEY BREWING in Boonville, California, is great for soaking up the sun and the brewery's Goses and other fine beers. Photo credit: Anderson Valley Brewing

CHAPTER 19

BAHL HORNIN WITH A BRIGHTLIGHTER

Anderson Valley Brewing—Boonville, CA

THE FIRST TIME THAT I HEARD ABOUT the Anderson Valley Brewing Company was on an early afternoon stroll along sparkling Glass Beach in Fort Bragg, California. Once a dumping ground for bottles and other city debris, the relentless surf had tumbled broken beer and soda bottles into a carpet of glistening gems.

Ted and Kim, a couple up from San Francisco for the weekend beach-combing the shiny shoreline, were carrying bottles of Anderson Valley's Barney Flats Oatmeal Stout. Curious, I introduced myself and asked about the bear with antlers emblazoned on Ted's black t-shirt. "It's a great brewery!" he enthused, ignoring the gist of the question.

When I mentioned that a buddy and I were headed to Santa Rosa-based Russian River Brewing to sample the brewery's renowned Pliny the Younger Triple IPA, Ted volunteered: "Anderson Valley is right on your way, in a town called Booneville. If you're headed that direction, you *have* to stop and try their beers!" Kim added that the locals there speak something called Boontling.

"Okay then, twist my arm," I replied, intrigued and wondering whether I might need an interpreter.

Before we parted, Ted sent me on my way with one of his beloved brown bottles filled with deliciousness. Barney Flats Oatmeal Stout is a creamy, ebony treat, with hints of espresso and a whiff of chocolate, like something hand-brewed by a beer barista, if there were such an artisan. It's not hard to imagine enjoying this malty-mellow, 20-IBU beer with a picnic basket of sliced deli meats, Gouda, sea salt chips, and oatmeal cookies.

My stomach suddenly rumbled, reminding me that it was getting late. So I thanked my new friends for the tip and kind gift, plugged a new destination into my smart phone, and we hauled ass down the pine-lined country roads to allow enough time for a quick stop at the brewery.

Lady luck had intervened yet again—I've learned to listen carefully when she whispers. The half-hour detour to Booneville was rewarded with an easy-on-the-taste-buds Boont Amber, a 5.8% ABV ale spiced with Columbus, Bravo, Northern Brewer, and Mt. Hood hops. The sessionable herbal amber checks in lean on the bitter scale, at 16 IBUs. Boont Amber is perfectly suited to its locale, a little on the fruity side, but with a nice, crisp, slightly sour apple finish that beckons you back for more. I was all too happy to oblige.

Never one to break a vow, I'm back in town several months later on a mission rather than a serendipitous whim. I have an appointment to visit Fal Allen, Anderson Valley's Brewmaster extraordinaire. Allen has concocted his creative beers in amazing places around the world, but probably none so original as Boonville, California. That is saying a lot for a guy who grew up on the lava-licked Big Island of Hawaii, migrated east to start his craft beer career in Seattle, and opened a few breweries in Singapore before ending up *back* at the Anderson Valley Brewery Company (yes, this was Allen's second stint in Booneville, but more about that a bit later). This quirky hamlet of roughly 1,000 people is tucked into Mendocino County's oaky hills, 115 miles due north of San Francisco. Based on looks alone, the place is special, but what makes it truly unique is that, as Kim had hinted months earlier, it has its very own folk language.

According to Wikipedia, "Boontling" was invented in the late 19th century and had quite a following at the turn of the 20th century. The jargon's roots drew from far and wide, from Scottish Gaelic and Irish to

Pomoan and Spanish, all rumored to contribute a little something to its roughly 1,000-word vocabulary (there is a comprehensive dictionary for you language lovers). For example, *Walter* translates to "telephone," allegedly named after the first man in town to own one. To keep things *really* local, Anderson Valley Brewing's bottles are labeled "Bahl Hornin," which means "It's good drinkin'" in Boontling. I'll learn to decode a few more choice phrases in this colorful language as my stay in Boonville progresses, but it's finally time to settle down with Allen for what locals call a *harpin' tidrick*, or a lengthy discussion.

I take a seat in Fal's office, just upstairs from the brew house. He looks young for his fifty-six years, reddish-brown hair and a face lit up by a puckish smile that makes you immediately want to drain several pints with him. Allen's black vest partly covers a dark grey striped shirt, rolled up to the elbows. He has obviously been hard at work. Allen kicks back behind his desk, and I notice that his computer monitor sits atop an OSHA safety manual. I already like this guy, and we've only known each other for five minutes.

"How did you end up at this place out in the middle of nowhere?" I start, giving him a rough time. As it turns out, after stints with iconic brewers Red Hook and Pike Place Brewing, Allen tried to launch his own brewery in Seattle. That didn't pan out, so he decided it was time for a change of scenery.

"In 2000, I packed up my car and my girlfriend, and we drove south and went to the breweries I knew," he remembers. "I stopped at a couple in Oregon and a few in California, and this was one of them. You know how beautiful it is here," he continues, looking right through me and the brewery walls to the natural beauty just outside. "It's quite easy to fall in love with this valley—oaks on one side and redwoods on the other. It's just stunning!"

The brewery has been around for about twenty-nine years, according to Allen. "In the beginning, they sold all their beer down the street, and it made sense—it was such a novelty," he points out. "There were only a handful of craft brewers back then, most on the east coast or west coast and hardly anything in the middle. If craft beer was what people wanted, then this was a real opportunity to pick up some craft beer not too far from home. The brewery became well known for making high-quality beers.

Allen knew the owner of the brewery, and as fate would have it, that contact led to his next gig. "We decided that it would be a good idea for me to come work for him," he recalls. "I started as a General Manager and did that for five years." Those turned out to be five tumultuous years wearing too many hats. As time wore on, the brewing guru and the original owner rarely saw eye to eye. When the relationship eventually soured, the restless brewer decided that it was time for a new adventure.

Little did he know what how much the next journey would influence and change him. "In 2005, a few months after I quit, a headhunter called me from Singapore and asked if I wanted to open a brewery there," recalls Allen. "I said, 'Absolutely not!' But it was a great opportunity, and I couldn't pass it up, so I went to work for Asia Pacific Brewing, which had about thirty regional big breweries throughout Asia. They wanted to get into craft-brewing in Singapore and be one of the first. There were already two there at the time. The job was to design a brewery, oversee its installation, design the recipes, brew the beer, and be the front man. I did that for about five years. I traveled all over Southeast Asia and got to work in Vietnam, India, and Indonesia, but I was based in Singapore.

"At some point, as an ex-pat, you have to make a decision to be an ex-pat for the rest of your life or go back home. After five years abroad, I decided it was a good idea to go back home to my family and friends, and I reluctantly gave my notice there."

Timing is everything. The new owner of Anderson Valley heard through the "hopvine" that Allen was coming back to the US and phoned him before someone else could snatch him up. "He said that he bought a brewery and was looking for a brewmaster," relays Allen. "I came to work for him here in 2010, and I've been here ever since. I didn't want to be the General Manager or oversee sales, and he was quite happy with that because that's what he does."

That leaves the Masterbrewer time to pursue his never-ending passion: experimenting with and perfecting his beer recipes. He loves the alchemy of brewing, and it's one part of the business that continues to keep him engaged. "One of the things that keeps it interesting for me is that it's so multi-dimensional—art and science, the chemistry, the physics," observes Allen. "The better you are at the science part, the better you are at understanding what's going on in the brewing process and controlling that and making a good product." He is a bit of a renaissance man, relentlessly exploring new possibilities.

True beer gurus absorb much more than the impressions of styles that tantalize their palates and olfactory receptors. Allen's time in Asia was particularly enlightening. "The woman in charge wanted to create beer that was a fusion between European brewing and Asian cooking," he recalls. "The first year, we had to build the brewery and design the equipment. While it was being built, I learned as much as I could about Asian cooking traditions. I toured the 'wet markets,' talked to suppliers, and talked to chefs who were there sourcing supplies. When it came time to brew, I fused European brewing and Asian cooking together, and it forced me to really think outside my comfort zone. I learned a lot of unusual ingredients, and it got me to think about beer differently."

He was forced to figure out how those odd additives would work while creating something that was still drinkable, maybe even desirable. "In Singapore, we made unusual beers," he shares. "We even made a beer with durian. It's this big football-shaped spiky fruit. The spikes are so hard that a few people die every year when they're struck on the head with durian falling from trees. It is a dangerous fruit. You have to wear gloves to open them. If you do it with bare hands, you'll bleed. Once you open it, the fruit inside is incredibly pungent. It's kind of a cross between bleu cheese, onions, and rotting fruit. Most Caucasians don't like it." Durian's smell is so strong that the fruit has been banned from Singapore mass transit and almost all the hotels.

Even in Singapore, it's a love/hate thing, according to Allen. "I got off work one day, got into a taxi, and as we were driving, started thinking, 'I can smell durian.' I said to the taxi driver, 'Uncle, did your previous passenger have durian?' He's like, 'No, never. I never allow it here.' We're riding along, and I'm thinking, 'Okay, but I smell it.' We're going down the freeway and about 100 yards ahead of us is a truck with durian in it. It is so pungent that in an air-conditioned taxi with the windows rolled up, on the freeway, I could still smell it!"

But Singapore is a very foodie kind of place, according to Allen. "Eating is the national pastime, and there is a lot of discussion about food," he continues. "Durian—known as the king of fruits—occupies a special place in the hearts of most Singaporeans." So much so that the brewery was asked to brew a durian beer for a local bar owner's birthday. "He said he loved durian and wanted a special beer for his birthday, and well, you can't really argue with what people like," observes Allen. "We made it. He loved it, I loved it. But most people hated it," he laughs. "I will say that it was a bit rich, and I could only drink three or four pints before I had to move on to another beer style."

Although Allen decided durian probably wouldn't be a fan favorite in the United States, he has managed to bring back the more open-minded thinking that he developed in Asia. That proved very valuable as the craft beer revolution began to win over the masses. "When I came back here in 2010, things were just beginning to take off again. The last five to six years have grown tremendously, and if I hadn't had that experience in Asia, Anderson Valley wouldn't have stretched the way it has. We're not well-known in the world stage of beer, but we are a reasonable-sized regional brewery in twenty-eight states and over ten countries, so we're somewhat known. The new owner, Trey White, has always been engaged, and he wanted us to push the innovation envelope." Given that green light, Allen has continued to test the limits as his brewery's resident experimentalist.

"I'll give you some examples," he volunteers. "We did a beer based on a beer brewed by Bryan Hunt who owns Moonlight. He makes a beer called 'Working for the Tips.' It's an unhopped beer with redwood tips. I wanted to use some local ingredients. We're in the redwoods, so why not, right? I didn't want to steal his idea, so I called him up, and he invited me down to show me how to do it. He said, 'Every time you talk about this beer, you have to tell this story.' He showed me how to cut redwood and what portion you use and what flavor you get from what portion—more cinnamon, more spruce.

"We came back here and made a batch of beer. We put the redwood in. Two weeks later, it's finished fermenting. We taste it, and everybody is like, 'I don't get it. No redwood.' So I cut down a tree from my yard and double the amount. We ferment it for two weeks and everybody again says, 'I don't get it.' We do this a third and fourth time. I've doubled it each time! By the time the fourth beer comes around, it's loaded with redwood. And everyone is like 'Whoa, way too much redwood!' Now I've got forty barrels of this beer that nobody is going to drink—one is too much and the other three are not enough.

"Our lab guy, Andy Hooper, says, 'We'll blend it all together, then separate it in two halves. We'll sour half in stainless, and we'll sour the other half in oak barrels. I'm like, 'Okay . . .' He's like, 'That's how they make Belgian bruin.' So we give that a shot, blend it all back together, carbonate it and keg it. It's fantastic beer! But it will never be repeatable. We have tried to recreate that using the redwoods and souring it, and it's good but it's never quite as good as that first time," he sighs.

Thankfully though, the other more consistent beers Anderson Valley brews don't require a chainsaw. "Our most popular, best-known beer is the gose, which is a style that, four years ago, I had never even heard of," confesses Allen. "We started tinkering around with doing a sour mash beer. In fact, making it was quite serendipitous. One of our guys, Andy Hooper, wanted to start a sour mash. I had done them before, but not very successfully. I didn't think they were a good idea. He made one, and it was terrible. I said, 'Well what do you think went wrong here?' Neither of us really knew, but Andy was going to try to figure it out. I thought, 'If he's going to try to figure it out, I should maybe do some research and see why I think it didn't work out.'

"We both came to the same conclusion: what you want to do is get the wort off the grain. The grain is covered in bacteria, and you've started this bacterial fermentation by letting it sit for a length of time. That's all well and good, but you're not just getting lactic acid bacteria. You're getting all these weird things that make unpleasant aromas. Then you also need to exclude oxygen as much as possible. We were no longer doing a sour mash." Step by step, learning from mistakes and successes, Anderson Valley's next product line evolved.

"As we were doing that experiment, a local homebrewer said, 'That would be perfect for making gose!' Both Andy and I were like 'Making what?' We did some more research and we agreed that it was a good process for that style of beer. We got as many goses as we could find from Germany and tried 'em. But who, outside of Europe, had heard of gose four years ago? We didn't think it would sell very well, but the owner tasted it and thought it could have wheels.

"We made our version, and it got people talking about the brewery a lot more. It sold very well for us!" That ongoing success story includes Anderson Valley's bewitching Blood Orange Gose, a wheat ale, kettle soured to perfection with lactobacillus with just enough sea salt and coriander stirred in to make it mesmerizing. This slightly citrusy beer isn't tart enough to make you pucker up and whistle, but its subtle orange hints help make it refreshing. I suggest to Allen, "This gose is so good that you could afford to rest on your laurels for a while."

He disagrees. "In this market, it's innovate or die. If you're not making new beers and coming out with new things, you won't survive. If we hadn't started innovating and coming out with new products, this brewery probably would have failed. My experience in Southeast Asia with innovation has kept me motivated to do more. We make forty to fifty new beers a year—probably a new one every week. A lot of them are one-offs. Some of them are weird and don't sell well. Some of them are delicious and just not economically viable. Sometimes, like gose, you get a home run. But we're constantly making new beers. I love that part of the process!"

After a behind-the-scenes look at brewery operations and a quality assurance tasting panel exercise where I am a fill-in, we *pike* to the tasting room to *buckeye* with Fal, Laboratory Manager Greg Knox, and Lab Technician Megan Jennings. We sample several beers that made the final QA cut.

An eight-foot-tall stuffed black bear, Barkley the Beer, dominates one end of the cavernous taproom, keeping a vigilant eye on the crowd under the vaulted ceiling. Puzzled, I ask again about the antlers, and everyone at the table laughs. "Bear . . . deer? Put the two together," smiles Allen. I swear I can hear the stuffed bear growling in Boontling, "*Neeble backdated chuck eesole* . . . run now, or I'll chew you up and wash you down with our Hop Ottin' IPA!"

I ignore his warning eyes, look across the table at Allen and think, "This dude has it made. After all, he can say that he's 'livin' the dream' without a touch of sarcasm."

"I'm proud of the beers we make," concludes Allen, finishing the last of his Brother David's Triple Abbey Style Ale. "I feel good when I hear about people enjoying them. That's what keeps me going." And that drive to be different makes Anderson Valley Brewing one of the *bahl*est breweries out west!

Fal Unfiltered

Don't Knock It, Until You've Tried It!

Allen likes to use unique regional ingredients in his beer, when they makes sense. Sometimes the open-minded brewer is willing to give something new a try, even when his experience and intuition warn that it might be a bad idea.

"The Little River Inn is a place on the coast, and the owner and her husband and I are good friends," he explains, and I immediately sense I'm about to hear something strange. Allen goes on, "He's the chef, and he calls me up and says, 'It's our seventy-fifth anniversary, and we want to make a beer.' I asked what he wanted to brew, and he didn't know, but he wanted to use Candy Cap Mushrooms. I had never heard of one. I said 'Okay, but I've made mushroom beers before, and by and large, they suck.'"

As is sometimes the case with chefs, his stubborn friend didn't listen. He brought some spices, plenty of locally foraged Candy Caps, and the daring duo brewed a beer. Allen pronounced it delicious. "It was very unusual," he remembers. "The beer had this maple syrup flavor and earthy mushroomness, and we decided to build it into a saison.

They served it for a year for the anniversary and liked it so much that he came to Booneville, and we brewed it again and again. Each year, it's a little bit different, but we always use local Candy Cap mushrooms. It's very interesting!" As the old saying goes, don't knock it, until you try it!

CHAPTER 20

RACING THROUGH BEER IN WINE COUNTRY

Bear Republic Brewing Company—Healdsburg, CA

BEAR REPUBLIC COO and Brewmaster Ricardo Norgrove races into his office with a smile on his face and makes a pit stop to shake my hand. Like the wide spectrum of fine beers that he and his crew craft, I find him immediately likeable. With his dad Richard Sr., Bear Republic's CEO, he founded the family-run Healdsburg, California-based brewery in 1995.

After our brief introduction, Marketing Assistant and PR whiz Kate Davis dutifully fills her boss in on daily details and a list of reminders. Super Kate, as Ricardo calls her, helps keep her high-octane hyperactive boss organized. That is important because he is interested in and good at so many things, from brewing to graphic arts to restoring and racing cars. "What they call it now is ADHD," he laughs. "Someone never told me that I couldn't do it all, so I just had to keep pushing on. I think I would go crazy if I wasn't constantly pushing myself in some shape or form."

It's hard to argue with his strategy. One need look no further than his office space, with signs of productivity in every nook and cranny. The modern-day Renaissance man welded the roll bar and made other enhancements to the beautiful blue pinstriped Factory 5 Cobra that sits at one end of this studio/garage. Norgrove has been into racing since he was a boy, getting hooked on the sport while watching his favorite Saturday morning cartoon, *Speed Racer*. He has managed to turn that boyhood dream into an adult obsession, driving in local competitions when he is able to take short breaks from the family's booming brewery business.

It has taken countless laps around the track to get to this point in his own success story. Like many in the industry, Norgrove was a home brewer first. "My dad's side of the story was that I was this kid in college drinking too much beer and having fun," he chuckles. "I had gotten into home brewing when I was in college at Sacramento State, and it was a means to actually make a little money on the side." While many in college were busy draining kegs, Ricardo was brewing them.

Eventually, Ricardo came to his dad with a business idea, but it was focused on a different kind of beverage. "I grew up with my father telling me all of the time that he was making tons of money for corporate America, and someday he was going to make money for himself," he recounts. "I took him to a coffee shop in downtown Santa Rosa and tried to convince him that we should get into making coffee. One of my first jobs was as a barista before they called it *barista*. I tried to convince him that we could sell a three-dollar cup of coffee. Well, look at where that got some companies," he grimaces. "He said no to that one," along with several other ideas that his son presented.

Fortunately, dad was willing to listen to another in a long line of pitches. Ricardo wanted to take the talent he had developed in school and parlay that into a brewery. "'This time,' I told him, 'I'm going to do it with you or without you,'" he remembers. "'Are you in or are you out?'" Ricardo didn't get an immediate "No" this time, which was a good sign. Instead, his father urged him to learn the business, and the aspiring brewer apprenticed with Marin Brewing Company. "I worked every Friday for free for a year," he says. "I learned the ins and outs of how to run a brewery and finally convinced my dad we could do this."

When the Norgroves finally got the "green flag" from the bank, it was with a caveat. "My dad and I started out with the intention of trying to have a production brewery," he notes. But lenders pushed the father/son team into opening a brewpub instead. Now Ricardo not only had beer to brew, but he had food to cook and patrons to serve.

"Early on in the company's history, I had to do a lot of different things," he remembers. "I was a one-man show for the first two years. I would be brewing the recipes in my head." One he had in mind from the outset was a house pale ale. But the process for turning his thoughts into good beer wasn't without jarring speed bumps. "I was half asleep because I had been putting in eighty hours a week, grabbed the wrong hop profile, threw it into the pale ale recipe, and went, 'Oh my God, what am I doing?'" he shares.

"The first time we made it, we called it Springtime Strong Ale." Norgrove rifles through a stack of drawings on the table, searching for something, and doesn't miss a beat. "I was trying to design what looked like a Chevy ss logo for it. Then my father reminded me of the negative connotations of the Nazi ss and said, 'No, we're not going to call it that.' Springtime Strong Ale, over several iterations, it became Racer. Then we called it 2, 3, and 4. When we got to 5, I wanted to call it Speed Racer Ale. We contacted the company that owned the name, and they said no. Some friends in business law from my fraternity suggested, 'Just call it Racer 5.'"

So the young entrepreneur dove headfirst into everything he could read about trademark law. "You look at a number in a NASCAR picture, and the number 3 is owned by Dale Earnhardt, Incorporated," he observes. "Dale Earnhardt is the first guy to take a number and say that is mine stylistically, and he trademarked it. I followed suit, came up with a number, designed my own font, and trademarked it. Speed Racer's number is basically Helvetica typeface, but the color scheme is reverse from ours. So, it's an ode to him."

Today, Racer 5 is a brand that is recognized by Bear Republic fans far and wide, and its faithful following has turned it into a big winner for the Norgroves. This precision-made, 75-IBU IPA is balanced with malted barley, wheat, and crystal malts. The unmistakable Columbus and Cascade hops accelerate smoothly across my anxious taste buds, leaving their mark without wrecking my palate. But be forewarned: this golden classic is so smooth it sneaks up on you, and its 7.5% ABV may leave you hitching a ride home if you aren't careful.

Ricardo is a modern-day da Vinci. "My dad and my partners get an extra bonus by having me be the brewmaster along with the creative art director," he smiles. "Back in the late eighties and early nineties, I went to school for graphic design." That training has paid off handsomely for Bear Republic. In this business, attractive artwork on a can or bottle is worth much more than a thousand words. Although you can't judge a book or beer by its cover, it might be enough to entice you to give it a try.

"Early on, when you looked at German tradition or English tradition, a brewery's name meant so much, then they would make a style," notes Norgrove. "Somehow in US marketing, you had to have not only a good brewery name, but then you had to have something that would catch someone's eye so that they might try the beer. The names for me were personal, and they were part of the story we would tell when we were a smaller brewery. For example, 'Where did Red Rocket come from?' Well, the logo for Red Rocket came from a head badge logo that I had designed for a mountain bike made for Sammy Hagar while operating as the Production Manager for Salsa Cycles, and it was rejected. So I went, 'I'm not going to lose this logo. I'm going to use this later on, for me!' Crazy stuff like that happens in this business."

Pressed to name his favorite beer, Ricardo winces, pauses, and confesses it is probably Red Rocket, and not just because he really likes the logo. "It's a dying style, and the base for many of my beers," he explains. It was one of his original recipes, developed in 1992. "For me, this started out as a traditional Scottish ale, wanting to create something like a Schilling 120 or a Schilling 90. It had all of these caramel malts, and it utilized single grains from English malts.

"I also have this love for hops. I might make ten gallons, and one might be made with Scottish ale yeast and another one with American ale yeast and then I would hop them differently." He mentions that he still has the original homebrew kit that he used to make the beer, which he fabricated himself while making homebrew stands for The Beverage People, where he first learned how to weld. "There are so many cool malts that are incorporated in that beer that if you took Red Rocket and you aged it for six to nine months, it would be a completely different beer than it would be at three months. It has legs and longevity to stay with you for a long time."

My amiable host is picking up speed as we round that turn and head into the straightaway. He is in storytelling overdrive and all too happy to continue regaling me with his tales. The momentum leads me to ask him about a beer that I know is near and dear to his heart. Bear Republic's Peter Brown Tribute Ale, a syrupy, red-tinged brown ale, is one of the brewery's best beers, medaling year after year in multiple competitions, including the Great American Beer Festival (GABF).

"Peter Brown was my first million-dollar salesman," shares Norgrove. "Right around my daughter Ryleigh's birth, we were developing this beer, and Peter Brown was working for me at the time. I made a beer called Ryleigh's Baby Brown Ale. Peter really loved that ale, but he kept telling me, 'If you did this or you did that, you'd have a winner, Rich!' And I thought, 'I don't know, man.' His favorite beer was our Big Bear Black Stout. We used molasses and brown sugar in that beer to kind of build the body up—it kind of gives it a chocolatey character. We even used a candy confectionary kettle." Resisting Brown's suggestions to blend in those bold, rich flavors wasn't easy.

Eyes watering, he remembers their final day as officemates. "Peter was having one of those days where it looked like he wasn't feeling very well," recalls Norgrove, who was a volunteer firefighter and EMT at the time. "He was fifty-three, and he smoked like crazy. I was sitting in the office with him, and said, 'Hey Peter, what's up?' He said, 'I'm just not feeling well, Rich.' I said, 'Well, let me check you out. I'll just run down to my truck and grab my med bag, and we'll take your blood pressure.' He's like, 'You're not touching me, kid.' I said, 'I'm your boss.' He's like, 'I don't fuckin' care. You can send me home, but you're not touching me.'"

Norgrove sent him home under the condition that he see a doctor. "I didn't say what kind of doctor for him to visit, so he went home and visited his chiropractor and got his back cracked. Stubborn! Then I get this terrible phone call from his wife. He had had a massive coronary heart attack sitting in his easy chair. I didn't know what to do."

The next day, the answer came to him. "I decided to do what he told me to do with the brown ale," he sighs. "It was real emotional. I'm going to take the elements from the Big Bear that he talked about, and I'm going to marry it to the brown ale. I'm going to make a beer for him.

"That same batch of beer, I send to the Great American Beer Festival, and it won the flippin' gold medal in the Brown Porter category in 2004. You want to talk about a bumbling crying idiot? We made this in loving memory of him, and we keep submitting it, and it keeps winning. Peter obviously knew his beer flavors."

No doubt, Brown had been on to something. The bitter characteristics of the stout and hops help balance the sugary sweetness swirling through this malty American brown ale. The dried fruit in the background hints at the date farm treats I've tried in California's Coachella Valley. That is the wonderful thing about beer. Close your eyes, and its flavors have the ability to transport the mind back to some of your fondest memories. The comfortable warmth generated by this 6.3% ABV ale has me dreaming of breezy boyhood days and walking barefoot in Palm Desert sands in the dead of winter. Smacking my lips, roasted coffee grounds break through on the back end of this little taste test, snapping me out of my daydream. Reluctantly, I'm back on track.

As the finish line looms, Norgrove shares his personal roadmap with me. He swears that the twists and turns ahead don't include selling the business to the big boys. "My vision for our company, and one that my father shares, is that we will be one of those old family-owned breweries," he concludes. "So not me, maybe not even my son, but my son's son or my sister's kids will keep the legacy going, because that's what all of the old European family breweries are. Our industry is so young that nobody has established that form of legacy yet. On my labels, I have printed 'Proudly independent since 1995.'" And there is no reason to believe Ricardo and his whole "racing team" won't be competing with the best in the craft beer circuit for years to come.

Ricardo Unfiltered
A Pit Stop for Changing Hop Profiles

The inventive Norgrove has taken his race car driver mentality and applied it to one of his favorite Bear Republic beers, Apex. "The term *apex* in racing is constantly ever changing," he explains. "I can start at the beginning of the race, and as I get more fatigued and my tires get hot or I'm burning down fuel, and I'm changing the weight ratio from front to rear, the apex on the corners changes. So, using that analogy, every year as brewmaster, I reserve the right to change the hop profile on our Apex Special IPA to establish what the new 'apexes' are." For example, the 2017 hop bill included Ella, Hull Melon, and Hallertau Blanc hop varieties, engineering a 100 IBU, 8.25% ABV strong IPA.

21ST AMENDMENT'S Hell or High Watermelon American wheat beer, stacked high at the company's massive San Leandro, California brewery and canning facility. Photo courtesy of Rob Palmer, On Location Photography

CHAPTER 21

CELEBRATING BEER WITH BREW FREE! OR DIE IPA

21st Amendment—San Leandro, CA

JUST OFF OF INTERSTATE 880 in a San Leandro industrial park, there is a party going on in a former Pop Tart® factory. It's December 5, and 21st Amendment Brewery is celebrating its namesake, the 1933 godsend that repealed the 18th Amendment to the Constitution of the United States and ended the cursed Prohibition. Nico Freccia, co-owner of the brewery, is running around in a period-perfect yellow-checkered gangster suit complete with matching tie and a black Fedora. He would fit right in with Al Capone, although Public Enemy No. 1 was forced to celebrate the newly won freedom in his chilly cell on Alcatraz.

Freccia isn't the only one dressed for the special occasion. A few of the ladies are decked out in sultry sequined dresses that show so much cleavage that one needs to find refreshment quickly to cool down. A combo jazz band plays relaxing tunes in the background and gentle breezes deliver tempting aromas emanating from the barbecued pig roasting just outside one of the bay doors.

But the real stars of the show today are not parading around in Big-Band-era costumes or spinning on a spit outside. They are flowing from the taps behind the long knotty pine bar that sits near the southeast corner of the massive brewery complex. Beers like Brew Free! or Die IPA, Fireside

Chat Winter Spiced Ale, and Back in Black are filling pint glasses and tulips under a cartoon of Lady Liberty lounging on the Golden Gate Bridge. The 21st Amendment website declares that Back in Black is inspired by Paul Revere's midnight ride. "We rebelled against the British style IPA, embraced the more aggressive American version and then recast it in bold, brave, defiant black," rings out the clever advertising copy. "Our Black IPA is a Declaration of Independence from the tyranny of the expected." I make a note to bring a few cans home to see if I am as moved by the beer as I am by the marketing.

Friends Freccia and Shaun O'Sullivan founded the 21st Amendment Brewery in San Francisco's South Park neighborhood in 2000. When the partners decided to start packaging beer in 2005, they couldn't find enough space for the kind of production they anticipated. Real estate prices were booming in the Bay Area, and they didn't have the capital to open a new operation. "We were spending a lot of time with Pete Slosberg, who is the founder of Pete's Wicked Ale, and Pete, along with Jim Koch from Sam Adams, pioneered this model in the '80s and '90s of contract brewing, where they used underutilized midwestern breweries that were big after Prohibition and were in decline," recalls Freccia. "We decided that the way to do this right, especially since we were canning and needed high-speed equipment, was to find a partner. We called practically everybody in the country. Part of the issue is we wanted to make beer with unique ingredients, and we wanted to bring our own yeast. A lot of these companies said, 'We won't allow this because it will taint our lines,' or, 'We only use these two yeasts.' But we found this company in Cold Spring, Minnesota, about eighty-five miles northwest of Minneapolis." They began canning their increasingly popular lineup of craft beer in July 2008.

Eventually, demand outpaced what their contractor could deliver. That was a good problem to have, according to Freccia. "Shaun and I always wanted to bring it back home," he shares. "We started in the brewpub where we could literally stand at the bar and talk about recipes for new beers, taste things, and talk about ingredients. And here we were, brewing 1,500 miles away and getting beer overnighted to us to sample it. We needed to be able to walk the floor, smell the tank, take samples, talk to the brewers, and feel the ingredients. And so that's what happened."

In August 2015, the founders took a giant leap forward, converting the 148,348 ft.² of industrial space that I'm standing in into a brewery and pub. To be honest, the place feels like it is about 90 percent brewery and 10 percent pub. The canning line hums in the background on most days, although nothing could compete with the band and crowd on hand this afternoon.

As my photographer Rob Palmer runs around capturing the moment, taking pictures of Freccia and his costumed buddies, I order a Brew Free! or Die IPA, find one of the few open tables and have a taste. It's a full-bodied, 7% ABV West Coast IPA that registers a hoppy 70 IBUS. A palate wrecker it is not, although I wouldn't suggest chasing it with the Hell or High Watermelon (more on that treat later) if you expect to taste any ingredient in the latter beer. This IPA, with its Amarillo, Cascade, and Simcoe hops, has the potential to overpower more timid flavors.

Savoring the citrusy pint, I think back to the first time I met with Freccia, nearly a year earlier. Although his wardrobe wasn't as snappy, his anecdotes and insights were another story, and those started flowing the minute we met. As the bartender lined up a series of tasters for us, Nico shared a little bit about the history of the massive facility pumping out the towering pallets of beer stacked just to my right.

"This is our newest addition, our pride and joy," beamed Freccia as I looked longingly at the mountain of IPA. "This building is a former Kellogg Cereal Factory, where they made Pop Tarts and Frosted Flakes for thirty years. When we first took over the building, we said the first beer we were going to do out here had to be an homage to Kellogg, so we came up with Toaster Pastry. It's an India Red Ale. We use biscuit malt for a crust-like, nutty character, and a lot of different imported English and American malts for this chewy, jammy middle. A number of relatively new, experimental hops give it a wonderful, fruity aroma."

Research has shown that our expectations can have an influence on the flavors our minds think they are detecting, and this was certainly the case the first time I sampled a Toaster Pastry. "I'm getting a tart cherry flavor," I said to Freccia at the time. "Well, there is nothing in that beer that should make it sour," he answered. Not one to offend my host, I took another taste. It was like biting through that flaky pastry crust and being greeted by a mouthful of Calypso hops, accented with a dollop of strawberry filling. Maybe my mind *was* playing tricks on me. Nevertheless, we were off to a good start.

Speaking of successful beginnings, Freccia and O'Sullivan met twenty years ago up the road at UC Davis while taking a short course on brewing. "We immediately became friends, started talking about what we wanted to do with the rest of our lives, and said, 'Hey, let's open a brewpub,'" recalled Freccia. "We were both home brewers, passionate about beer. Shaun was brewing professionally at Triple Rock in Berkeley. I had been working at restaurants for ten to twelve years. We had the right mix. We worked on a plan, and back then, you didn't have access to the resources, information, and money that's out there now. It took us about five years to write our plan, get funding, and get a building."

It's not surprising that Freccia likes to talk about the past. History is central to the whole 21st Amendment marketing strategy, from the company name to the mischievous artwork and brand names adorning its packaging and cans. "We thought it would help us differentiate ourselves, and with cans, we had all this extra real estate to tell our story," he explained. "You literally have a 360-degree canvas. We also started to do the six-pack boxes, which are like little billboards. The whole idea of using the American iconic image was born out of that impulse to tell stories." These guys wove graphical tales that took product branding to a whole new level.

"Back in those days (2007-08), there weren't as many breweries, and it was common to see a beer named by brewery name and beer style—Sierra Nevada Pale Ale, for example," he continued. "We thought there's a missed opportunity to come up with something unique, fun, memorable. A lot of it was, 'What does 21st Amendment mean to people? American values, history, and government.' So we thought we'd take images that everyone's familiar with, like Mount Rushmore and the Statue of Liberty, and put our own unique twist on them. We've got our Hell or High Watermelon beer, which is our summer classic." So is the artwork covering the cans and boxes. The tall tale that Freccia weaves to describe the product brand/

mini-masterpiece goes something like this: "The Statue of Liberty had a long walk across the country and is resting on the Golden Gate Bridge, where she picks up a giant watermelon on a barge passing by." He forgot to mention that she has set her torch and tablet down on the bridge and her crown hangs from one of its towers. "Hell or High Watermelon Wheat Beer comes out of that American, industrious, can-do attitude," he continued, taking the tale into the outer limits. "It's about manifest destiny, and we want to have fun with it!"

Damn straight! "It is all about freedom and independence, isn't it?" I ventured, perhaps a bit overexcited. Propelled by the tasters, we were getting downright patriotic. If one throws down enough shots of high ABV beer, he begins to imagine that good healthy beer consumption helped inflame the courageous souls depicted on this noble brewery's cans to successful revolution and many other feats of wonder that have shaped this great nation. Before I could belt out "God Bless America," Freccia brought me back to reality and the glass in front of me, none other than Hell or High Watermelon.

"We've been making this since the first spring we opened fifteen years ago," he said, as I emptied the juicy taster. "It's a home brew recipe I did sixteen to seventeen years ago in my basement. It's an American wheat beer with 100 percent fresh watermelon puree that's fermented. This is available April through September. We've kept it on tap here for novelty's sake, but you normally don't get it this time of year. It goes down easy, light. You can drink three to four before a Giants game." That is a bad subject if you happen to be an A's or Dodgers fan.

The refreshing, bright watermelon and wheat combination reminded me of a picnic in the park on a sunny afternoon. The watermelon is just enough in the background that it doesn't run roughshod over the Magnum hops. For me, this is definitely more of a summer beer, but I made an exception and enjoyed it in in the dead of winter. It's a mellow 4.7% ABV, 17 IBU wheaty treat that would be a great choice for a day at the beach when the weather finally cooperates.

Next in the lineup of tasters was the Session IPA, Down to Earth. "You can see compared to the El Sully (the brewery's Mexican Lager), it's got a lot more of the orange color," he pointed out. "We use the imported heirloom malt called Golden Promise from England. The problem we found with the lower-alcohol beer is that they taste like dirty, hoppy dishwater. They are incredibly bitter but they have no backbone, so the way we combat that is that we use this British heirloom malt, deeper-orange color, it has a nuttier flavor. You want to make a pretty bitter beer that mimics an IPA without the alcohol. It's heavily dry-hopped, with Mosaic, which gives it that kind of spicy flavor."

About that point in the visit, Nico finally broke my grip on the bar and lured me away on a tour of the plant, with the promise we would be back. I followed him around the corner. Yes, this certainly qualifies as a brewery, but it is as massive as some of the industrial manufacturing plants that I've wandered through. The king-sized operation includes two 60,000-pound grain silos and augers that mill and feed the brewery pale malt. "We have room for future stations to add more bag stations, grist cleaning, and grist hydration," pointed out Freccia.

"This is a four-vessel, hundred-barrel brewhouse. We have mash, lauter, kettle, and whirlpool. Four vessels allows us to move brews through this system at about a brew per every two hours, once the initial brew is done. Full capacity is about eight brews a day or 800 barrels. By comparison, that is about what we brew at our pub in San Francisco in a year. We have space for a fifth vessel, added down the line, which will bring us to between ten and twelve brews a day." Today, the brewery produces over 100,000 barrels of beer per year, with space to expand to 250,000 barrels if needed anytime in the future.

As we made our way back to the bar, Freccia took us on a detour to the packaging area, a strangely hypnotic place in the brewery. There, cans are fed into the German-engineered, Wisconsin-manufactured assembly line, race up an elevator, and run single file through the efficient system at a blazing 500 cans a minute. In the process, each can is X-rayed for fill levels and date-coded. Fully loaded, the aluminum soldiers are paraded to an accumulation table that can package them in four-packs, six-packs, and even twenty-four-can cartons for big box stores. The tray packer and palletizer finish the job, shrink-wrapping and readying the beer for shipment.

"When this is humming and working, which is most of the time, it's really a beautiful thing to watch," observed Freccia, with a grimace that indicated there are occasional challenges with the equipment.

After we wrapped up the tour, it was time for a Fireside Chat. It's a good way to end most any day, whether that is beside a hearth or at a table in a cavernous cereal factory-turned-brewery. "Fireside Chat is our winter seasonal, which has FDR on the label," noted Nico. "He's sitting by the fire having a famous fireside chat, talking to an elf. This is a beer we've been making since we opened fifteen years ago. We called it the Holiday Spiced Ale at that time. It's basically an English-style strong ale base with a couple of nontraditional holiday spices as well as some cocoa nibs to give it a nutty flavor. The idea is that it's a nice, well-balanced, bitter, English-style ale with just enough spice to make it interesting without beating you over the head. You can smell a bit of a cinnamon character to it."

"I can taste it too," I replied. For me, this ale is aptly named. It is a delicious dessert beer that I can imagine having with a log crackling in the fireplace.

The great thing about this universally loved beverage is it relaxes everyone so much that there is time for comfortable moments of silence and reflection. After one such pause, Freccia summed up the brewery's philosophy with historical flare: "Before Prohibition, there were literally thousands of breweries in America: the neighborhood gathering places where people got together over a pint to talk politics, social issues, and religion. This whole culture was wiped out with Prohibition. Today, the 21st Amendment is allowing us, as a culture, to start the slow climb back to reclaiming the essence of this neighborhood gathering place that had been lost."

Back in the present at the rollicking "Repeal" celebration, I take a long pull on my pint of Brew Free! or Die and realize just how right my host and tour guide was when he made that observation many months ago. I've witnessed the magic created by craft breweries on islands, in cities, in garages, and now here in a former Pop Tart factory. Craft beer brings us all together, no matter our gender or color or other differences, and it has people smiling again.

Nico Unfiltered

The Value of a Good Education

"To me, the enjoyment of beer has always been about education," shares Freccia. "It's like learning about ingredients in food, learning about wine. I used to read *Wine Spectator* when I worked in restaurants. It's very elitist and exclusive, and if you don't understand the terms and flavor descriptors, you could feel really lost." That bothered him.

"When we opened, we wanted to spend a lot of energy on education," he continues. "We did Beer School every week. It was a free event about the history of beer. We would do a different style every week: how did that style develop, how did pale ale morph into IPA, how did Irish ale and other things fit in?"

Freccia enjoys teaching people about the brewery, the equipment, and the beer it produces. "When we first put beer in cans, we thought there'd be a big educational curve," he points out. "We had a lot of people who would say beer in a can was the crappy beer their grandpa used to drink. We had to get past the myths and perceptions. So to me, it's a collaboration between us and our consumer. It's about doing an effective job telling our story, educating the consumer so they could become better about their choices."

The volume of canned beer being produced here indicates he, Shaun, and the whole 21st Amendment crew have been successful evangelists. And it sure doesn't hurt that beer is the most widely consumed beverage in the world after tea or water.

CHAPTER 22

BEER SANCTUARY BY THE BAY

Faction Brewing Company—Alameda, CA

DRIVING DOWN A ROAD flanked by abandoned military buildings in Alameda, California, I start to imagine that I've accidentally happened on a movie set. Rolling alongside rows of impersonal grey rectangles, you half expect to encounter a hundred-foot-tall alien machine stepping out into the street, barring your way to the brewery. Or maybe a band of hungry zombies will swarm your vehicle, drag you and your beer buddies into a dark ally, and eat you alive before you ever get the chance to try Faction's A-Town Pale, Moon Germs, Antidote To Reality IPA, or other ales.

"Did my engine just sputter?" I wonder, mouth too dry for a nervous swallow. "Man, I would really hate to break down here. OMG, was someone watching me from that rooftop?" Maybe it's the late afternoon Bay Area daylight playing tricks on my eyes. But just as I begin to believe my imagination, a sanctuary looms on the horizon. And what a breathtaking horizon it is! As I pull into the parking lot at Faction Brewing Company, the Bay Bridge looms due west in the foreground of a postcard-come-to-life backdrop that includes the San Francisco skyline. It's stunning, even more so considering the stark eastern-bloc-like neighborhood I just left behind in my rearview mirror.

The brewery is actually located in an old military hangar at the edge of a wildlife sanctuary. Inside, you can still see Marine Corps helicopter skid marks' cross-hatching on the floor. The 25,000 ft.² building used to be part of a Navy base in the 1990s, before the Clinton Administration shut it down. A Coast Guard dance party is in full swing as I walk past shiny conditioning tanks on my way to the tasting room.

There I meet with co-founder Rodger Davis, who opened the brewery with wife Claudia Pamparana in December 2013. Rodger is wearing a smile beneath a mostly salt with a sprinkling of pepper beard and a navy-blue Faction baseball cap. He is tall and lean, probably from working his ass off in the brewery for several years. Looking down toward my shoes, I make a note that a little hard work hauling hops wouldn't hurt my belly.

Those grandiose plans will have to wait for my next set of resolutions. The goal today is soaking in everything I can about Faction. Rodger starts the process by shaking hands and trying to talk over the din of the crowd in the tap room. "This view is spectacular," says me, master of the obvious, spreading my arms toward the windows. "That field between us and the bay must be priceless."

"Not so much priceless as it's billion-dollar land," he corrects me. "They had developers come in who said they would put in high rises and shopping." But the field next to my beer sanctuary is apparently a bird sanctuary for the *Sternula antillarum browni*, and the protected species zone is responsible for killing those Black Friday sales dreams. Davis describes the way it came down in his own words: "The bird people came in and said 'You can't do shit out here!' It's habitat. It's endangered." He explains that there's a height restriction on anything built nearby because the California least tern (as it is commonly called) nests in the ground and predators can nest up high, swoop in and take the young. "That's why our grain silo is all the way in the back corner of this building. It's a unique situation, but at the end of the day, we have that view."

From the looks of things here, the wild neighbors are not hurting business. In fact, the Coast Guard revelers and local regulars are having such a good time this winter's day that we decide to make our way through the production facility to a quieter break room. We plop down and dive into the interview.

The red beer on the table is enough to nourish me until supper time. Faction Red is a 5.6 ABV, 40 IBU American red ale, dry hopped with Cascade, Centennial, and CTZ hops.

"What do you like to pair this with?" I ask Davis, taking my first taste.

"I like to pair the glass with my mouth," he cracks.

"Oh, so you're a purist!" I fire back, before taking second taste to confirm my first impressions.

It's easy to see why Faction Red is a popular choice with the patrons here today. Hops are in the spotlight in this rust-colored, slightly bready beer, leaving an unmistakably citrusy but not overbearing aftertaste. In fact, hops are the stars of the show in a lot of Faction's beers, and that makes me wonder if there are enough to go around for small breweries like Rodger's.

"Are there enough hops being grown that you see no supply chain issues?" I ask.

"We had a heart-to-heart with one of the farmers in Yakima when I was up there last year for harvest," reports Davis. "He said, 'Something has to give. There's not much land left where we can put hops.' Granted, we're talking about Washington, which legalized marijuana (since our interview, California and Oregon have joined Washington in that regard). Idaho, a Republican state, will never legalize it. There's always going to be hops in Idaho. But what's the soil going to give to the hop? There's a reason that Oregon is very famous for their wine grapes and hops. California was the same way for a long time until they started to rip out the hops and put in wine grapes because they were making way more money per acre.

"Breweries like Sierra Nevada are focused around a lot of hops, and they're moving into new markets. Those guys use a shit-ton of hops. It's stressful for me, as a smaller person, to be able to get the hops that I need to produce the beers that I want. Most of these farmers are growing apples, too. They're not going to pull the apples. What does it take to get a yield on an apple tree, ten years?"

Rodger worries about this stuff because he has been to the school of hard knocks and learned a few lessons along the way. There were points when he wasn't sure if he would ever get a shot to open his own brewery, let alone be able to procure enough hops for his delicious IPAs. "The window (of opportunity) was busted for years," says the witty brewer, "but the door cracked open finally." In 2011, he bought a twenty-barrel system from a buddy who was expanding his brewery. "We brought it out here and started hitting snags. One would say it's a roller-coaster ride, but it's not one of those roller coasters that lasts for three minutes. It lasted for like forty-five minutes, trying to figure out the permitting. The city wanted to see everything stamped by an engineer because they didn't know what a brewery was. We're the first production brewery since 1898 here. The last one was The Palace Brewery.

"We were literally on the verge of just jumping ship. We were asking, 'How do we get out of this?' because we were losing money. Eventually, you're going to have to start paying rent. We wanted to get a one-way trip to Mexico! But we persevered, and slowly but surely we started to move onto bigger things. We started with the kegerator—a $2,000 piece of equipment—then that paid for itself within two to three weeks. Then we had a tasting room and that snowballed into twenty beers on tap. Everything I look at nowadays is, 'What's the return on investment?' When we were building it out, it was just money going out the door. It was so stressful. I didn't have any gray hair before we started this."

"You're probably waking up at 3:00 a.m. with your mind racing," I empathize with him. It makes me wonder what else keeps him and his peers up at night. "Can the country sustain this growth?" I ask him.

"It's not the country so much as the community," Davis corrects me. Back before the 1920's and Prohibition, most people enjoyed beer that was brewed in their own neighborhoods. "That's the small brewery mentality of 'Hey, let's bring this back to the small towns,'" he shares. With beers like Faction's 007 Pale Ale, Summer IPA, Vandelay Wit, and Anomaly Milk Stout among other intriguing options, Faction has assembled plenty of good reasons to unite.

The challenge of gathering the area's unlike-minded craft-beer enthusiasts under one tap room roof seems to be propelling the rather rebellious

Davis and his successful business forward. He is in this for the whole roller-coaster ride, terrifying hairpin turns and all. "We dropped in six new fermenters, but I don't want to blow up and sell this brewery for a billion dollars," he concludes. "I want to be a part of this brewery at seventy years old, not necessarily graining out," but at least dropping in now and again. I ready myself for a parting one-liner. "As it turns out, there are roundtrip flights to Mexico," he finishes with a grin.

Rodger Unfiltered
Yelped into Conformity

"We got called out on a Yelp review by some guy who Yelped the whole brewery," reports rebel Rodger. "He said, 'Hipster conformant-beers are drinkable, at best.' I respect that. Our beers aren't for everyone. Then he went on 'With the cutesy little names, maybe they should focus more on making beer than coming up with names.' Next day, Hipster Conformant went into the tank. It's a PBR knockoff. We fermented it at forty-eight degrees for like ten days. It's got a lot of corn and rice, and is lightly hopped."

"My eighty-eight-year-old father-in-law would love that," I suggest.

"We put that story on our Facebook page, and it literally went viral," continues Rodger. "Normally it goes to 2,000 people, and this went to like 48,000 people."

He asks me if I want a taste, and for once, I decline. "I've gotten spoiled because I'm going to all of these places with amazing beers," I respond like a true snob.

"Til you got here," he laughs.

"I like your beers," I protest.

"Fuck off," responds the ornery brewer. "You don't even know what you're talking about."

"You're a real wiseass," I smile.

"It's what I get paid for," he smirks. I'm laughing so hard that I need to pause and wipe tears from my eyes; then we resume tasting Faction's anything-but-average IPAs. As good as the comedy is today, it's time for a parting shot of Rodger's Red Ryder (7.8% ABV) imperial red ale.

CHAPTER 23

NOW YOU SEE IT, NOW YOU DON'T

Firestone Walker Brewing Company—Paso Robles, CA

IN 2001, ADAM FIRESTONE and his brother-in-law David Walker bought the remnants of a bankrupt brewery in Paso Robles, California. They moved their tiny craft brewery ninety miles north of Los Olivos, where Firestone and Walker had been running the smallish operation in their spare time on the famous family's vineyard since 1996. Paso Robles, with its moderately arid Mediterranean climate, was already building a reputation for a growing number of noteworthy wineries, but the recently shuttered SLO Brewing Company had never managed to take root in the region.

The entrepreneurial partners were intrigued with the idea of expanding their small brewery (9,000 barrels per year at that time), with hopes they could sell enough craft beer to make a go of it. They managed to do much better than that. Firestone (aka "The Bear"), great grandson of tire and rubber company founder Harvey Firestone, and Walker (aka "The Lion") acquired the beleaguered Paso Robles production facility and enlisted the help of a gifted young brewer to work his magic on their beer.

Fast forward a couple decades, and I'm standing in Firestone Walker's tasting room on a comfortably cozy winter afternoon in Paso Robles. My host is busy behind the brushed-metal bar, eyeing the stream of dark liquid flowing from the tap and creating an enticing foamy head millimeters from the rim of his glass. As it turns out, the Masterbrewer's nickname is Merlin, and he is extraordinarily meticulous about the details as he puts a new spin on one of Firestone Walker's legendary beers.

As the story goes, Matt Brynildson has been the brewery's resident alchemist since 2001, the year it moved operations from Los Olivos to Paso Robles. Merlin earned the nickname over time as he piled up top honors at prestigious beer competitions. One of his inventions, the soft and smooth Velvet Merkin Oatmeal Stout, was subsequently renamed Velvet Merlin in the brewmaster's honor . . . and because "we got cold feet," according to a cryptic reference at firestonebeer.com (plug in *merkin* at dictionary.com if you must have the original definition but be forewarned).

Now, I'm here just in the nick of time to watch the wizard at work on his latest showstopper. Today, he is in the process of transforming his chocolate-brown namesake into a nitro milk stout. It's safe to say getting the process down is not as simple as pulling a rabbit out of one's hat or sawing an assistant in half.

"You've got to have that perfect three-quarters to one inch of foam stay on the beer," Brynildson observes, coming out from behind the tasting room bar. "I had out a little ruler earlier and was measuring foam depth." He is exacting when it comes to getting the style just right: "Three-quarters of an inch is what I'd like. A half inch would be minimum, and a full inch would be maximum."

The precursor to what will become Firestone Walker's Nitro Merlin Milk Stout looks so good that I wonder if it's an illusion. One taste confirms that is not the case. Beneath the velvety, lactose-laden head is a coffee-colored treat that has a sweet, roasty finish. With hints of vanilla and oatmeal and a dash of chocolate, this milk stout is the perfect partner for a late afternoon cookie or can stand on its own, come dessert time. "Now you see it, now you don't," I quip, having emptied a taster. However, Brynildson isn't quite as mesmerized with the result of his latest craft brewing experiment.

It takes time to get it right. Merlin was once an amateur himself. While working on his senior project at Kalamazoo College and interning with a spice extraction lab, he was exposed to research being conducted for major brewers around the world on light-stable hop extract. "Then, I just fortuitously got placed in the hops lab while I was finishing my organic chemistry degree," he remembers. "I ended up working for them for three years, and they sent me to the Siebel Institute for a short course so that I could get up to speed, interface better with customers, and learn more."

While studying at the renowned brewing sciences school, Brynildson met Greg Hall, co-founder of Chicago-based brewery Goose Island. He ended up quitting the hops research gig to become a brewer and assist the growing craft brewery fire up its new QC laboratory. "I was a brewer by day and a lab guy by night," he smiles. "It was getting that program going that got me to be head brewer later. I probably did a lifetime's worth of learning in the first one to two years. In those days, everything that was taught in the brewing schools was about how to make American light lager. There wasn't a dry-hopping class or a barrel-aging class. We had to learn how to make craft beer ourselves. I was young enough then that I didn't have anything else to do but just live for the brewery." What better apprenticeship for a budding beer virtuoso?

Not everyone was fond of Brynildson's choice of vocation. "My family thought it was crazy," he laughs. "I was supposed to go to medical school or something, and they are like, 'You're going to be a brewer for $9 an hour?' And I'm like, 'Yeah!' Now they say, 'Can we come out and visit?'"

Who wouldn't want to visit Firestone Walker? The stylish tasting room, accented with the brand's signature metallic grey tones, provides plenty of elbow room and a rotating assortment of craft beer styles for parched visitors. The friendly bartender pours me a pint of golden Pivo Pils, and I'm immediately impressed. It takes more than sleight of hand to make a lager that really stands out like this 5.3% ABV, quaffable beer. Magnum, Spalter, and Saphir hops boost this mildly fruity, 40 IBU beer well beyond your average pale lager. The herbal and lemon zest undertones in Pivo Pils make it the perfect partner for an outdoor barbecue or picnic fare. If it were possible to turn sunshine into fermented liquid, I imagine this is what it would be like.

Truth be told, consistently brewing high-quality beer is more about science than art. "There are living, breathing scientists that work in this brewery," reports Brynildson. "We have analytical, microbiological, and sensory labs. We pretty much have the lab staffed seven days a week, and we have a packaging lab that has to be staffed anytime we're bottling or canning, so there's two shifts."

Detecting flavors and faults in beer is a challenge for the brightest minds and the most sensitive tongues and noses. "In terms of sensory, what you're trying to do is turn a group of trained tasters and use them like an analytical tool," he explains. "Everybody is trained in the off flavors and speaks the same language like describing what they're tasting in an analytical way, such as: 'This is the chemical constituent that I'm tasting and the intensity level is this.' You can use that data for quality." Brynildson shows me a score card. "You can see all the green lines, which represent people that are what we call 'validated.' So they have to score a 70+ on the test. People in the red still are allowed to taste, but their data is not statistically relevant, since they're not a good enough taster yet. The goal is to keep your key panelists tuned. They're spiking beers weekly, if not daily, to see if you can hit your off flavors. If you miss it, your score drops. I'm not the best taster, I'm kind of embarrassed to say." Merlin is being humble.

Signs of the magic he, Firestone, and Walker have worked are everywhere. The original 15,000 ft.^{2} footprint was never designed to make more than 30,000 barrels a year. Now, the brewery is doing roughly ten times that volume. "We figured out how to basically get it up to eighty barrels a turn," states Brynildson.

That said, Firestone Walker's growth strategy was never about mutating into another manufacturer of ubiquitous mass-market beers. Take, for instance, its 805, a kick-back blonde ale and relaxed 4.7% ABV beer that was originally distributed only to the 805 area code. The brewery has always been mindful of its carbon footprint and impact on the environment. "But it kept getting bootlegged into the Central Valley and Los Angeles, so we decided we'll just make it available statewide," he shrugs. It's also on tap here at headquarters, so I decide to try a half pint. "Not bad," I think. In fact, it kind of grows on you. The subtle malt and tropical flavors in this 20 IBU beer make it a safe bet for those who aren't crazy about hoppier options.

Although I'd like to sit down and relax with several pints of this session-able ale, it's time to put away my pen and follow Merlin through a maze of tanks and pipes, deep into the brewery's catacombs. He wants to show me something he and his crew have been conjuring up that is a bit more bold.

"In 1996, Firestone Walker released its inaugural beer, Double Barrel Ale (now known as DBA), which was fermented in a 'union' of oak barrels, inspired by the famed Burton Union system that dates back to the late 19th century in Burton-on-Trent, England," explains my guide as we pass another tour group. "We've been fermenting beer in oak for so long that we forget to talk about it." Now his captive apprentice for the next hour or so, I'm treated to an outpouring of details.

Firestone Walker's founders' fascination with old wooden barrels goes beyond the brewery's fermentation program. Brynildson notes that a new wrinkle was added in 2006, when they began aging Strong Ales in bourbon and other spirits barrels. As if its two successful programs weren't ambitious enough, seven years later, Firestone Walker established its Barrelworks wild ale facility ninety-three miles down Route 101 in Buellton. Barrelworks uses recycled oak barrels and foeders for secondary fermentation and maturation of its wild, largely sour, ales. "Now we've got three distinct barrel programs," he clarifies as I struggle to keep up.

By now, we have wound our way through the Brewhouse to the Barrel Room. Dozens of steel-striped, worn wooden containers rest on metal racks in the cool, dimly lit, cavernous space. Brynildson winces and points to a group of "800-pound gorillas" in the room. "We've bought these new barrels that we're trying to age things in, and I think it's funny that they're leaking more than the twelve-year-old ones," says the painfully amused brewer. Not everything works out as planned.

However, try hard often enough, and you might just discover a novel approach that you can't poke holes in. "When we first partnered up with Duvel Moortgat Brewery (which has since purchased controlling interest in Firestone Walker), you have this one hundred-plus-year-old Belgian brewery," he reports. "They were extremely curious about barrel aging and asked our help in jumpstarting their barrel-aging program. To have them come and ask me how to do barrel aging? Never in my wildest dreams!

You'd think the Belgians would have that down. In the '70s, if you had said, 'American beer' to a Belgian, they'd have laughed you out of the bar." My, how times have changed.

As good as the brewery is getting at aging beer, there is always something new to learn. Firestone Walker has leaned on old ties in the wine industry, oak experts in their own right, to refine its barrel-aged vintage program. "Our Anniversary Program is cool because we pull everything out of the cellar, and we sit down with a dozen local winemakers," he shares. "We give them the components, and they help create our anniversary ale blend." That is collaboration at its pinnacle, especially when you consider that winemakers and brewers aren't always on the same page.

"Another thing that we're really proud of, though I don't like to tout it too much, is that we've done so well in competition," says Brynildson. "Not only does the Great American Beer Festival and World Beer Cup give the opportunity for accolades, but at least once a year, every brewer in the country is focused on making sure that the beer they send is good. It's the one time you get to see how your beer stacks up against your brothers' in the industry. If it wasn't for those competitions, some breweries might not focus as much, maybe. I like to think we have that focus all year round. But competition does give you the chance to look and say: 'Oh gosh, I should make something like that, for sure.'"

At some point, even intoxicating beverage magicians deserve to retire to their castles and rest on laurels of gold and silver medallions with a good craft beer book. I wonder if the still red-bearded Merlin has thought ahead to the day when the grey and white whiskers show up. He admits that the day-to-day grind can be stressful at times. "It's like a bakery," says Brynildson. "You can't let anything break down. That grind can get you, you know. There are days I say, 'I wish I worked in a brewpub, where I could kick back.' But I have eighty staff in the production brewery, and every one of those people's families rely on this brewery functioning and continuing to grow. We always say that we're one bad beer away from bankruptcy. You can sink the ship pretty fast making a couple of bad batches. There's a lot of pressure. If anything gets old, it's that, but I think you'd have that in any industry."

Yet here he is as engaged as ever, content to be at the brewery on a Saturday afternoon. "What's cool about working at Firestone Walker with Adam and David is that they have allowed me and the brew team to innovate freely. Our brewing program dictates the beers that we make, not the marketing or sales teams. I think this must also be true for other successful craft brewers—our customer base is demanding innovation, and we need to react to that." That keeps him on his toes. "The breweries that have kept playing the same songs, like a band that keeps playing the same hits, find themselves left behind," he sighs. "You can't get away with that anymore. What keeps me up in the middle of the night is, 'What's next?' Trying to figure it out. That's the challenge." No doubt Merlin has plenty of other tricks up his sleeve, and his audience can't wait to see what he pulls out of the tap tomorrow.

Merlin Unfiltered

The Importance of Fresh Beer

There is nothing magical about beer that has been aging in a warm garage or as part of an unrefrigerated store display left on the floor to move those last few cases. "Craft beer consumers have keyed into freshness," according to Brynildson. "That is something that we can't emphasize enough: seeking out and finding fresh beer, pushing retailers to rotate stock, and demanding freshness and cold storage. If people start treating craft beer like they do their milk or another perishable item, then everyone's going to be enjoying good craft beer. If and when we get calls on quality, 9.9 out of 10 times, they didn't read the date, and they don't understand why it doesn't taste good. Then we clue them into the beer being six months out of code, and they just didn't realize beer went bad.

"We keep a cold library and a warm library, and we do most of our sensory out of the warm library because worst case scenario, it's sitting on a grocery store floor, the consumer takes it home, warm-stores it and throws it in the fridge right before they drink it. So we want to know what the worst case scenario is. It's unbelievable the difference between sixty-day warm-store beer and sixty-day cold-store beer. If everybody cold-stored it, we could double our shelf life. We put 120 days on everything that we do. Even some of our sales staff tastes the 120-day beer, and they're like, 'Tastes perfectly fine to me,' and I'm like, 'It's not, man! We have to tune you up!'

"Ten years ago, I'd say that, and it was a problem because no one understood the perishable nature of beer. Nobody was clued in. More people are now." It doesn't take a seer like Merlin to wave a wand and turn swill into pure golden goodness. All that's needed is attention to the sell-by stamp and access to a functional cooler.

CHAPTER 24

GETTING A GOOD BUZZ ON AVOCADO HONEY

Island Brewing Company—Carpinteria, CA

RAPIDLY SCANNING THE DOZENS of craft beer options on the refrigerator shelf at a Ventura, California supermarket, my eyes stopped on a pale green label. It wasn't just the color that drew my attention, but three magic words: Avocado Honey Ale. That's because I spent the first fourteen years of my childhood climbing trees and picking the rough-skinned green fruit from the orchard that was my backyard in nearby Santa Paula.

Forty years later, and I'm still obsessed with avocados. I scoop them, slice them, and infuse them into every recipe imaginable. I thought I'd tried this fruit of the gods in every possible combination, yet here it was in liquefied form and much easier to guzzle than guacamole. I picked up a few irresistible bottles of the Island Brewing-made beer, raced out of the parking lot, and headed to a reunion with an old buddy whom I hadn't seen in decades.

Avocado Honey turned out to be everything I'd imagined and more. My friend dutifully tasted the cold ale and, not being much of a beer drinker, placated me with a polite smile and nod. Meanwhile, I sighed and savored the ripe creamy Haas that I was sure I detecting. This certainly wasn't the avocado aroma sometimes associated with acetaldehyde (an unwanted chemical that can hang around due to incomplete beer conditioning). The heavenly retronasal effect a split-second after each delectable, slightly sweet taste reminded me of the ubiquitous fruit I'd tolerated as a kid and grown to crave like a rare treat as an adult.

It was nearly a year later when I learned the truth from Island Brewing founder Paul Wright behind the brewery at his beach town taproom just off the 101 in downtown Carpinteria (roughly sixteen miles northwest of Ventura by surfboard). The now-white-haired seventy-five-year old owner and beer aficionado picked an incredible spot to turn a longtime dream into reality. He celebrated the Fourth of July weekend in 2001 by opening his microbrewery along this stretch of eye-candy-beautiful Santa Barbara County coastline.

Now, nearly 16 years later, I'm sitting on the pub's patio with only train tracks and a grassy park separating me from a strip of soft warm sand that is continuously kissed by the Southern California surf. The temperature is climbing on this hot April afternoon, but the ocean breeze makes things perfectly comfortable as we get started.

After brief introductions, Wright informs me that I'll have to wait to learn the secrets of his Avocado Honey. We have a lot of other ground to cover first. We grab a flight of beers and head for a private tasting room he has set up away from the happy crowd of customers.

I start with the Island Blonde, a mellow, straw-colored Kölsch-style ale brewed with Pilsner, Vienna, and wheat malts as well as a dash of Saaz hops. This 17 IBU, 5% ABV, bready beer is easy to drink in the warm weather. It's also not going to overwhelm the other stronger beers lined up on the table awaiting their turn.

Meanwhile, I turn my attention from the full-bodied blonde and those tempting tasters to my knowledgeable host. It's time to hear his story.

Wright began brewing in the Bay Area back in the late 1980s. "My wife gave me a home brew kit and that was all canned extract, including hops," he recalls. "You just dump this in a container and add water, throw in dry yeast, and two weeks later, you have beer." Miraculously, the neighbors liked his first forays into brewing (or they had damn good poker faces).

That promising approval rating fed Wright's ambitious nature. He joined a local homebrewers club, Mountain Hoppers, which later merged with MASH, another Bay Area group, to become Homebrewers of Marin and Elsewhere, winners of California Home Brew Club of the Year in 1998. At MASH, Wright learned the intricacies of the craft from President Mike Riddle and others in the club. "If you're a runner or in a competitive sport, and you have someone who is really good at it, you try and do your very best to keep up with him or be in the same league," he points out. "That really helped me to move ahead and to be willing to brew as much as I did and get that good education when it was available."

Some of Wright's concoctions weren't right at all. "I put together a small 5-gallon system and started brewing some weird stuff," he remembers. "I was bringing it to the club and saying, 'What do you think? What's this weird taste?'" Then he just listened to the experts and took their helpful hints home, plugged it into his computer database, and went back to work brewing in the garage.

Those critiques, along with Wright's unbending focus on recipe formulation, helped him improve to the point that he was winning more than his fair share of awards by the end of his home brewing days. "I was doing fifty-four batches a year for two years, primarily for competition," he says. "I think that really helped give me a good basis in how to put a beer together. Brewing is something you have to learn by doing."

By no means did the lessons stop when Wright and his family opened Island Brewing. Some discoveries were painful, but bound and determined to turn his passion into something bigger, he persevered. "There were a number of nights early on that I slept on the couch and didn't leave for days, trying to get this thing going," he recalls. "It was difficult to brew, process the beer, and go out and sell it. I suppose if I were a sane person, I probably wouldn't have continued.

"I remember one Monday, we came to work and there was black stuff rolling out the front door." That high tide turned out to be stout that had overflowed from the fermenter blow off. "It went across the brewhouse and out the front door," he winces. "We spent a lot of time cleaning up messes because the slope of the room wasn't very beneficial, and we just didn't have enough drainage." Eventually Wright added drains and tweaked his processes to the point where the flood of start-up problems subsided. Success freed him to stop mopping and start focusing on his recipes.

"It's interesting because the new breweries coming along have their mission statement, and it always says, 'We use the very best ingredients,'" observes Wright. "We've always tried to use the best, and as a result I do more English and European grains, especially the specialty grains." He has always been a fan of English ales. "That's kind of being traditional," adds the meticulous brewer, "but we've certainly experimented and gone in different directions, too."

Although Wright is a bit of a traditionalist when it comes to ingredients, he also believes that you have to take some chances. "You can't just rely on a stout, a porter, and a couple of pale ales," he says. "You have to continue to experiment and try new things. We're always doing that now, but always with an idea of, 'What is the public going to enjoy drinking and come back for another?' That's part of the equation, too."

We pause for a taste of one of Paul's personal favorites, Jubilee Ale. This Scotch-style ale has taken a silver at the GABF (2002) and first place at the LA County Fair (2003). I ask him for his evaluation. "Caramel, caramel, caramel," he says, looking past me as he focuses on the roasted malt flavor.

Maybe it's the influence of the deep-copper-red liquid in my glass, but I'm detecting dark fruit over top of the malt in this relatively potent 6.8% ABV beer. "It leaves a slightly sour, plum-like aftertaste on the sides of the tongue," I observe.

"It's a really a wee heavy (a 6%+ Scotch ale)," he adds, enjoying the double entendre and the relatively thick, gut-warming beer.

Island Brewing also makes a Barrel-Aged Coffee Jubilee, which conditions in coffee-spiked oak barrels for three months before the nutty, dark-roast treat is ready for prime time. It's a wee bit heavier than the Jubilee Ale at 7.2% ABV, so plan on catching a ride home or you may find yourself passed out under the stars.

As the late-afternoon sun melts into the Pacific, we finally get around to the secrets of Island's Avocado Honey Ale. It takes a several sips and a few minutes to rinse the lingering film from the bourbon-barrel stout. I wonder what type of avocado he is infusing in his award-winning beer. "Where do you introduce the mashed fruit in your process?" I ask. He just stares across the table with an amused look on his face. His eyes crinkle at the corners, and he chuckles.

Wright proceeds to tell me just how wrong my initial evaluation of his prized beer was. "There is no avocado in the beer," he explains with a wry smile. But he quickly lets me off the hook. "We did think about throwing avocado in the mash or even in the brew kettle, but our experience with avocados is that they're sort of oily. We even thought about maybe putting some pits in the mash, just to say that we made an avocado beer, but that wouldn't have been much of a beer either." This makes perfect sense, but it's a little like discovering a magician's secret and realizing that it's all just an illusion. I'm left disappointed, flat as a week-old, half-empty growler, but just for a minute.

As it turns out, Wright and his team were trying to develop a recipe that would tie into the local Avocado Festival. "All of a sudden, it occurred to us that there is a honey derivative from the avocado tree," he says. "It is a fruit that requires pollination. There's not much of a flower, but it does require that bees are pollinating and bringing back the nectar; then the beekeeper would develop the honey."

Fortunately, there just happened to be a few people working at the brewery who were amateur beekeepers. "We were able to get a third of their production, one bucket, and make some avocado-honey beer," Wright shares. "It's dark, intense, mollassesy—one of the darkest and most intense of the honeys."

Ultimately, Wright had to abandon the amateur beekeepers and look for a source that could keep up with the growing demand for his popular Avocado Honey Ale. A healthy sixty pounds of thick, viscous honey goes into every fifteen-barrel batch. "We have partnered with one local honey producer now for a number of years," he says. "It's been a good combination for us."

I feel the same way about this afternoon's fruitful meeting. I've acquired a few precious pints of Avocado Honey to take back to my room and a recorder full of Wright's good stories. As we finish up and wander back into the busy pub, Paul's place is abuzz with guests enjoying laughs and libations.

"Beer is a conversational thing, a community thing," he observes. "I'm not sure if it's because of the (affordable) price or the perceived history of beer that makes it fun, but it certainly is. Our goal is to just make people happy."

He has certainly accomplished that mission with at least one customer today. It's just another case of serendipity: this time stumbling on something special in a supermarket cooler and following the trail to its even more remarkable source. In Craft Beer Country, all it takes to get there is a little curiosity and a sense of adventure.

Paul Unfiltered

Similarities in Pairing Wine and Beer with Food

"A light beer, like our Tropical Lager, and maybe even the Blonde, are more akin to a white wine, so you can think about pairings in the same way," suggests Wright. "People have done a lot of work about pairing with wine, so why not use some of those same attributes? The lighter beers would pair well with lighter food, such as fish and cheeses. As you get into IPAS, you can pair them with more hearty foods—maybe a steak. Does it complement the food or help balance it out in the other direction? You want to try and pair like things or maybe dissimilar things. I've been to some beer tastings where the chefs came out with wonderful pairings, but it was nothing I'd ever think about, like a big roast with a Hefeweizen. Of course, you might go with our Jubilee or more malty beers for your big roasts and things that are heavy.

"Let's say tomorrow morning, you're going to be hung, and it's your last supper tonight," I interrupt. "Tell me what beer and food is on your table! You've got to pick something, cowboy."

This question clearly pains him, and I can see the wheels turning, trying to resolve this quirky prisoner's dilemma. "I do a lot of fish, so something to do with fish," he says. Then his eyes light up. "Or the Avocado Honey," he smiles, "that's a good in-between beer. I'd drink it all night and not go to bed!"

CHAPTER 25

A PLEASANT SURPRISE IN PLACENTIA

The Bruery—Placentia, CA

PUSH PINS COVER much of San Diego County on my Craft Beer Country map, but oddly enough, the breweries I've visited end in San Marcos, California and pick back up again along the coast, 113 miles northwest in Carpinteria. In between lies sprawling Greater Los Angeles, the second largest urban region in the United States. I finally pinpoint a brewery to visit in Orange County and schedule a tour and tasting.

After navigating a tangle of SoCal highways, my GPS puts me on the 57 North, where I immediately peel off at the Orangethorpe exit. After a quick left at the bottom of the ramp and a sharp right just a block later, I pull into an older, single-story office park that has been revitalized by The Bruery. I wander past a black Chevy Impala lowrider, shiny trunk inches from the pavement, slick hood pointed skyward. "It's time for a cerveza," I think, as I head for the door.

The tasting room is already humming at 4 p.m. The Bruery is apparently the place to be on a semi-sunny Monday afternoon in Placentia. Just like a complicated beer recipe, the room is a mixture of ingredients, a melting pot of people enjoying each other's company, rainbows of beer on their tables.

I meet with Senior Director of Operations, Jonas Nemura, who orders a colorful flight for me to sample. I'm pleasantly surprised at the first taste of Or Xata. "What does that remind me of?" I ask. He looks at me quizzically and raises his eyebrows as if to say, "You tell me and we'll both know." So he's not a mind reader. "This smells like a cinnamon roll," I volunteer. "Well that makes sense," he replies. "Or Xata (or Horchata for gringos like me) is a slightly sweet Mexican drink that has a cinnamon and vanilla flavor." I know that this sounds strange for a beer, but the retronasal cinnamon scent is pleasing, not overpowering. Am I imagining it or is that icing I taste as I savor a sip from the taster? This is one of those beers that borders on addictive, and I have trouble moving on to the next glass waiting on the wooden tasting tray.

Nemura is crazy about beer too. He fell head over heels for brewing after leaving New York for New Zealand, where he discovered his true calling. During a gig with a real-ale pub, he juggled brewery and bar duties and loved it. Upon returning to the US a year later, he met restless Patrick Rue, who had abandoned his original plan to be a lawyer and was busy working on turning his dream to launch a brewery into a reality.

"I loved his concept of high-end, full-flavored specialty beers and asked him for a job after sticking around far too late following a BJCP (Beer Judge Certification Program) exam at The Bruery," remembers Nemura. "Fortunately, he liked me." He became the second full-time employee, doing everything from brewing to packaging to warehouse work to working with distributors. "With the rapid expansion of our distribution program, it became clear pretty early on that I was the best suited to handle that side of the business, and the rest is history."

I'm starting to think that this brewery, just a few miles from Disneyland, might be one of the best kept secrets on the West Coast. In the nine years since launching The Bruery, founder Rue, Nemura, and company have built a lineup of some of the most fascinating flavors in the country. Although they maintain a beer club with a fanatical following, shipping is limited to the California-based members. Mention The Bruery outside the state, and most people respond, "Yes, I've heard of lots of breweries. In fact, I'm putting together some great stuff in my garage! Want to try some of my killer IPA?"

The fermentation process for Rue's destiny actually began during his first year of law school at nearby Chapman University. "My wife, Rachel, told me to get a hobby—or perhaps it was, 'Get a life, Patrick!'—after complaining about the early days of my law school career," he recalls. "Home brewing is a hobby I've admired for some time. I had a good-sized garage that wasn't being used for parking, so I converted it into a ten-gallon brewery with a five-tap kegerator. In those three years of school, I became a great homebrewer and a mediocre law student. In 2006, right after graduation, I won Best of Show at the San Diego County Fair, Orange County Fair, and runner-up at the LA County Fair homebrew competitions. I took that as a message of what I should be doing with my life."

At first, Rue thought he might become an attorney for craft breweries but figured out that wasn't what he really wanted to do. "I decided my best, yet risk-laden option was to open my own brewery," he says. "While I was studying for the bar exam, I was also putting together my business plan."

With backing from his family, he leased a warehouse in Placentia in 2007. "We brewed our first batch in March 2008 and started selling beer in May 2008," he shares. "I was twenty-seven years old at the time we opened and generally had no idea what I was getting myself into." Those types of business adventurers often ultimately lead to spectacular failure. But there are also instances when bull-headed persistence ends up in a resounding success.

Sometimes, Lady Luck plays the role of Ninkasi and magically comes to the rescue. "There have been quite a few happy accidents," according to Rue. "The original batch of Black Tuesday was a fairly terrible idea. The idea was a kitchen-sink beer to use up a bunch of random sacks of malts I had ordered to test recipes on my homebrew system before we opened." It's often a cascading series of missteps rather than one significant mistake that leads to a big problem. Such was the case at The Bruery in the wee hours one morning in 2008, and here is what ensued.

"The first mistake was waking up at 3:00 a.m. to brew beer," confesses Rue. "I didn't have a clear head going into my day." Driven to turn the leftover ingredients into something drinkable, the young, sleepy brewer forged ahead. After all, doesn't fortune favor the bold?

"The second mistake was putting too much grain in the mash tun," he continues. "The grist was very dry and the mash stuck repeatedly." Rue points out that he should have brewed smaller batches of high gravity beers or done two mashes. In retrospect, he adds, "You'll save time in the end."

"The third mistake was allowing visitors while I'm brewing a beer I've never brewed before." The mash stuck, the sparge kept running, and the mash tun overflowed while Rue was paying attention to his guests rather than the equipment working away at the wort.

"The fourth mistake was after ten hours of brewing, I decided there was plenty left to extract out of the mash, so we should do a second-runnings beer (reusing the mash to make a second, lower ABV beer). No big deal, right? Just another four hours, best-case scenario. After collecting a few BBL's (barrels), the mash had cooled down, became gelatinous, and we had the mother of all stuck mashes on our hands. The mash tun was completely full, and no liquid would come through. We had to dump the whole thing, approximately 700 gallons of hot water and grain."

This was fast developing into to the mother of all microbrewery nightmares. "The fifth mistake was using a tool that would fit into the spent grain chute valve," he reports. "We had a difficult time getting the grain/water mixture out of the mash tun. It was that stuck! So, we took a small paddle and poked a hole in the grain bed to send the grain and water out of the spent grain chute, which is a large butterfly valve on the bottom of the mash tun. Without us knowing, the paddle got stuck in the valve, and we couldn't close it. We thought it was the strength of the rushing grain-water mixture that was keeping the valve open. About half of the mash tun emptied itself on the brewery floor, most in areas without floor drains. After sixteen-plus hours of work, this was the last thing I needed. I remember shoveling grain and mopping up water with a blistering hand."

"The good news is the beer turned out great!" In fact, The Bruery still produces Black Tuesday, although the process has since been cleaned up and doesn't involve Rue fighting sleep deprivation and a flash flood of wort.

Over the years, stories like these and a growing lineup of well-made unique craft beers have set The Bruery apart. It isn't easy to stand out here, a few miles from some of the area's famous amusement parks, but this somewhat inconspicuous brewery has made a name for itself with out-of-the-ordinary beers like The Traveling Plum. This unique sour is unlike anything I've tasted during my trek. It reminds me of sneaking wild plums from the neighbor's orchard and eating the sweet-and-sour fruit down to the pit. The Traveling Plum also has subtle spice notes to it and a hint of prune. "I love that beer," agrees Nemura. "We certainly didn't know it would be a hit. Quite the opposite: we were concerned about making too much, and honestly, it wasn't that great of a seller initially. It has picked up a bit with time and developed more of a following, though." Count me among the growing fan base. In fact, I've special ordered several bottles since my visit, sharing The Traveling Plum with friends from San Diego to Denver.

Many of The Bruery's beers are unique works, modified styles that you aren't likely to find elsewhere. "We focus on flavor profiles rather than styles or even ingredients, and I think that makes a big difference in how the beer comes out," says Rue. "It sounds simple, but I find that most breweries try to achieve a certain flavor, but try to get there by following a certain style. Brewing concepts on the pilot system allows us to try out a lot of different recipes and see what works."

The process is working so well that I'm faced with a paradox of choice. There are simply too many great flavors, scents, and textures here, and not enough stomach capacity to accommodate them all. A sampling of the many temptations includes pucker-up sour Frucht: Boysenberry, a bubbly pink-headed Berliner Weisse, barrel-aged at the company's new Bruery Terreux facility, and Tart of Darkness, an oak-barrel-aged malty stout, spiked with sour cherries. Picking a favorite is a little like asking me to choose my favorite child. Nemura plays along: "The bigger problem in this case is that we have literally hundreds of children. I'm incredibly proud of lots of the beers we've made, but if I had to pick one 'desert island' beer, it would probably be Humulus Terreux. It's incredibly drinkable, but also complex enough to think about, pairs great with a wide variety of food, and changes a lot depending on age and serving temperature."

Rue credits at least part of The Bruery's success to having had an all-star team of mentors in the industry, including Greg Koch and Steve Wagner from Stone Brewing, Tomme Arthur from Lost Abbey, and Vinnie Cilurzo from Russian River (among a long list of others). "All come to mind as people that inspired me and who helped me personally in the early days." Half-joking, he says, "I may have stalked all of them."

Much of their advice traveled north from San Diego, where craft brewing caught on quicker than in greater Los Angeles. But that slower start also helped The Bruery stand out early on. "There weren't many breweries in LA or Orange County in 2008, so it wasn't too hard to get recognized at that point in time," notes Rue. "It was very difficult to find beers like ours. When we first started, Rachel and I would work the tasting room and serve perhaps up to twenty people in a day. It was slow, and we've gradually built the business. Most of our customers learned about us by word of mouth, and they'll seek us out.

"LA is an interesting place," he continues. "I don't quite understand why craft beer has taken so long to take off here, but it's well underway. Having local breweries in LA has really helped develop a market for craft beer, as there's more awareness around craft beer with local brewers. Craft beer is here for the long run, and just like fine wine and good whiskey, it will continue to exist."

As I prepare to depart the crowded parking lot, I can't help but believe that Rue has nothing to worry about. Here in the heart of this late-blooming craft beer country frontier, he and his team are consistently cranking out intriguing beers that have people talking, and then walking into his tap house. In fact, it's been such a pleasant surprise in Placentia that I'm already looking forward to my next visit and another taste or two of true Southern California paradise.

Patrick Unfiltered

Mood Pairings

"I can't say I have a favorite beer style," shares Rue. "It's dependent of a lot of things. I have a better sense of 'mood pairings' than I do 'food pairings.' Am I hot and thirsty? Then a hoppy, very cold pilsner is ideal. Have I had a difficult day and need to unwind? A dank double IPA would be perfect. Is it autumn, and I'm in a celebratory mood? A Rauchbier from Schlenkerla (a historic brewpub in Bamberg, Germany) would be my choice. Am I watching a movie late at night, and want something to sip and savor? A barrel-aged imperial stout would be my choice."

CHAPTER 26

SEARCHING FOR ARTHUR'S LOST ABBEY

The Lost Abbey—San Marcos, CA

INTRIGUE AND IMAGINATION took over the minute that I stumbled across The Lost Abbey on the Internet. Visions of enjoying a deep golden Tripel on a sun-drenched San Marcos, California courtyard danced in my head. It would be like visiting one of Europe's lovely Trappist breweries, only in the laid-back style of Southern California, wearing sandals, shorts, and shades, while soaking in the radiant rays. My mind's eye quickly converted an old adobe mission into a beer-garden oasis flowing with malty delights, their micro-bubbled heads bursting with fragrant esters!

Now it was a promisingly warm December afternoon, and I hoped my dream would come true. Rather than breaking through woods to find a hidden glen, I made my way down a freeway frontage road and into a light industrial jungle. "Where is that church bell, anyway?" I wondered. A few office parks later, and The Lost Abbey appeared between inconspicuous buildings, not a monk in sight . . . at least yet.

After friendly greetings from the brewery brethren, I was ushered to a conference room, where I met Tomme Arthur. Dress Tomme in a brown habit, and he could double for a monk. Arthur has a sturdy, friar-like look to him, bald on top and sharp studious eyes under spectacles that make me a little nervous. He is as serious as his intense focus is on making consistently delicious craft beer.

Arthur, who grew up Catholic, found brewing in 1996 at a little pub in downtown San Diego called Cervecería La Cruda. "It means the hangover brewery in Spanish, or at least it's loosely translated what they were," he explains with a smirk. "It lasted less than a year."

After a short stint at White Labs, a San Diego-based company that produces brewing yeast and provides lab services to the industry, Arthur spent eight years honing his skills as head brewer at Pizza Port in Solana Beach. "I put in a lot of time crafting very interesting beers at the brew-pub level," he recalls. On a road trip with Pizza Port owner Gina Marsaglia, Arthur learned that her brother and partner Vince had a concept in mind called The Lost Abbey. "Nobody really knew how to make it fly," he remembers. "So I spent a lot of time just imagining what that would look like, what it would be as a brand." Ultimately, Arthur saw the light, and a new brewery was born.

"We opened our doors here in 2006, expressly with the purpose of giving me a chance to run a facility and grow the brands," he says. "Most people think about breweries as brands, but as a brand, what would we invoke? It's an artistic impression, a real sense of the biblical struggles of good and evil. Are we good? Are we bad? Are we going to hell? Is there a heaven? It became very obvious to me how easy it would be to brand a beer and a label like that because of the ability to dig into the Bible or to dig into the allegory. There are lots of places to look for that inspiration. It's all about the picture and the story and the message."

It's also about producing beers the appeal to an ever-growing audience of enthusiasts. "Our ability to appeal to women is massively important," shares Arthur. "It's historically been sort of a manly beverage, but there are a lot of women that really want to be involved in beer because the range of flavors is just so exceptional, and it can do so many things. It's exciting because it is a whole different sensibility. Women have great palates, and they have the ability to perceive flavors and aromas that sometimes men can't—different thresholds, so I welcome it." Those traits enable them to identify and appreciate an exceptional beer when they see, smell, and taste it.

Although Arthur has turned The Lost Abbey's branding into artwork, he knows that the frescos covering his bottles are nothing without the magical ingredients sealed within. "The quality of the beers exceeds the branding in some ways," continues Arthur. In fact, the Abbey's approach is much more refined. "Now with respect to some of the more esoteric things that we do that are very unique, a lot of the barrel-aged beers that we produce are world class. I'm very proud of our sour beer program. We make some incredibly rich and deep beers that are highly sought after."

Professional and amateur chefs have taken notice of food-beer pairing opportunities, thinking beyond brats and burgers. "We make a beer called Cuvee de Tomme," says Arthur, eyes lighting up. "It's a barrel-aged sour with cherries. Some friends of mine created a pairing for a dinner one time where they took duck confit, rolled it into a spring roll and deep fried it and then served it with a cherry dipping sauce. It was fantastic with the Cuvee—a lot of acid, lot of bright flavors, some crisp texture, and then the duck fat." Ah! "It was a spectacular, sort of home-run thing."

Arthur is adventurous by nature. "So we always talk about the four components of beer, but I always talk about the fifth one being the passion for beer," he reveals. "Then really looking at how you can innovate and how you can experiment. We're not in chains, and because of that, our numbers are really based upon bold flavors and smaller case total runs. We get a chance to really not be beholden to making the best pale ale in our town or the best wheat beer in town or the best of this or that. We get a chance to make some pretty good leaps at experimentation." One such experiment led to a beer that drinks like a liquefied cookie, a treat I will soon get to sample.

We move from the office to the tasting room, which is a little like a cross between a chapel and a bar in decor, sans any pews. *Tapists* run behind the counter. One young monk (okay, bartender) pours me a Track #8, a powerful, 13.7% quad that has been aged in bourbon barrels. "When I tasted the beer in the lab environment prior to packaging it, I said, 'This has got this oatmeal-raisin-cookie quality to it, and I think we should chase that sense of flavor in a beer,'" remembers Arthur. "So when we went to texture the finish of the beer, we definitely ended up with this carbonated oatmeal raisin cookie. It's got the coconut essence to it, and it's got some really cool flavors. But the process of actually adding the cinnamon and chilies to the barrels brings out a coconut note in the beer, yet there is no coconut in the beer. It's incredible to think that the barrel process, the toasting of the barrel itself creates a compound. But it's almost like the cinnamon and the chilies act as a catalyst and then bring that forward. That was sort of a truly happy accident."

Back then, parts of the artisanal process were painfully slow and labor intensive. "We actually caramelized the raisins prior to them getting into the beer," notes Arthur. "When we were brewing on the small scale in the pub level, we used to do it in a pan, and we would just sort of almost caramelize it like an onion, then deglaze it with some port and sear it, and flash it off. Then we would add it to the beer." Times, they have changed.

"The scope is so much bigger here," emphasizes Arthur. "We couldn't have a guy out there tossing raisins in a pan all day, so we ended up buying a commercial flamethrower. Now when it comes time to brew the beer once a year, all the guys take turns flamethrowing the raisins." You can't take the boy out of the man. "It's really fun to watch," he smiles. "The guys get excited about playing with fire and stuff like that." No kidding! One could make a case that "playing with fire" is the unofficial mantra here at The Lost Abbey.

But Arthur is careful not to get too cute with his beers. "I don't believe in esoteric for esoteric's sake," he confides. "I don't believe that we need to create a beer that has thirteen ingredients in it just to have one more than the guy down the street. So while we do have experimentation, I think it's more of like a classic pianist who knows how to play that sheet perfectly and then goes off when they want to." He and those brothers and sisters in the industry worthy of being called his peers have come a long way.

Today's craft beer world bears little resemblance to its humble beginnings. "When I first got into this in 1996, we were having to bang the gong," shares Arthur. "We were having to run around and tell people what these things were. There were beers that are being brewed today that you couldn't even imagine that would have been brewed back in that time. We spent an enormous amount of time and energy educating the masses and really trying to cultivate a deeper sense of beer drinking. There was a hardcore set of people that knew about beer, and they were really into it, but we had to get it outside of that really tight circle."

Now the circumference of its reach is growing daily. "The volume of people in the craft beer community is so much larger than I think any of us could have ever imagined," reflects Arthur. "And with that now brings the sense of commodity. We're bringing some serious dollar bills into it, and that has definitely changed the landscape in the last couple years, and it's not done. But at the same time, you can still start a brewery for $100,000. It's not ideal, but if this is your passion, and you want to max out your credit cards and chase a little system in a garage somewhere, you can still do it. Some of the best breweries in this country started on shoestring budgets. The entrepreneurial spirit is still very well alive in this space!"

There is no question that the creative flame burns bright in Arthur's realm. "We don't think there are many breweries in this country that have the range of expression of flavors that we do from the front to the back," he contends. "We just do so many different things, and hopefully, we do a lot of them well."

Although one of craft beer's kings has been at it more than two decades, his burning passion for brewing hasn't burned out. "The business has gotten to be a far larger enterprise than we set out," points out Arthur. "We have far more employees, more regulatory concerns and all that. But when 4 o'clock rolls around, I still have that shift beer and get to revel in what we've accomplished."

After so many years in the business and plenty of beers under his belt, he still appreciates the little things, like a cold, 8.5% Mongo Double IPA, at the end of the day. "I've been at it a long time, but I'm not thinking about the exit anytime soon," he claims. "I'm thinking, 'Can I be doing this at sixty-two?'" And I'm thinking, "Why the hell not?"

Soon enough, it's time to leave Tomme's magical tap room at The Lost Abbey, and head back to the reality of rush hour traffic. While I crawl along the Southern California freeway on my quest looking for the next ale oasis, Arthur goes about his daily mission: spreading good beer to those in need of a little comfort.

Tomme Unfiltered

Beer Tasting Tips

I asked Arthur what the average beer drinker doesn't know about beer tasting that they can do to improve the experience. "Do you have any tricks or anything you can share with me as far as tasting to pull the flavors out?"

"A lot of us get very deadlocked in drinking that same thing, but I'm a professional judge," he says. "We work really hard at being incredibly astute with our observations. So I think that it's useful to develop a library of terms that you use, not to be really preachy about it, but just as a matter of nailing some of those things." There are a number of great reference books and websites out there for the lexicon (try *The Beer Bible* or *Encyclopedia of Beer*), but Tomme offers some practical advice to experiment with.

"I often recommend that people take and buy a six-pack of a specific beer that they really love and then abuse it," he says with a straight face. "So keep one cold, heat one at a certain temperature and maybe put one in the sun. Then maybe even keep one for three months and go back and visit it later. You'll see, in just that regard, what heat does to something, what light can do to it, and what oxidation can do." Although it sounds nearly criminal to me to destroy good beer, I understand the method behind the madness.

"From my experience over the years, the one thing that most consumers are pretty blind to is old beer because a lot of the beer that's out in the market place isn't as fresh as they may have ever tasted it. In that way, if I go out and drink Mongo off the tap every day, and every week we change the keg, that's really fresh Mongo!"

CHAPTER 27

GUARDIANS OF THE CRAFT

Stone Brewing Company—Escondido, CA

THE FIRST TIME I VISITED stonebrewing.com, a gargoyle with a beer stein stared me down from the home page. I entered my birth date on the page and cautiously proceeded deeper into Stone's virtual lair, where I discovered the following explanation for the brewery's ominous logo: "For centuries, gargoyles have been known to ward off evil spirits. Since 1996, our gargoyle has helped us ward off cheap ingredients, pasteurization and chemical additives . . . the modern-day evil spirits of beer!" Okay, I get it. Stone's grotesque guardian hoists a pint with a muscle-bound right arm, obviously pumped up over its eternal role in quality assurance.

Safely past the gate keeper and mandatory legal-drinking-age check box, the deeper I delved into Stone's web site, the more mesmerized I became by the long list of tempting craft beers. Its inner sanctum is a realm of shades, covering the entire SRM color chart from straw-hewed IPAs to dark porters. Pictures may be worth a thousand words, but they aren't worth a damn when it comes to tasting beer. It was time to plan a visit to Stone Brewing, turn temptation into reality, and verify that the gargoyles were indeed doing their job.

A few days later, and the taste test is just getting underway on the brewer's lushly landscaped patio in Escondido, California. The process starts with a glass of Stone IPA, a 6.9% ABV gem made with Magnum, Chinook, and Centennial hops. The nicely balanced ale, with hints of citrus and pine, makes me wonder if the clever brewer found a way to graft a lemon branch to a Douglas fir. Not that the day is particularly hot in perpetually perfect San Diego County, but it's just warm enough for an Oregon boy that this cold, 77 IBU beer is particularly satisfying. Stone IPA isn't exactly lawn-mower beer, but it would certainly help alleviate the pain in lieu of ibuprofen after a hard day in the yard.

As leaves rustle in the breezy beer garden, I wonder whether Stone is using any of the region's indigenous goodies. As it turns out, the gargoyles apparently turned their heads just long enough for the brewers to dose a cask of porter with local avocado honey and jasmine. No doubt they would have scowled at the notion, but not its creators, who enjoyed the odd combination. In another experiment gone right, grapefruit peel somehow found its way into a Ruination IPA cask program, and the results were anything but ruinous. And its Saison Du Buff included local parsley, sage, and thyme, and rosemary, some of it picked right here on the brewery grounds.

Stone's workforce includes many with culinary backgrounds, team members who suggest new combinations of ingredients for the company's cask program. Every few months, the brewery staff taps and compares a lineup of their experimental beers. That leads to interesting conversations . . . and sometimes, clever new ideas.

Although countless pints from its employees' inspirations haven't quite made their way into Stone's mainstream of beer, they are clear indications of the bold characters of the brewery and its founders, Steve Wagner and Greg Koch.

It took more than guts for Koch and Wagner to launch a brewery in the mid-1990s. From the very beginning, lady luck intervened. "It was a time in my life when I realized one career was coming to an end," says Wagner, who was a traveling musician. "I was looking for the next thing." That turned out to be something just as fun. "On one of the last bands I was in, I was with a guy who brewed his own beer. He got me pretty interested in it. So I started brewing on my own and learning about it and started thinking maybe this is the next chapter of my life."

Little did Wagner know that the following pages would bring him back together with an old music buddy, Koch. "In my pursuit of more brewing knowledge, I went up to the University of California Davis in 1993 and was attending some extension classes on sensory evaluation of beer and advanced home brewing, and ran into Greg at one of those classes," he recalls. "It was one of those 'What are you doing here?' moments, and then we realized we had a mutual interest in craft beer. I think it was later that day, over a beer, that we said, 'We should start our own brewery.' I'm good at turning hobbies into careers—that's my thing," he quips.

Wagner ended up landing a job at Pyramid Ales in Kalama, Washington, where he worked a little under two years and absorbed the day-to-day details of the brewery business. "It was a fantastic learning experience, just a fire hose of knowledge," he says. "I realized that I really did love the work. You don't work overnight shifts if you don't really like what you're doing."

At one point, Koch called Wagner and asked, "So, are we going to do this thing or not?" The two decided it was now or never. "We decided on San Diego as the place we wanted to start Stone," remembers Wagner. "We weren't the kind of guys to do a lot of market research and analyze San Diego as the right place to start our business. It was more, 'Hey, there are some cool things going on here, and we like the weather, so let's do it here.'" The partners' intuition appears to have been spot on. "It ended up being a great place to start the brewery for reasons that we didn't know at the time. It's small enough geographically that you can make a big impression. In the case of our start-up, we were a draft-only brewery, and we found that if we got our beer on draft at a couple of influential places, then pretty soon everybody in town knew about it."

Wagner remembers when the microbrewery made its first sale. "We had made friends with the people at Pizza Port in Solana Beach, Gina and Vince Marsaglia, and they made their own fantastic beers. When we finally got up and running and we had our first official keg of beer that we wanted to sell, they said 'We want to be the first place to have Stone on tap.' Not only did they want to buy it, but they came and picked it up from us. And that gave us a completely unrealistic view of the brewing business at that point in time. We thought, 'This is great. We just make the beer and everybody comes and picks it up!' We quickly learned that there is this thing called distribution that is an entirely separate career that involves a lot of hard work and not a lot of money to go along with brewing, which involves a lot of hard work and not a lot of money. But you'd never start anything if you knew what you were getting yourself into. As Greg likes to say, 'It was a twenty-year overnight success,'" laughs Wagner.

Stone's gargoyles still guard a few secrets, and I try to pry one out of Wagner that hasn't been featured in his book with Koch, *The Craft of Stone Brewing Co.: Liquid Lore, Epic Recipes, and Unabashed Arrogance.* "How do you resolve disagreements between you and Greg?" I ask. "Usually it's a cage match," he fires back, stone-faced. "Last man standing gets his way. I'm actually on a losing streak the last five." Don't laugh; it's plausible in this day and age. "Actually, one of the strengths of our company is the push and pull," shares Wagner. "He has a million ideas all of the time, and a lot of them are really great. I kind of help focus him and pull him back a little bit sometimes. He drags me along when I want to go slower and maybe not grow so fast. We end up in a middle spot, which is a really good place to be for our company."

The brewery's branding is anything but middle-of-the-road. Take, for instance, Arrogant Bastard, an American strong ale that has been one of the brewery's juggernaut beers. Koch says the beer told him what its name was. "We did not create it," he contends in his book, *The Craft of Stone Brewing Co.* "I did not name it. It was already there. We were just the first lowly mortals to have stumbled upon it." Good story, anyway.

But if tales are true, the dynamic duo did stumble on the recipe for Arrogant Bastard Ale. Wagner believes that while triangulating the recipe for Stone Pale Ale, he unknowingly miscalculated and added malt and hops in the wrong percentages. In two weeks, when the beer was ready, Wagner tasted it and immediately knew something was wrong. He went back and discovered the miscalculation. He was so disappointed in the mistake that it took him awhile to realize that they had created something really special. The 7.2% ABV ale, with its "classified" hop profile, has since become a favorite here in Craft Beer Country, and I've even found it on tap in Amsterdam. One sip of this hop bomb (let me guess: Columbus,

Chinook, and Centennial in generous abundance), and you might start imagining that the Arrogant Bastard did name itself.

Although Koch has come up with many of Stone's creative brand names, Wagner is not shy about sharing a few of his favorites. "We actually released a summer seasonal beer called our Stone Citrusy Wit, which is a wit beer with some kaffir lime leaf," he shares. "Internally, we came up with a name many of us preferred, but we ended up not going with it, but it was called 'Stone Gives a Wit'. I think we missed a big opportunity with that one. That's the way it goes sometimes. I don't always get my way." Even cage fighters get their ass kicked every now and again.

On the other hand, Wagner's refusal to cry uncle has led to big wins as well. "There are probably two of our beers that I'm most proud of coming up with the recipe," he shares. "One would be Stone IPA, just because it has been so important to the company for so long. It's nineteen years now that we've been brewing that beer. That was not an overnight-success type of beer back then. A lot of people tasted that beer and said, 'What the hell is this all about?' It's been kind of a long palate shift for the beer-drinking public, but it's still one of our best-selling beers, and it has been for a long time.

"Probably the recipe I'm the most proud of is our Stone Imperial Russian Stout, just because I was inspired by an English Russian stout that John Courage made that isn't available anymore. I did a lot of research on it and was inspired by that recipe and tried to get some of the similar flavors as I recalled that recipe. It's been one of our most popular special recipes for a long time. I also really like the way that that beer ages. We've done ten-year vertical tastings here, and the way it develops over time is pretty incredible."

You hear a lot of good things about Stone Brewing in the craft beer community. The edgy Southern California brewery seems to pop up in conversations everywhere I go. Not everyone takes collaboration as seriously as Stone. Maybe you can do that when you are confident that your products can stand on their own. It makes sharing ideas and ingredients with others less threatening. Stone has co-brewed beers with well-known competitors like 21st Amendment, Firestone Walker, and Sierra Nevada.

"In general, there are some really cool people in the craft beer industry who we like to hang out with," explains Wagner. "It pushes you out of your comfort zone and gets you to try something you might not have considered. That's always a good opportunity to grow your perception of what good craft beer can be. Usually we come up with something great that people get to try, so they win too."

Some worry that as competition increases, collaboration will decrease. "It's one of the special things about craft beer, and I hope it can continue," sighs Wagner. "Obviously, it's getting more crowded with more breweries. I think there is still good growth there for everybody out there. My fear is what happens as it gets more crowded and more competitive, people will try to differentiate themselves by saying negative things about other brands instead of telling their own unique positive story. I hope that doesn't happen because we've got something really special going on."

There are plenty of things to worry about, and one of the great things about craft beer is the escape route that it provides. We move onto a subject near and dear to every human not on the paleo diet: food and beer. "There is nothing like a good IPA, whether it's Stone IPA or any of the other wonderful IPAs out there, to drink with good spicy ethnic food," says Wagner, who certainly picked the right spot to call home. "In San Diego, we have a lot of great Mexican food, and for me, an IPA and chile rellenos is really nice." Okay, that is hitting below the belt for a guy based in Oregon, a thousand miles or so due north of Baja.

My gut gets ready for the cage fighter's next punch, but he goes easy on me this time. "Our Imperial Russian Stout with a not-too-sweet chocolate dessert is pretty incredible," he says. "And that's a good beer to pair with a cigar too. We do beer and cigar pairing dinners here at Stone quarterly in our outdoor gardens." It's hard to imagine that the Garden of Eden could have been any more tempting. It's a good thing the gargoyle is around somewhere, ready to drive off any evil spirits.

The thought plants me back in the present, shaded by poplar oak and white sage trees in a quiet courtyard next to a tranquil pond that is home to red-eared slider turtles. I'm relishing a pint of Arrogant Bastard as I watch Wagner's customers inside the bistro eagerly digging into their food and tasting golden craft beers. Although I can't hear a word through the floor-to-ceiling glass window that looks out on the patio, it doesn't take a lip reader to deduce that they are enjoying their afternoon. For a change, I'm content to be the fly on the wall, watching them from my hiding place in paradise, savoring this audacious ale, tucked away behind boulders in a Stone garden.

Steve Unfiltered

Working with Water

With a hop-forward beer like Arrogant Bastard Ale, maltier alternatives like Stone Smoked Porter, and yeast-driven Stone Saison, does water play a bit, but obviously vital part in the process? How do you use H_2O to enhance your flavors at Stone? "Historically, water was very important to brewing, and I think a lot of the great brewing cities and unique beer styles grew out of the water supply in those places," points out Wagner. "These days, water is pretty easy to manipulate. You can get the mineral profile that you're looking for—the hardness, the softness or those sorts of things. It's not as difficult to make it the way you want it to be. Yeast is much more touchy. Barley and hops are annual crops, and you get what you get; you just have to deal with it. So you have more ability to control water than the other ingredients." Well, almost, anyway. "Now the issue, at least in California, is just acquiring water," he adds. "It's much less about the quality of it. It's, can you get it?"

ALESMITH CEO and craft beer connoisseur Peter Zien in the San Diego brewery's spacious tasting room

CHAPTER 28

SMOOTH LANDING IN FIGHTERTOWN

AleSmith Brewing—San Diego, CA

IT'S BARELY NOON, and I already need a drink. After my not-so-smart phone navigation app leads me to the chaotic parking lot of a bustling Asian specialty-food market, I make a quick phone call, readjust my course, and punch the gas pedal in my Jeep. I'm running late for a highly anticipated visit to AleSmith Brewing.

Jets thunder in the distance as I make my way south through a maze of busy streets in nearby Mira Mesa. That's nothing out of the ordinary this afternoon, or any other for that matter. The beckoning brewery is located just a stone's throw from Marine Corps Air Station (MCAS) Miramar, sandwiched between Interstates 15 and 805 in the San Diego suburbs. I'm on a mission to quench my thirst in Fightertown!

I make my way to the brewery parking lot on AleSmith Court, zip my jacket to shield me from an uncharacteristic Southern California downpour and make mad dash for the tasting room. Inside, CEO Peter Zien has built a state-of-the-art brewery, a spotless stainless steel network of tanks, pipes, and valves that is the backdrop for his contemporary yet comfortable social space. Just this side of the floor-to-ceiling windows, a stylish blue-lit stand-up bar zig zags the length of the floor. Patrons inside enjoy pints of blonde to black liquid at the rustic barrel-top tables spread across a creamy beige, brown, and copper marble floor. The 25,000 ft.^{2} room is big enough to accommodate a whole squadron of F-35 Lightning II fighter pilots dropping by to cool down after a day in the cockpit.

The fifty-five-year-old owner greets me with a warm smile. I might have mistaken the lean, clean-cut Zien for a military man except for a little online research. His boyish face belies the many years of hard work he has put into building AleSmith. From its humble beginnings in 1995, he has helped forge this brewery into a force to be reckoned with.

"My friend Skip Virgilio started this in '95, and it just sort of didn't grow that much," recalls Zien, who was a homebrewer and AleSmith volunteer at the time. "To his credit, he developed a great reputation from the get-go, but the market was just different. Some of these beers were just hard to give away in the '90s." But there were just enough adventurous souls interested in trying new flavors to keep the brewery kettles boiling.

"In the early days, we were only open to the public Thursday and Friday, 4 to 8 p.m.," continues Zien. "You had eight hours to come see us. You'd open the door, and you wouldn't see anyone because we're in the tanks. Once someone saw you, we'd take our safety goggles off and say hello. It was a working brewery, plain and simple. There was no seating because unfortunately, our goal was to get you to leave so we could get back to work." Customers had to walk by a fermenter, and the brewers would tell them, "Don't touch that, it's hot!" Retail sales were less than a half percent of AleSmith's gross. "It was small potatoes," he says.

Ultimately, Virgilio decided it was time for a change and sold the brewery to his passionate homebrewing friend, Zien. "I tell everyone who will ask that I'm standing on his shoulders," he smiles, eyes creasing at the corners. Having built the business from a modest three-person staff, back in the early days, to seventy-plus employees in 2017, it's kind of him to share so much credit.

As I pause to take in the million-dollar-plus tasting room, "the house that Zien built," our bartender delivers a bowed silver caddy of four generously poured tasters to our table, a beckoning arch of golden, amber, brown, and black beer, each topped with a quarter-inch bubbly protein head.

I reach for the Lil' Devil, a golden, 5.75% Belgian-style wit. "It started its life as a yeast propagator for Horny Devil, which is an 11% version of this beer," notes Zien. "It's a Belgian, so you get that big, fruity bubblegum flavor, but then you get the coriander and the orange peel. It's extremely drinkable. It's a nice entry level beer for people who don't think they like typical beer flavors. I get people that say, 'I don't drink beer.' I'm like, 'Just humor me and try this.' In all of our beers, we really strive for a balance of all the raw ingredients and also drinkability. I know that term has been stolen by a big mass-produced beer, but we really want you to finish one of our beers and want another one. That's kind of our very simple plan." He's succeeded with Lil' Devil, and I make a note to try the nearly double ABV hornier version later on.

By now, the rain is rattling the roof so hard that we need to raise our voices to talk over the din. "We so need it," sighs Zien. "But it's overflowing the gutter." He points outside. "If you were standing right there, it would knock you over. I mean, the building is 105,000 ft.^{2}, and there's only two points where the rain comes off. That's a large volume. I could probably brew a batch with all of that water! We do have to monitor this. If we exceed a half-inch event today, we can't dump anything in the wastewater." AleSmith and the neighboring Marine base share the same wastewater system, and there is only so much volume that it can handle.

Zien is obsessed with water for other reasons as well. "You have four ingredients here, and one of them is water," he explains. "It has given me an edge. If I was going to make a Scottish ale, I was writing to the water authorities in Edinburgh asking for their water profiles. I wanted to know their calcium, magnesium, sodium, sulfate, chloride, carbonate values, and I was altering my water. I became a crazy chemist! I was adding food-grade acids to change molecular things."

I volunteer: "You are a mad scientist, Peter," and he gets this sinister look in his eyes that melts away to a grin.

"Good time for another taster," I think, and carefully remove the Nut Brown Ale from the caddy. "We premiered this beer in 2002 at the end of the year, it has just had meteoric growth!" he gushes. "It's got a cocoa note to it, but there's no chocolate in it. It's just a combination of the dark malts. It's low alcohol at 5%, our way of showing people that dark beers don't have to be big and scary. In the case of the Nut Brown, the color is pushing a little bit darker towards brown porter." I feel right home sitting next to a fellow beer geek. Peter's picture might well be in the urban dictionary next to the definition.

"I've always been kind of a beer nerd," he admits. "In tenth grade, I had a 300-bottle beer collection in my room. My dad was taking me to Europe at age fifteen. We would always go out at 11 a.m., have a beer, and I just watched how it was treated. When you go to Europe, beer is treated like an elegant beverage. I remember being in Vienna and ordering a Gösser, and a waiter in long whites with a silver tray and a Gösser glass. The beer arrived, and it was so cool!

"Belgium is a whole other story. Beer is *the* beverage. You can walk into a bar at 10:30 in the morning, and there might be a group of eighty-five-year-old ladies, and they've each got big Duvels in front of them, each one. It's just a wonderful sight."

Zien believes that beer can be an elegant beverage. "Bottles like this belong on the finest tables in the finest restaurants and bars," he insists. "We don't want you to just fall in love with the packaging. It's what's inside that'll keep you coming back." As if on cue, the next taster in the procession on the table in front of me draws my attention.

I've been anxiously awaiting the third glass in the lineup since I spotted it on the menu. The .394 is named after San Diego Padres baseball legend and Major League Baseball Hall of Famer Tony Gwynn, who once finished the season with that incredible batting average. I'm betting that it's a home run, since the detail-oriented Gwynn was involved in creating the recipe.

"My wife and I had the pleasure of meeting him and working with him and the family, making a beer that was from his initial instructions: 'light with a kick.' It's not your typical beer-judge vocabulary, but I understood. I got to sit with a Hall of Famer and drink beer. It turns out he wanted it very hoppy, but he wanted subdued bitterness and more of a malt character. I explained to him, 'You know bitterness comes from those hops you love? But there are some procedural things that we can do to make a beer low in bitterness but extremely hoppy that will still capture the imagination of hop lovers.'"

Pardon the predictable cliché, but this coppery-colored beer is a hit. Why would I expect anything else from an all-time great? The Cascade-hopped, 6% .394 has that recognizable pine-citrus flavor with the subdued bitterness that Gwynn specified (13 IBUs). This slightly sweet-finishing, well-balanced treat would be the perfect teammate with mustard-and-relish-smothered foot long hot dog.

Alas, when the beer came out for sale on June 6, 2014, it premiered at Petco Park (home of the San Diego Padres), and Tony was too ill to come out and enjoy it at the ballpark. Zien takes a deep breath, "He went to bed the night of Father's Day and ended up not waking up." I wipe the corners of my eyes and fumble for another question before I make a fool of myself in public. "How did you come up with the AleSmith brand?" I ask.

He thinks back twenty-plus years: "Our motto is "Hand-forged ales," and for the longest time, we did things the absolute hardest way possible. We had nothing designed for the brewing industry in the original brew house. Being home brewers, that was right up our alley. We bought pumps from other industries. We had our tanks from the dairy industry. The boil kettle was not from a brewery.

"We made it work, and we actually backed into some really good ways to produce beer by having to do it the hard way. Duct tape and milk crates were our best friends, and we just made it work. I think we got kind of got lucky for a while. We had open fermentation. These weren't properly sealed tanks, but it just made us that much more careful. It made us more anal about sanitation and procedure timing. We knew we had very little margin of error or we're going to lose the whole batch. So, it just had us on our toes.

"That imagery of the blacksmith and hard work, and dirty-faced workers, really fit AleSmith for the longest time." Now the memorable brand is recognized as one of the best in the west. "Sometimes, I forget how we got from there to here when I look at this shiny, beautiful new brew house. It's making our beer better than it's ever been."

AleSmith is a classic, style-oriented brewery that is not out to invent flavors of the week, according to Zien. His goal is to put a West Coast spin on world-accepted styles. He freely admits that his beers sometimes straddle style categories: "We take liberties, and in some of our beers the raw ingredient may be stylistically correct, but we might choose a different yeast strain. Even with that nontraditional mentality, the brewery has taken home more than its fair share of top awards over the years."

Although Zien enjoys the accolades that come from winning at competitions, he doesn't seem too concerned when his beers don't medal. "Speedway is probably the beer we're best known for, and I can count the awards on one hand because it's a coffee beer," he points out. "But we strive to layer it in there, so if you enter it into the Coffee Stout category, the judges will come back not quite getting the coffee. And if you just say, 'Forget the coffee, let's enter it into the Russian Imperial Stout category,' they'll say, 'I'm getting a coffee note, try entering it into the coffee category.'" He sighs and shrugs his shoulders—with new categories added to beer festivals every year, knowing what to enter where is becoming increasingly complicated.

Instead of the frustrating exercise of trying to funnel beer into a competition classification, I stick to judging it right here at the table. Before me is AleSmith's Speedway Stout, a potent, 12% ABV beer with a creamy, tan head. Under its bubbly cover I pick out bitter chocolate, sweet caramel, and dried fig flavors, as well as abundant coffee notes. The only thing missing here is an edible partner for this midnight-black beverage—maybe a steamy stack of sliced barbecued brisket on a toasted-butter bun.

"I think what I love about the beer and food pairings is that I can actually bridge flavors for you," observes Zien. "Here, I am in control of direct flavors, like roasted and caramelized, which are huge flavor components going back to the dawn of time when we held meat over fire, and we developed a sense of taste for roasted. So I can make a beer black-dark with roasted malt that's been brought nearly to the point of combusting by the maltster. It's brittle, it's burnt, and you pair that with any roasted or charred dish.

"Caramelization is a process of the brewing, when you're boiling the wort. Wort is a fancy word for sugar water. So you're boiling sugar, and you're developing caramelized flavors. I can tie that in with the Maillard reaction going on in cooking. I think it's a little bit of a slam dunk. Chefs get in here and their eyes bug out, and that's how we do this. We usually invite them in, and we put out a number of our beers. I love watching the wheels go. A lot of times they're thinking, 'Oh, I love that caramel, I'm thinking of a something savory, maybe a mixed spring mushroom dish. There are all sorts of pairings you could do. With the cocoa in here, you may want do a cocoa-rub lamb and so forth. I think it's tied to the farm-to-table and eating-better movement."

One of his favorite combinations came as a pleasant surprise during a special dinner prepared by an old friend. Guest chef Schuyler Schultz paired his grandmother's dessert with AleSmith's Barrel Aged Decadence 2005. "It just caught me so right that night," remembers Zien. "The toffee notes of the old ale, the bread pudding, and this really old recipe from an East Coast grandmother. I like to call it where one beer plus one food equals three. You've now elevated the experience. Each item has been enhanced beyond its sole characteristics by the pairing. The bread pudding benefited from the boozy nice barrel aging, and the barrel-aged benefitted from the wonderful sweet finish that came back in the toffee notes. I want a little more creativity than a Speedway float, where you just throw beer over some ice cream."

The longtime brewer believes that beer deserves a place at any table in town. "I try not to offend the wine people, but you got to let us play," he insists. "For so long, it was wine and food pairing dinners. I'll give them credit, too, for getting everyone warmed up to it and to allow us in. But I encourage people to go to beer and food pairings and just learn more about all these wonderful beverages."

When it comes right down to it, Zien is an artist. Although he is focused on the business, he is often absorbed in the creative element of his craft. "I was inspired by the very Renaissance-like people of Belgium," he recalls fondly. "I have to admit, you get a little bit of an extra intro when you own a brewery, and I got to know some really great brewers in

Belgium. Many of them were just real Renaissance people. You're sitting on a chair they made. They're serving smoked salmon that they caught and smoked for you, jams, cheeses, everything. And that's why I fancy myself similar in a modest way. I try to do as many different things as I can." Thank goodness this mad-scientist/Renaissance man has been able to turn his dreams into pint-sized masterpieces.

Pete Unfiltered

A Match Made in Heaven

Zien knows his beer, but he is also a bit of a cheese connoisseur too. Why should anyone be surprised? "My mom was a Wisconsin girl, and I was born in Minnesota in the heart of cheese country," he reveals.

Now he is a bona fide fromager: "Cheesemaking started when I lost my beloved home-brewing hobby because I was doing this all week, and my weekends were going to be beer-free, other than drinking," he chuckles. "The farmers who take our spent grain were bringing me back jugs of raw milk from the animals that were eating the grain. At first, I didn't really know what to do with it. I'm not really a milk drinker, unless I get a nice bunch of chocolate in it. But I started researching about cheesemaking, and it scratched the same itch for me as home brewing. I got excited about it.

"I think brewing is the blend of art and science. It's unparalleled. But cheesemaking is fairly procedural because you're limited to one raw ingredient, milk. I geeked out on it and started taking cheesemaking courses at Cal Poly San Luis Obispo. I was serving underground cheese for years at our little parties. I would just make very simple Fromage Blanc with pasteurized, homogenized milk. My standards are higher than any FDA ones, so I never worry about serving my cheeses. So that developed into a real business plan, and CheeseSmith is a registered company. Our logo is the same anvil, but it has a cow sitting on it holding a pint in her hoof."

Beer and cheese go hoof-in-hand, according to Zien. "I've done many beer and cheese pairings over the last fifteen years and love them all for the seemingly endless variety of flavors that can be created." When pressed for some of his favorite pairings, he mentions Balsamic BellaVitano (manufactured by Sartori Wisconsin) with AleSmith Grand Cru. "Young or aged, this cheese is a true masterpiece. Nutty and fruity flavors are married to a sweet finish from the vinegar. AleSmith's Grand Cru completes the cheese by adding plum, prune, raisin, and over-ripened fruit flavors and aromas and is bold enough at 10% ABV to stand up against the flavorful backdrop of this amazing cheese!"

CHAPTER 29

MORE FUN THAN A BARREL OF MONKEYS

Karl Strauss—San Diego, CA

SCROLL THROUGH THE RESULTS of the Great American Beer Festivals (GABF) from year to year, and you will find a mid-sized Southern California brewery that somehow wins awards again and again, yet flies below the radar of most craft beer fans. Karl Strauss Brewing Company is the Olympic equivalent of a small country that keeps showing up on the medals stand, but at the annual US craft beer competition in Denver rather than on world stages like Rio and PyeongChang. In 2016, Karl Strauss, which hauled in a pair of golds to go along with two bronzes, was named Midsize Brewery of the Year.

"This Karl Strauss must be one hell of a brewer to win so many awards," I thought. "I'd better fly to San Diego to investigate."

When I arrive a few weeks later, Karl isn't there to greet me for reasons that I'll reveal a little later. Instead I meet up with Matt Johnson, Brewmaster of Brewery Operations, and Kiersten Winant, Public Relations Coordinator. Winant is dressed in tiger-striped pants, which seems appropriate for this semi-casual Friday on the southern fringe of La Jolla, twelve miles north of the world-famous San Diego Zoo.

Johnson and Winant lead me into the quiet brew pub, which won't be hopping with guests until it opens later this afternoon. As we settle in at the bar, I get my first look at the brewery's long lineup of colorfully named Zootopia tap handles, including Baby Burro Saison and The Tijuana Zebra American Stout.

"I let the brewers name their beers because they come up with some very creative names," laughs Johnson, who joined Karl Strauss Brewing in 2008. "It started with a batch we called Unicorn Tears, then another person came up with Bear's Growl, so they all started getting on this animal thing. Now there is stuff like Thumping Rabbit, Show Pony, Barrel of Monkeys, and Juice Tiger, which is our juicy and delicious Vermont-style IPA. If you don't keep it fun, people lose interest."

Although the brand names are wild, the recipes are just tame enough that they meet my creative host's high expectations. "A lot of these beers are excellent, and you're going to see them in the future," predicts Johnson.

One citrusy swig of Juice Tiger, and I can't wait to get my paws on a whole growler. "Is that a pink grapefruit hiding there in the hop jungle, ready to pounce on my olfactory sensors?" I raise my eyebrows, shrug, and smile. Johnson probably already thinks I'm bananas, and I've only just begun with the monkey business. But he is stuck with me because Mr. Strauss won't be available for this or any subsequent interviews.

As a matter of fact, the amazing man that the brewery was named after died in 2006 at the age of ninety-four. "I think what a lot of people don't realize about us is that Karl Strauss was an actual guy," shares Johnson. Sensing something good here, I dig a little deeper into the backstory.

"What's the connection?" I ask.

My hosts explain that Strauss was born in Feldschlösschen Bräu, the brewery that his father operated in Minden, Germany. There are probably more than a few beer lovers who wouldn't mind taking their last breath in a pub. But who ever heard of a baby gathering its first lungs' full of O^2 in a brewery, even if he was delivered in the Administration building? This was clearly a child destined for greatness in the beer business. Ultimately, he made the decision to climb that steep path. After helping around the brewery as a boy, Strauss went on to study malting and brewing science at the Technical University of Munich at Weihenstephan. He augmented that degree by earning a Master Brewer Certification. Strauss quickly put his schooling to work, perfecting his craft at a variety of breweries from Detmold in Westphalia north to Lübeck near the Baltic Sea.

Unfortunately (or fortunately, depending on how you look at it), that is where his career path ended in Deutschland. "1938 was not a good time to be in Germany, and Karl Strauss was Jewish," says Johnson. "So he and his sister fled and left his parents for America. On his way to San Francisco, he stopped in Milwaukee to visit a cousin, who worked at Pabst. His cousin went in one day and said, 'Hey, we have a certified German Brewmaster. We can't let him go!'" The boss listened and hired him to work on the bottling line.

Strauss eventually worked his way up to become Director of Brewing Operations and then Brewmaster for Pabst Brewing Company. "Karl is the only brewmaster to win the three major awards given by the Master Brewer's Association," Johnson proudly points out. Strauss, who was president of the Master Brewers Association of the Americas from 1961–63, won the what amounts to the industry's triple crown, receiving the MBAA Award of Merit in 1981, the Award of Honor in 1992, and the Distinguished Life Service Award in 2003. Oh, and according to Johnson, he also created a relatively popular beer called "Pabst Blue Ribbon" while he was at it.

This tale *is* going somewhere, I promise. After Strauss retired from the Midwest brewing giant, he began consulting, helping a Chicago start-up called Goose Island take flight. About the same time, Karl's cousin Chris Cramer, a recent Stanford graduate, was touring the world, figuring things out, and ended up near the edge of civilization in Perth, Australia. There he stumbled on a small bar where he tasted the best beer he had ever come across. The bartender led him on an abbreviated back-of-the-house brewery tour for a look at the small operation. The visit led to an epiphany for young Mr. Cramer. He knew what he wanted to do when he headed back to the States.

When Chris returned home, he caught up with former college roommate Matt Rattner in Pacific Beach. There, under lifeguard tower 10, they started plans for a new craft microbrewery that could make the kind of beer Cramer had fallen in love with on his overseas adventure. There are times in life when the stars align and everything magically comes together like ingredients in a brew kettle. Cramer approached his legendary cousin and asked him if he wanted to help. Karl agreed, happy that someone else in the family shared his passion for brewing. As the project developed, Cramer suggested naming the brewery after Strauss. He said, "Why not?" and so the Karl Strauss Brewing Company was born. The rest is history.

"We've been in San Diego for almost thirty years now," says Johnson. "We were the first brewery to open here after Prohibition. Since day one, we pretty much started with just a whole myriad of different beers, so people could come and enjoy different styles. We love the variety because it's something for everybody. If you come in and say you don't like beer, I'm going to give you some of the Windansea Wheat and say, 'This tastes like banana and clove, give it a try.' Or maybe if you are lucky enough, Johnson will offer you his Queen of Tarts, with its hint of Michigan cherries—winner of GABF's gold medal for the American Sour Category in 2016.

Despite Karl Strauss's impressive GABF winning streak, the company doesn't have plans to conquer the world; but growth is still an option. "Right now, we want to stay local," explains Johnson. "We have been here for a long time. We also want to have controlled growth. A lot of places get too big too fast. That's what we're worried about. We want to be able to provide consistent, quality beer to our customers and to our fan base and not run out. If it tastes the same on tap as it does in the bottle, that allows us time here to focus on the quality and make sure that there is enough to satisfy our fans.

"Do we have plans to go further? Possibly. We're looking at building a larger brewery. But until that happens, I think we're going to stay in California and keep the quality consistent and have enough to satisfy everybody who wants it. I want everyone to enjoy our beer, like I did when my friends used to drink my home-brewed beer. I love the fact that they enjoyed a product that I produced."

Johnson, who started his career as a bored business consultant in LA, once faced the ultimate pressure cooker of making drinkable beer for a friend's wedding, so he certainly isn't afraid of trying something new. That includes working with nontraditional partners, including one from the music industry. "(San Diego-based) Taylor Guitars produces a guitar made of maple wood," he tells me. "We did a Saison that was aged with maple wood scrap, leftovers from what they use for their guitars. The maple is very subtle. It's kind of like the wood flavor that you get from oak barrels. You taste the little bits of wood in it, but it's not overpowering at all. Taylor Guitars loves doing it with us because they get beer in exchange." He adds that it's a newer way of looking at collaboration.

Meanwhile, time is running out on this joint venture, and my eyes slide down the colorful row of taps to what Johnson calls the brewery's core beers: the workhorses. "We have our original amber that we've had for twenty-nine years," he shares along with an accompanying taster. "Red Trolley is our number one seller. We live in San Diego, so you'd think an IPA would be the best seller because we're hop-forward here. No, Red started out as our first holiday brew back in 1989, and it has always been our workhorse."

As it turns out, this is one of Karl's recipes, mingling Glacier and Willamette hops with four malts to make a nice, balanced, 30 IBU Irish red ale. The 5.8% ABV, plum-colored beer is warm-fermented, drawing out flavors like raisins and dark fruits. It may not be an exact match with industry standards for what an Irish red ale should taste like (malty sweetness), but it's a damn fine beer, so who cares? Plenty of others must agree, since it remains the brewery's favorite to this day.

I've found a way to connect with the old brewer after all. "This is a beer that I could come back for again and again . . . if only I lived a thousand miles closer," I wish out loud. Johnson nods his head in agreement. He, like so many in the industry, are following in the huge footsteps of guys like Karl Strauss and the craft beer pioneers who came before them. At the same time, the company's head brewmaster and his staff of "zookeepers/ brewers" are busy blazing their own new trails. Johnson appreciates nearly every minute of it: "I love what I do," he beams with a grin as authentic as the brewery's beers. "To have a passion like that for something, it sure beats working every day."

Matt Unfiltered

Matching and Contrasting Food and Beer Flavors.

As you might expect, Johnson's favorite food and beer pairing tend to lean a little to the wild side. "Our Mosaic with a good plate of Penang Pork, a Thai dish—probably No. 7 spicy because I can't take No. 10, with a side of Pad Thai and fried rice," he rattles off, as if he's ready to sit down for dinner right now. "That spiciness would probably be enough that it would make my eyes water and my nose run, but as soon as I drink my IPA, it would kind of cool it down and kill some of that so that I can keep eating."

It takes a bold beer to stand up to some spicy dishes. Johnson believes it is often a more compatible partner than other adult beverages. "I think food almost goes better with beer than it does with wine because there are so many flavors of beer that complement or contrast and cleanse your palate when you're eating food," he observes. "You can pair beer with tater tots with cheese on top all the way to filet mignon with bolognese sauce on it."

Sometimes it's just fun to experiment. There are times when Johnson likes to match like flavors. "We have a dish made with Red Trolley Barbecue sauce, and what goes perfect with it?" he quizzes me. "A Red Trolley because that sweetness in the barbecue sauce and the sweetness in the Red." As I reach for one last taste of Karl Strauss's Penguin Pale Ale, his comment leads to an epiphany: birds of a feather flock together, and not just when it comes to food and beer pairings.

CHAPTER 30

SOAKING UP SUDS IN SIN CITY

Big Dog's Brewing Company—Las Vegas, NV

BREWMASTER DAVID PASCUAL BOUNDS into Big Dog's Brewing in North Las Vegas, smiles, and apologizes for being a few minutes late for our interview. Pascual explains that he had to make the three-hour round-trip to the China Ranch Date Farm in south Death Valley and pick up 120 pounds of dates for the brewery's new Belgian-style quad. "What? A date farm in Death Valley?" I ask in mock disbelief. "Come on! You were downtown playing a little blackjack, weren't you?"

The hottest surface temperature on record, 201°F, was recorded in Death Valley in 1972. It's hard to believe anything could grow in such a harsh climate, but it turns out he wasn't bluffing. The family-owned date farm mocks the elements, a green oasis thriving in the middle of the hottest spot in the Mojave Desert. But an eighty-five-mile drive through hell and back for a few boxes of sweet brown fruit? Ah, the lengths that a determined brewer will go to create a good Belgian-style beer!

Back here in the air conditioning at Big Dog's, far from the allure of desert date palms, we are a mere sixteen miles from the twenty-four-hour action of the Las Vegas Strip. Yet I still find this place entertaining. There aren't any beautifully lit high rises or high flying circus acts out here—just fast food joints, retail outlets, and a great little brewery.

Pascual, who looks Polynesian and turns out to be Filipino, has been a Las Vegan since his dad retired from the military and moved two of six kids to the city in 1994. David went to UNLV, studied biology and chemistry, and started working at a local brewery called Barley's. Initially, he learned the ropes from a brewer nicknamed Mufassa. "I got into brewing because of him," he says. "He convinced me to try and intern for him. He told me he was an ex-engineer, doing this for a living, that it was life changing, but that I'd love it. He said 'It's not one of those jobs that you ever want to look back and wish you had made another choice.'"

The hardworking, open-minded brewer learned to appreciate other beer styles. "Coming from college, I was drinking Newcastle, Hefeweizens, or things like that," he remembers. "I thought they were odd, different beers that most people weren't drinking." Back then, Sin City was lawnmower-beer country. "Vegas was six or seven years behind the trends," he says.

His new training ground offered something traditional too, just not "born and raised" here in Nevada. "The brewery I first interned at was a German-influenced brewery, so we brewed cleaner type beers. I was appreciating a lot of German Hefeweizens, which shared similarities in some Belgian beers. I think that's where it segued for me. I thought that these beers have so much character to them—a little bit of banana or a touch of spice!"

After six months of unpaid but priceless training, Pascual decided it was time to gain more than experience and tapped into a paid position with Chicago Brewing Company (about 1,750 miles southwest of the real Windy City). "I was the head brewer there from 2008 until I jumped ship when this position came open," he notes. "They're a smaller brewery, yet collectively they won so many awards! It was a cool environment, but I needed to take the next step to run a bigger brewery, do production on the side and run a barrel-aging program."

Which brings us to the present moment, right here at Big Dog's, where Pascual is making the most of that opportunity. "Not many people can say they produce something from start to finish and understand the hard work that goes along with it—just having that passion to keep pushing yourself," he says of brewing.

The evidence of that hard work is poured into the tulip of Tripel Dog Dare Belgian-style Tripel that I'm enjoying this afternoon. In 2017, the spicy, noble-hopped treat won a GABF Gold Medal in the Belgian-Style Tripels category. This bright, golden beer, with its beckoning bubbly white cap, looks innocent enough, but at 9.1% ABV, it is sinfully sneaky. If you like the retronasal aroma that you whiff after eating a warmed slice of banana bread, you might like this estery treat as well.

"Belgians are something I really love," confesses Pascual.

"I have a friend in the Netherlands who says the same thing," I reply, and he does his best to ignore me.

"There's a lot of character to each one—sours, tripels, and dubbels. I was trying to think of anything local to source that we could impart in the beer," he continues. That is when Pascual came up with the idea of adding dates to create a new recipe for the cleverly named seDATEd Belgian Quad. It's a whopping 9.5% ABV that pours dark amber with a foamy, light-brown head. Not surprisingly, the quad is a slightly sweet beer with hints of dates, raisins, and fig. "You get a sugary character that's partly due to the dates as well. It was in a red wine barrel," he adds. Like with most of Big Dog's beers, you will need to make a road trip to Vegas to take your own tasting notes (although the brewery does ship to some beer to northern Nevada).

The Big Dog's bark may not stretch far, but its brand is popular enough that the place is busy on this Monday afternoon. I soon learn that this is a Green Bay Packer bar and wonder how much business this remote, forest-green and gold outpost could possibly count on from roving cheeseheads. "Aren't the Raiders moving here from Oakland?" I ask. "How will fans who dress for Halloween every weekend in the fall feel about date and banana brews?" My patient host has apparently been asked this question before.

"One of our beers is a Silver and Black IPA," he laughs. "That was our brew-school beer, where we teach a class on how to brew and the science behind it. We brewed it with Galaxy, Amarillo, and Simcoe hops and debittered black malt, crystal, and rye. I know we're a Packer bar, and a lot of people are like, 'How are the Raider fans going to take it?' The running joke is, 'Well, we're technically the Silver State and it's a black IPA, so there you go.'" I'm betting that the Raider Nation takes over the bar on any given Sunday and adopts the dark and malty, 6.8% ABV namesake as one of its own. He won't take that bet.

Pascual isn't much of a gambling man when it comes to brewing. "Having the science background, where you control variables and you line up the equation, you try to minimize mistakes," he explains. "Then you keep yourself in a bubble when you don't take those chances. But having those in the back of my mind, where I don't want to fail or ruin something, it haunts me. I don't get as much sleep as I used to!"

There are times when the brewer/scientist is willing to experiment and roll the dice, but only when he is reasonably sure the brewery will come out ahead in the game. "We're doing some barrel-aging here," he reports. "We've been blending some of the beers that we've come across and are finding some surprising characteristics that worked really well. We did a sour stout with blackberries from Oregon. We soured it and put it in a barrel for some secondary fermentation with wild yeast."

Pascual has gotten so good at his craft that he has been taking home awards at some of the world's biggest beer festivals, including the GABF. "Winning does feel good, I won't lie to you," he admits. "Going to the beer festival, I feel like I've only been in the industry for a blink. Looking at how much the industry has grown and how much beer is out there, it validates the work that you're doing. Someone who really knows beer can validate you. It doesn't mean that beer will be the biggest seller, but it's nice to get that recognition."

He shares all the accolades with his brew crew, including one of his brewers, Amanda. Not only is she indispensable around the brewery, but she has also helped formulate and name one of the beers, Underbite IPA. The logo is taken from a picture of her big dog sprawled on the ground, eyes shut, a ragged row of buck teeth jutting up under his upper lip.

Most of the creative brand names here (Tailwagger Hefeweizen, Dogtoberfest, Sour Hound, Black Lab Stout—you get the picture) have a canine twist in honor of the former proprietor, the late Tom Weisner, a Badger State native whose nickname was Big Dog.

Perhaps the biggest, baddest dog of them all sits on the table in front of me. Red Hydrant Brown Ale is an English-style brown, appropriately named for its ruby-red fireplug hue. This beer's oval logo includes a white hound sniffing a red hydrant, complete with a tap handle. With hints of toffee, caramel, and mild roast coffee, it's easy to understand the attraction. The rich, creamy, brown head has me lifting a pint (rather than a leg), enjoying the brewery's award-winning Fuggle-hopped recipe. I'm not the only admirer. Red Hydrant won gold medals at the 2006 and 2010 World Beer Cups, silver at the 2012 Great American Beer Festival, and gold again at the 2015 Great American Beer Festival.

Like so many breweries I've visited, I'm right at home shooting the shit with Pascual and the pack of artisan brewers in back. Nearly everyone in the industry has been approachable, so why should this "pack," named after man's best friend, be any different? Truth is, making about 3,000 barrels of beer a year and pleasing your patrons is all that any Big Dog needs to be happy.

"Everyone comes from different walks of life and seems to fall into brewing and in love with it," he says. "It's such a rewarding job. There are so many things that you can pour in a glass that will just blow your mind! And the community—everyone is so warm, so welcoming, so inviting. I look at other industries, and nothing is like what breweries are. I hope it stays that way and the newer crowd follows through with that." He goes silent for a second, and the pause is filled with happy chatter from guests and their clanging beer glasses. "Those who don't do it right will go out of business . . . or get sucked up by someone else." After all, it's not the size of the dog in the fight, it's the size of the fight in the dog!

David Unfiltered

Every Dog has Its Day!

Big Dog's pedigree traces back to the Holy Cow! Casino Cafe and Brewery, which launched its own microbrewery in 1993. Because of its location on Las Vegas Boulevard, Holy Cow! Casino Cafe and Brewery was always impacted by the ebb and flow of the tourist season in Las Vegas. "Big conventions, big fights, and holiday weekends always were busy times at Las Vegas's original brewery," says Pascual. "But nothing prepared us for our first encounter with the throngs of Deadheads that descended upon Las Vegas in May of 1993 for the annual Grateful Dead weekend of shows.

"Upon learning that Las Vegas now had its own microbrewery, the Grateful Dead fans would come spend their nights after the show into the wee hours of the next morning, enjoying our Pale, Red, Cream, and Wheat Ales. This was really the brewery's first test at being able to handle a large crowd, and we ended up falling a little short. In fact, by the end of the weekend, the crowds had drained the brewery completely dry of all its beers and we remained a brewery without beers for another ten days, when the next batches finally could come back online."

When the Deadheads returned in 1994 and 1995, Holy Cow was utterly full of craft beer and never ran completely dry again . . . not even when the café and casino closed in March of 2002. Nearly everything was sold, including the property's fourteen-foot cow statue, which was purchased by the owner of a Nevada automobile dealership. But the little brewery continued to operate. Big Dog's Hospitality Group ultimately moved its brewing operations to its current location in North Las Vegas. Every dog has its day!

CHAPTER 31

A HIDDEN GEM UNDER THE NEON LIGHTS

Brasserie St. James—Reno, NV

RENO, NEVADA, The Biggest Little City in the World, is best known for its bright lights and slot machines. Visitors flood northern Nevada's casinos in hopes of making their fortune (or at least not losing their asses). The town was established in 1868 on the western edge of the Great Basin, an area that has always been associated with silver and gold in one way or another.

Now I was in the shadow of the Sierra Nevadas, hunting for a different kind of treasure. I planned to stake my claim on a bar stool at Brasserie St. James, about a mile and a half from the Peppermill Hotel. Some of craft beer's most adventurous fans have discovered liquid gold in these here parts. The microbrewery, which opened in the historic Crystal Springs Ice and Water Building in 2012, was named the GABF's Medium-sized Brewery of the Year in 2014 and has won numerous medals for its European-influenced beers.

Worn out by the long drive from Vegas via a tortuous but spectacular detour through Death Valley and then Lone Pine, California, it felt like I had finally reached the Promised Land. I quickly made my across the hardwood floor, past the river rock fireplace, and to a line of taps set against a red brick backdrop, like a parched man who had wandered out of the desert and into an oasis. There, in a space that reminded me a little of an Old World brewpub, I met Josh Watterson, head brewer at the time.

After the customary handshake, we gathered several samplers from the bartender, then wandered out to the enclosed patio to take advantage of the nice weather. We were joined there by Madison Gurries, then Waterson's right-hand man and Brewery Operations Manager. Gurries studied at the Siebel Institute and Doemen's Academy, then spent a few years apprenticing under Watterson's watchful eyes. (With Watterson's departure from Brasserie St. James in November 2017, Gurries now runs the brewery day-to-day).

One of the beers bubbling up at me from the sun-bleached picnic table that afternoon was Daily Wages, a gold-medal-winning saison. The dry high-desert air made me eager to "collect up" from the taster of the acclaimed, hazy-yellow pale ale. Three quick sniffs and a sip confirmed that the judges know their business.

I imagined I could live on Daily Wages for a month or more if I had to, maybe with bacon, lettuce, and tomato sandwiched between a few slices of ancient-grains bread just to keep things honest. At 6.7% ABV, it has enough alcohol in it to help me forget my worst day on the job. It's delicate, dry, and floral flavored by the hard work of three proprietary yeasts. There is a medium fruit-tart flavor that had me remembering a quaint countryside café on the outskirts of Bruges. "I like the spicy, sour finish," I complimented my hosts at the time.

When he hears that I admired the brewers' and yeast's hard work during my visit months ago, Brasserie St. James owner Arthur Farley is pleased. Farley has had an appreciation for Belgian beers for many years, having toured some of the renowned breweries in the birthplace of his favorite style. "I like complexity and nuance of quality beer, and Belgium reigns supreme in that regard," he shares. "I always get a kick out of people who say they're huge craft-beer fans, but mostly drink hoppy beers. It's like someone saying they're a serious oenophile, but mostly drink California cabernet or chardonnays. Tripel Karmeliet, Orval, Rochefort and Saison DuPont were early game-changers for me and sparked a love that has lasted!" A passion for craft beer that started in Portland, Oregon was stoked in Europe, and eventually ignited his desire to move operations from garage to limelight.

Farley, who grew up helping out in his mother's restaurant and continued to work in the industry in food and beverage hotspots like Los Angeles, Dallas, and Portland, first decided to start his own bar. An avid homebrewer by then, he launched the St. James Infirmary in 2008, bringing rare ales and lagers to the northern Nevada city known more for gaming than beer-tasting opportunities.

Four years later, the beer connoisseur opened Brasserie St. James, and hired European-trained Watterson away from Bridgeport Brewing in Portland. "We met and discussed our shared love, not just for the great lagers of Eastern Europe, but especially that of the saisons, lambics and Trappist ales of Belgium," recalls Farley. "We also discussed our frustration with the craft-beer scene, and how it seemed stuck in IPAS —a frustration I still feel. We also shared a love of the great sparkling wines of France, Italy, and Spain, pinot noirs and Chablis of Burgundy, German rieslings of Mosel, Alsatians' dry white wines, Sancerres of Loire and cab francs of Chinon. This has influenced a more nuanced and varied drinking palate and has greatly influenced the beers Brasserie Saint James makes." He adds that it's also why he is still a little frustrated by the flood of green hoppy beers.

Fortunately for Farley, his brewery sits directly on top of another ingredient that may be less sexy than hops but is essential to beer nonetheless: pure mountain water. "I brewed my first homebrew with Crystal Springs water when I was renting a house three doors down," he informs me. In fact, the brewery taps into a massive underground lake, hundreds of feet below its foundation.

Yeast may play the most important part in Brasserie St. James's saisons and other European-style beers, but these meticulous brewers are plenty proud of their local water. "Water is so important because treated water goes through municipality cleaning where they add chemicals like chlorine," pointed out Watterson as we walked the production floor. "When we get out of the pool, and we smell like chlorine, we want to take a shower. The yeast doesn't like swimming in that either. It's the same thing. It affects the flavors. If you get a delicate, light lager, you'll taste what I put into it, which includes the water."

Brasserie St. James is taking full advantage of its subterranean natural resource. "There are no additives, and the salts are natural," he noted. "When you add salts, you're adjusting pH. Even if I add the exact same mash salts, it's not the same water because it's not blended the same. We're stripping these minerals over hundreds of years. I think water plays a huge part. It's 98 percent of the beer you drink!"

H_2O isn't the only local product that finds its way into the brewery's beers. Brasserie St. James's White Downs, a barrel-aged saison, incorporates fresh-picked white sage from the area. At 9.0% ABV, this seasonal beer is capable of turning a rough day around quickly. "White Downs was sort of my F-U to pumpkin beers, a style that I found silly, sweet, and overdone," says Farley. "I had the idea to do a beer with butternut squash and whirlpool it with some local white sage for aromatics. Then we decided to sour it, so it's still a farmhouse-base beer." He named it White Downs as an obscure nod to Middle Earth. "White Downs was the borderlands of The Shire," he confesses. "I know, really nerdy."

I wonder how Farley and his brewers come up with their wild-ass ideas. As it turns out, they have developed a system. "When we decide to brew something, we bring three or four of our favorite examples of the style and we blind taste them," he reveals. Next, Farley and now Gurries make vigorous notes on what they liked and didn't like and design their own versions of a style, incorporating some of the traits of their personal favorites. The deconstruction/reassembly process has worked in spades. "We did that with Daily Wages, and right out the gate, it took a gold at 2014 GABF." That is proof enough for me, but he has other tricks up his sleeve and deals me yet another tale.

I've found that there is often a good backstory that bridges creative thinking and hard work to a great beer. Take, for instance, Brasserie St. James's Red Headed Stranger. "Red Headed Stranger started as a beer in my garage that I brewed for my bimonthly poker game," shares Farley. "I was drinking a lot of saison, but was also geeking out on some small, lesser known Biere De Gardes from France. I decided I wanted a beer somewhere between the two, and that's how Red Headed Stranger came to be. Josh perfected it for a production scale, and to this day, it's our most popular beer and has been named as one of the best beers in the world!"

This red-hued Belgian farmhouse ale flows out of a tap in the Reno brewpub or, if you're like me, you pour it from a 750 mL wine-style bottle into a curvy tulip and park on your living-room couch. The yeast has done its work on this stranger, turning it into a familiar saison, with the trademark fruit and spice hints. At 6.6% ABV, it's possible to drink an entire twenty-five ounces in one sitting . . . if you can't resist its delicate, sweet charms.

It takes a special care to make beers worth talking about, and I learn just how much finesse goes into each bottle. Just down the street from the brewery, Farley opened an environmentally controlled barrel-aging facility specially designed to store and monitor beers like its sour ales. The majority of Brasserie St. James's barrel program relies on Belgian-style fermentation and oaks. There is a lot of back-and-forth blending that goes on here, as Gurries slowly creates wonderful old lambics, tart gueuzes, and other flavorful European-inspired beers.

The brewery also combines ages-old techniques with modern technology. Brasserie St. James's newly remodeled facility doubles as a beta site for a company that does barrel monitoring. Originally, a barrel was just a vessel, not meant to be monitored by anything other than touch, taste, and smell, but now there are temperature probes available that can measure things like barometric pressure and humidity. These instruments can sense a 1°F difference in the temperature from the top to the bottom of the room we are standing in. "There's this Old World thing—beer, which has been around for thousands of years—and then technology that syncs to your iPhone to tell you how your beer is doing," mused Watterson during my first tour. I thought, "It's a damn good thing that these guys don't have to keep a constant vigil over these barrels." This beer needs so long to mature that talented brewers, like Watterson, sometimes change jobs before they get a chance to enjoy the fruits of their labor.

Brewing great Belgian-style ales requires the patience of a saint, waiting for just the right time to unveil another classic. "We don't rush any of our beers," says Farley. "Even our ales take seven to eight weeks in a fermenter. That's something I saw and heard a lot of in Belgium: Give them time." Truth be told, that is Brasserie St. James's real secret ingredient.

"You're like the monks of Nevada," I volunteered to the brewers before I ended my first visit and reluctantly left their pseudo abbey in the heart of Neon Babylon. Okay, maybe not, but these guys won't be rushed into releasing beer below their high standards. I tasted the artisanship in every delicious drop.

Watterson laughed at the notion of being an abbot, then shared a final parting thought: "The beer tells us when it's ready, not the other way around." They may not be monks, but these are certainly three wise men.

Art Unfiltered

The Best Kept Secret in Reno

Growing up in Reno, where the big beer brands have ruled for decades, hasn't been easy for the craftsmen at Brasserie St. James. Although the brewery has developed a local fan base, many of its patrons are still curious visitors from out-of-state. "I would really like to see Reno emerge as a viable other option to cities like Portland, Oregon and Austin, Texas, where young creative types will come and build a life," wishes Farley, who I've learned doesn't mince words. "Reno still has a little redneck culture and those who celebrate a sort of scumbag ethos. While I find some of that charming to a point, it makes it difficult sometimes for those of us that would like to elevate Reno from its past negative image. I have to remind people that liking quality food and beverage doesn't make you a snob. All in all, there are some really great people here. It's just a great quality of life, and it's less than four hours from the ocean, the Bay Area and wine country. We just need to find the balance with a young, progressive, and more urban mindset and the old-schoolers. The biggest challenge is that it's a small market, and when everything is drifting toward 'buy local,' you need your 'local' to grow and expand." For the time being, Brasserie St. James is still one of Craft Beer Country's hidden gems.

ALASKAN BREWING in rugged Juneau, Alaska, is accessible by car or on foot after you ferry or fly in to the land-locked northern city

CHAPTER 32

FINDING BEER IN THE LAST FRONTIER

Alaskan Brewing—Juneau, AK

THERE ARE NOTEWORTHY BREWERIES in the West that are off the beaten path but worth navigating the maze of country roads that leads to beer nirvana. Then there is the fabled Alaskan Brewing Company. I've found Alaskan Amber everywhere from hotel bars to mini-mart walk-in coolers, and I've always wondered about the source of this delicious craft beer that flows south to the lower forty-eight. When I Google the journey from Albany, Oregon to Juneau, Alaska, it maps out to a thirty-six-hour, 1,850-mile drive zig-zagging through Washington state, British Columbia, and the Yukon Territory to Skagway, Alaska. From there, it's a mere six hours on two ferry boats and a half-hour drive to the brewery. Being a bit of a dreamer, I briefly consider turning that challenging itinerary into another travel-writing adventure.

Then I come out of my beer buzz and to my senses. There may be a day when I have time for an Alaskan Highway road trip, but it's not now. The more sensible option is to drive to Portland International Airport, catch an Alaskan Airlines flight with a short layover in Seattle, and land in Juneau about three hours later. As the 737 flies, it's about 909 miles from SeaTAC International Airport.

Just over a month after plotting the journey, we break through the cloud cover and land in what appears to be Middle Earth on an uncharacteristically chilly July evening. There are forest-covered mountains, white-capped peaks that touch the cotton canopy of clouds, and deep-blue waterways everywhere. Tucked into the nooks and crannies in a setting straight out of a Tolkien novel is Juneau. I've finally arrived in one of my bucket-list destinations, the wilderness-locked capital of the forty-ninth state.

Three-and-a-half miles from the city's tiny international airport, steam rises from the Alaskan Brewing industrial complex on the edge of the rugged Coast Range. I meet founder Geoff Larson outside the tasting room, and we take the scenic route through the parking lot to the business offices. Larson points out a bald eagle perched high in a pine about a hundred yards from where we walk, scouting its next meal. It's the first sign of just how much he cares about all the wild environs that surrounds him.

When we arrive at a conference room, Geoff's wife and business partner Marcy joins us by speaker phone, so she can tell her side of the story. Founded in 1985 by the nature-loving Larsons, Alaskan has been a dream-come-true for the couple—a brewery that has been creating award-winning craft beers for going on thirty years.

During a summer gig at Glacier National Park in Montana, a friendship that developed while hiking eventually warmed up to dating. Ultimately, that romance led Geoff to follow his heart and Marcy all the way to Juneau. But first, the then homebrewer/beer hobbyist made a slight detour on his way west to visit Anchor Brewing in San Francisco. As fate would have it, he ended up meeting craft-beer legend Fritz Maytag during his tour, and the two ended up talking for hours. The conversation had such an impact on young Larson that he began considering a different application for his chemical engineering degree, one a little out of the ordinary.

"It was interesting because it was the day before Thanksgiving; so afterward, Fritz drove me to the bus station and on the way, he picked up a turkey for his meal," laughs Larson. "I liked to say he picked up one turkey and dropped another off. From there, I took the bus to Seattle, got on the ferry and moved to Alaska." And everyone lived happily ever after . . . except for a few potholes on the road to success.

While Marcy held down two jobs in Juneau, Geoff focused on planning the brewery. "Between the two of us, we got all the planning done, and started raising money," he recalls. "I figured I talked to 1,000 people one-on-one. We would go to Chambers and Rotary meetings, and I'd tell them about beer. It's an interesting investing subject, but also one that no one really knew about, like the history of brewing. We thought we would be able to raise the money with just a few large investors. Instead, it ended up being a whole mess of small investors—eighty-eight of us total in the end." That included all types, from Democrats and Republicans to loggers, fisherman, and park-service people. "Nobody agreed on anything except for beer," he chuckles. "It took work to keep everybody in sync," adds Marcy.

The Alaskan Brewing Company officially launched in 1986 and has been brewing popular craft beers ever since. In fact, the brewery, which started by producing under one hundred barrels its first year in business, filled 150,000 barrels in 2017.

I ask the entrepreneurial couple, "Were you ever nervous? Did you ever think 'Oh my God, what have we gotten ourselves into with eighty-eight investors in landlocked Juneau, Alaska? We're not going to make it!'"

"There's laws that prevent you from treating others as we treated ourselves," answers Geoff. "Were we scared at times? Oh my God!"

"We were so close to the edge that if we had sneezed, we'd have gone out of business," interjects Marcy, who remembers tight times in 1987. "We didn't know we were at that edge. Thank goodness we were that naïve because we never gave up hope. There was one point in time when we had sold all the beer that we made. There was no more beer coming out of the tanks for at least another week, and I had to cut payroll. When you cut payroll and you're in a small business, you have to make sure those checks are going to clear." She went downtown and sold fourteen Alaskan Brewing t-shirts to local merchants to put enough money in the account to pay the staff. "Cash flow is the big problem—it catches you off guard.

"You just don't give up. Geoff and I are both pretty stubborn. We were ready to give all and everything to make this happen. We couldn't afford rent so we lived on a boat. One of our investors, a local fisherman, let us live on it for the winter. There were a whole lot of sacrifices. Our crew was with us every step of the way. I didn't bounce any of their checks, which helped."

Making good beer sure didn't hurt either. While doing a little local history research at the library, Marcy stumbled across a 1907 newspaper article on a turn-of-the-century brewery. "It must have been less than twenty-four hours later, a fellow from Juneau called and said he had found a bunch of stuff in an old collection, and it was all from the Douglas City Brewing Company," she shares. That fortuitous connection eventually led to information on a particular type of hop that Geoff was brewing with at the time called Bohemian.

"Now it's called Saaz," notes Geoff. "You think about this guy, and he got these hops from the Old World to Juneau, Alaska in the early 1900s. He was using the hop in a way to balance the beer, not to overstate the hop character. Of course, this was from behind the iron curtain then, in Czechoslovakia.

"So we tracked it down and started getting the hops from there." If the beer could be recreated from Saaz alone, Geoff would have been home-free. The glacier water hadn't changed much over the eighty-year span, but other ingredients were more difficult to duplicate. He had to find the right crystal and pale malt from the obscure historical references. That was difficult because there are many different types. "Of course, we didn't have the yeast either," points out Geoff. He pieced together the recipe for Alaskan Amber from various sources, and started experimenting. "Essentially, we felt comfortable based on the flavor descriptors and some of the fermentation characteristics described in the article," he says. "We wanted to ferment at as cold a temperature as our yeast could take. The brewmaster was having a difficult time keeping the beer warm enough for the yeast. We used the term 'old style' because that was the old way of brewing ales, that cool fermentation."

Although they worked out the kinks, there were casualties. "We destroyed quite a few batches," Geoff winces. But practice makes perfect.

Eventually, through trial and error, Alaskan not only had an Old World amber beer to sell, it had a good story to tell. "We've come close to what was being produced at the turn of the century," he says with a little pride.

Alaskan Amber is an Alt-style ale, or a slow, top-fermented beer. Its copper color reminds me of the wild sockeye salmon swimming in pristine streams created by the nearby Mendenhall Glacier. Slight sweetness from the first sip fades quickly from this well balanced, not-too-bitter, 18 IBU beer. My mind floats away for a split second, imagining the creamy smooth microbubbles in the ale with the fleshy halibut fillet and berry chutney garnish that I had the night before at downtown Juneau's Twisted Fish Company. The sessionable, 5.3 ABV amber, a GABF gold-medal winner in the 1980s (ancient Olympics in terms of the US craft-beer scene), seamlessly fuses European and Northwest hops with two-row pale and specialty malts. The damp, chilly weather outside paired with this German-style ale has me longing for Oktoberfest in July.

Then Geoff reels me back into the conversation. "It was so special to be able to manufacture something different in a state that was known for raw materials, timber, oil," he shares. Being somewhat isolated creates a few challenges, but sourcing ingredients for Alaskan Amber isn't one of them. "Quite frankly, it's just a hop, skip, and a jump to go to the hops selection," he jokes, adding wryly, "What's interesting is there's another layer to the onion that's appealing to us; appealing maybe isn't the right word."

"Geoff is stuck on the pun," sighs Marcy.

"The challenge is interesting," he continues. "We want to keep the highest-integrity product for as long as possible once it's packaged. You're on a road of possible oxidation, no matter how careful you are." Heat increases chemical oxidation reaction rates, which can lead to the wet paper or cardboard taste often associated with beer past its prime. According to the American Homebrewers Association, fusel alcohols, acetaldehyde, and trans-2-nonenal are responsible for the majority of off-flavors associated with stale, oxidized beer.

Alaskan sidestepped the problem with an innovative, green solution. "We use carbon dioxide to purge out the bottles and purge out the kegs," reports Geoff. "The difficulty in getting carbon dioxide here pressed us into thinking about alternatives that other breweries don't think about." Alaskan learned to capture its own CO_2 off of fermentation. The brewery started purifying, liquefying, and using the gas for other parts of the plant back in 1998. "We were challenged, by our locale, to be sourcing CO_2 in a way that was appropriate for us," explains the chemical engineering student turned brewer. "We couldn't just say, 'Well, it was always done this way.' We had to make our own way."

Now, Alaskan has been self-sufficient when it comes to CO_2 for two decades. "The CO_2 that we captured is from plants, so it's renewable," notes Geoff. "Over 70 percent of CO_2 that is supplied is from fossil fuels. So inadvertently, what we've also created, is something that is mindful and appropriate for not only our locale but for the greater world community for which we are a part of. You can always call up the CO_2 supplier, but they don't deliver to Juneau."

There are also homegrown ingredients that you can actually pick out in some of the brewery's beers. A storyteller at heart, my knowledgeable host explains that none other than Captain Cook was the inspiration for another Alaskan beer. He dove into the famous explorer's journals and found that the good captain was brewing beer while mapping the area during his search for the Northwest Passage.

Larson's sources also reported that the HMS Resolution had an extraor-dinarily healthy crew. "In earlier times, other captains would leave with three times the crew that they needed because by the time they made it, two-thirds of the crew would die," says Geoff.

"Captain Cook would send his crew out to gather fresh edibles, and in his journals, he has fourteen references to the use of spruce in making beer. The two spruces that he used were Sitka Spruce in Alaska and White Spruce in New Zealand." Geoff had the Sitka analyzed and found that the oil fractions are extraordinarily close to Noble hops. "It's acidic, tart, aromatic, and has a fairly high sugar content," he points out.

"What is remarkable to me is here was Captain Cook using spruce tips in 1778, and he made reference to the spruce tips being 'especially fine.' I think of that as a man who is extraordinarily attentive to his senses. Maybe in some ways, that's a neat thing about the discovery of a beer. Beer was relegated to being a bland, low-flavor product, and here we were, presenting something with a huge amount of flavor and unexpected delight. Spruce tips are something that we've used, but we've used a whole manner of different botanicals."

One of the most successful products developed from such experiments is the brewery's Old English ale, appropriately named Alaskan Winter. It's a crisp, golden beer with enough alcohol, at 6.4% ABV, to warm a local fisherman. Noble hops add a pinch of bitterness (22 IBU) to help offset the sweet floral flavors extracted from the evergreens' new growth. It's easy to see why customers anxiously await this slightly malty seasonal beer just about the time the kegs run dry each spring.

You might get lucky and find a stray spruce-infused six-pack of Alaskan Winter Ale when the bears come out of hibernation in April. However, from my own frequently fruitless expeditions, you would be even more fortunate to discover Alaskan Smoked Porter (another of Geoff's gems) at your local taphouse. The tobacco-brown beer, first released in 1988, has won forty-one total awards and fourteen Great American Beer Festival Gold Medals since then. "It has won more awards than any other American beer," brags Geoff, who has earned the right. "We use the same recipe every year," he shares. That includes smoking the beer with local alderwood, an epiphany that bubbled to the surface while hanging out with a local fishmonger.

"There was a smokehouse across from us and a guy who was making great smoked fish," recalls Geoff. "He'd come over on Friday afternoon, and we'd have beer and smoked fish. We thought, 'What would be a great complement to this food?'"

"The smoked fish needed to have a beer to stand up to that," adds Marcy. "You wouldn't taste the amber that much. That is kind of where it started—as all great things do—in the taproom."

Some beers deteriorate with age, but not this one. "We'd taste the smoked porters after a year or two, and we started to see that it was changing, but changing in a positive way," continues Geoff. That observation led to an experiment.

In 1993, the Larsons pulled together a group of craft-beer legends that included renowned beer writer Michael Jackson and Charlie Papazian,

Founder of the Brewers Association and the Great American Beer Festival, inviting them to participate in the enviable task of tasting Alaskan's older smoked porters. "I asked, 'Could we, should we vintage date these?' There was a resounding affirmation, 'Yes!' Michael Jackson suggested afterward that we not filter it and let it be live. So from that date on, we've dated them and talk about vertical tastings. We have a library of beers that goes back to 1993!"

A sampling of that collection was available in the Alaskan Brewing tasting room, although it didn't stretch all the way back to 1993. Just as Geoff explained, the smoky flavor fades with time. I start with the 2008, and hope the beer is much better than that year, when the economy tanked and left the US in a recession. With the phenolic curtain pulled back, other flavors, like coffee and a hint of tart cherry take the stage. Good stuff, but it's time to move five years into the future. That proves to be a whole different experience, just like the brewer predicted it would. Only coffee and caramel notes poke through the much-heavier smoke screen in the 2013.

By the time I reach the last bottle, I've started nibbling on a block of ten-year-old Canadian cheddar to add to the experience. There is no escaping the burnt wood pouring from the 2016 Alaskan Porter. The first whiff immediately reminds me of nights drinking dark beer and smoking cigars beside a bonfire on the beach. Of course, the smoke is what makes this vertical tasting possible. It's hard to imagine it working with aged peanut butter porter, but I guess you never know.

The interesting thing about smoke is that it's an antioxidant used for the preservation of food. "There is no question that as time progresses, the smoke character tends to mellow and diminish," notes Geoff. "The more interesting sherry and dry fruit-type characters can come out with the roasted malts. You can still taste the smoke. When people do vertical tastings, I highly recommend starting with the oldest vintage first. If you start with the youngest, your palate will become blind to smoke." Just like a jacket that you hang up in the closet after coming inside from a nice campfire, it doesn't really smell smoky until you reach for it the next morning.

Alaskan got so good at making smoked beers, that the Brewers

Association asked Geoff to write a book on the subject with noted industry expert Ray Daniels, who ultimately developed the Cicerone Certification Program. It's now part of the Brewer's Association Style Guide.

While researching smoked beers in Bamberg, Germany, Geoff was overwhelmed by the fact that some of the breweries, like Spezial, were nearly 500 years old. "What right do I have to write about their beer?" he wondered. "I was humbled by the fact that we were a fifteen-year-old brewery at the time. But in those 500 years, they reinvented themselves over and over again. All of the sudden I realized, 'Okay, we're a young brewery. So what? That shouldn't diminish what we can do as an integral part of our industry.'"

That kind of thinking has led the brewery to innovate. "Our location basically does put us in a different viewpoint with different needs than some other brewers," explains Marcy. "That's made us jump ahead and do things quicker than others. We think of different problems earlier than other brewers in the lower forty-eight."

Not only does the brewery conserve two million gallons of water per year with its mash filter press, which Geoff describes as a giant espresso machine (it presses all the good stuff from the grain), but it helps turn its spent grain into fuel. "The interesting thing is that one man's trash is another man's treasure," he observes. "We produce so much of the grain that we have to deal with it. It never entered our mind to put it in a landfill. I know other breweries do."

Instead, Alaskan created a patent-pending system that enables it to replace 60 percent of fossil fuel power with its dried grains. "What's going to be interesting is here we are, a tiny brewery using spent grain as a primary fuel, and we have an opportunity to change the industry. That trash is no longer something you have to get rid of. That trash is something that has value."

Most of Juneau had been mined out of precious ore by the time the Larsons started creating their brand of liquid gold so many years ago. They are still the dreamers that they were when they fell for Mother Nature and each other—just more settled into this magical place and their role in the world around them. "When John Muir came up to this country, he was mesmerized by glaciers," Geoff muses. "He created the tourist industry by describing something unique and different. That's part of this culture. It's not an easy place to live, but for those that have the appeal to live here, there's no place like it. I drive home, and I cross salmon streams. I saw a brown bear yesterday. I look at where I live, and it's pretty remarkable. People pay thousands of dollars to come here where I live. It's pretty rewarding. And we're able to brew beer!"

Geoff Unfiltered

It's All Good

"People ask me what my favorite beer is," says Larson. "I always say that 'The best beer in the land is the beer in your hand.' I'm not going to sit there and cry about somebody's tastes. That's their tastes, and it's great. I think that's important."

CHAPTER 33

EXPLORING CRAFT BEER COUNTRY

A Few of the Many Other Great Breweries Out West

THE EVER-GROWING NUMBER of good to great breweries from the South Pacific to the West Coast made it impossible to write a chapter about each and every one, let alone cover them all in a paragraph or two here. Had I tried to include every noteworthy brewery in these regions, it wouldn't be time to write this happy ending. While tasting every delicious ale or lager out west sounds enticing, it's just not feasible given the shadow that my belly is now casting after visiting 70 pubs, taprooms, and beer gardens.

Truth is, I saved some of the very best for Craft Beer Country's last call. Many of my favorite people, places, and beers make a cameo appearance in this grand finale.

On that note, I'll start one last journey just down the street from a Washington State ferry terminal, at **Anacortes Brewing**. Anacortes isn't just easy to remember because it's in a unique location near the tip of Fidalgo Island in the San Juan Islands; it's home to this cool little brewery and its selection of enjoyable beers. General Manager Rick Star, who was inspired about beer at an early age by his Bavarian brewmaster uncle Peter, is serving beer worth the twenty-five-minute drive from I-5. Although I was on a mission to try the now tapped-out Broken Link Sour, winner of a gold medal in the Wood & Barrel Aged Sour Beers category at the 2015 Washington Beer Awards, there are plenty of other great options available. The European influence on Star and the brewery crew is evident on the menu, with its 6.5% ABV Mai Oh Maibock, a golden, malty, bock-style beer with German Perle and noble hop notes, and 8.4% ABV Aviator Doppelbock, a dark, rich, bready beer with noble hops thrown in for a little balance. Other more sessionable options include a 5% ABV, Saaz-hopped Czech Pilsner and a light-bodied, 4.8% ABV Helles lager.

A stone's skip from Seattle's Lake Union is wonderful **Freemont Brewing**. The Freemont neighborhood hangout seems like *the* place to be on a Saturday night. Barrels line the walkway that leads through the spacious patio to the tasting room. Inside, my hostess Emily recommends that I try the Lime Gose, a small batch on tap tonight. I can't decide whether it reminds me of key lime pie in a glass or a mellow margarita. All I know is that I want to spend the entire night here, drink many goblets of this deliciously tart beer, and come to a decision. But sleeping in the taproom or on the patio is not an option. A local favorite, Freemont has many beers worth dreaming about, including the slightly piney Interurban, an 80 IBU IPA that is lit up with Chinook, Centennial, and Amarillo hops, and a variety of imperial and barrel-aged beers. Still, ten minutes after I pull away from this popular brew house, a pleasant hint of lime lingers on my palate and makes me wonder what other surprises this creative brewery has in store for its fans.

The jagged Seattle skyline is so close that it nearly casts a shadow on **Georgetown Brewing**, a fantastic brewery located a few blocks from Highway 99 in Seattle's industrial Georgetown neighborhood. Tasters are free, and friendly bartenders Max and Sam take good care of me on a busy Thursday night in July. Patrons are stacked two deep behind the bar, while others wait in line to purchase growlers of their favorites. You can't go wrong with Manny's Pale Ale or Roger's Pilsner. The pils, with its Sterling hops from Crosby Farms, is a bit more dynamic than your average lawnmower beer at 34 IBUs. Yet it's still a sessionable 4.9% ABV. But my favorite Georgetown beer tonight is the Gusto Crema, a golden brown ale made with 2 Row Pale, Munich, and Sterling Hops, English Ale

Yeast, and a mountain of medium-roasted coffee beans from Caffè Umbria. The aroma is strong enough that you can close your eyes and imagine it was made by your favorite barista. Max mentioned that this beer was a gold medal winner in the Coffee Beer category at the Great American Beer Festival in 2016. It's difficult to disagree with the judge's taste buds.

Right around the same time, in the fall of 2016, the skies have opened, and it's pouring on the rollicking crowd in the parking lot at Elysian Fields (the north lot of Century Link Field) in downtown Seattle. But these fans aren't headed to their cars celebrating a Seahawks football win. Instead, this festive bunch is waddling between craft-beer tents at **Elysian Brewing's** 12th Annual Great Pumpkin Beer Festival in early October. Pumpkin ales have actually been around since colonial times, but I'm convinced that this style of beer has matured to near perfection at Elysian.

My first taster at the event is filled with Night Owl, Elysian's first pumpkin beer and most popular seasonal ale. The slightly spiced pumpkin-nutmeg-cinnamon flavor shines through without the sweetness you'd taste in Grandma's Thanksgiving day pie.

Next I'm treated to Dark of the Moon, a GABF Silver medalist, and its 7.5% ABV warms my spirit on this damp, chilly fall night. Dark of the Moon tastes just as enchanting as it sounds. It's a seductive stout brewed with seven different malts, balanced with Magnum and Saaz hops, and topped off with a microbubbled cinnamon-spiced pumpkin head that you smell well before your lips ever find glass. When mouth and mug do finally meet, bittersweet chocolate, coffee, and the subtle squash flavors come together in perfect harmony.

My personal favorite, though, is Elysian's Punkuccino, another noteworthy pumpkin stout. The 6.0% ABV beer is jolted to life with a shot of Stumptown Coffee combined with chocolate and kiln-coffee malts and other delicious goodies. Sipping this irresistible ale is like pairing homemade pumpkin loaf with a mug of bitter, jet-black coffee. Just like a decadent holiday treat, it draws me back for seconds, but without the guilt.

As I finish one last precious pint of The Great Pumpkin Imperial Pumpkin Ale (a boozy 8.1% golden-orange delight) before calling it a night, I silently mourn the coming nine-month drought before I can drink these delectable seasonal beers again. Alas, Elysian's pumpkin ales and stouts start showing up on select grocery shelves in the late summer and begin disappearing not long after midnight on Halloween.

ENine is a unique brewery about a 40-minute drive south of Seattle in Tacoma, Washington. Engine House No. 9, built in 1907 to provide fire protection for Tacoma's north end, was converted into a tavern in 1972 and later became the city's first craft brewery in 1995. Since then, E9 (as it is further abbreviated by fans) won Mid-Sized Brewery of the Year at the 2017 Washington Beer Awards. The quaint old former firehouse was a real hot spot during my visit, and most everyone on hand appeared to be enjoying pints paired with a meal. For the famished (as is too often the case with me), food options like "Not Your Mama's Meatloaf" pair well with the slightly hoppy, 65-IBU India Pale Ale. For those into something a little different than the ubiquitous IPA, E9 usually has a broad selection of saisons, sours, witbiers and other interesting styles on tap.

Across Puget Sound in Poulsbo, Washington, former auto mechanic Mike Montoney has permanently moved his wrench sets to his appropriately named **Rainy Daze Brewing** operation. It is pouring outside, and stepping inside the little pub not only warms the body, but the good vibes immediately warm the soul. Only the Tip is a 9% ABV, 95 IBU double IPA brewed with spruce tips from Sitka, Alaska. Montoney mixes in hops to complement the piney characteristics of the spruce. Given the pine-covered setting near the Olympic National Forest, this brewpub is a great choice if you want to immerse your taste buds in the region and immediately wipe out all hints of a rainy day outside. Now, there are sunny days in the area too, and Mike's cask-conditioned, coppery English Pale and hoppy but lawn-mowing-approved Sod Slayer ISA, which both check in at a sessionable 4.5% ABV, are great when the weather finally gets warm. This was definitely one of my most memorable stops and worth an overnight trip up the Olympic Peninsula.

When I found out the former Fish Brewing beer artisan Paul Pearson had taken his mad skills a few blocks down the street to **Well 80** (a new brewery in Olympia, Washington), I had to give his new digs a try. At the back of the brewery is an artesian well (designated Well #80 during a 1939 survey) that pumps out thirty-five gallons of 53°F water per minute from an ancient subterranean reservoir. This magical H₂O has been the area brewers' claim to fame since the late 1890s. One hundred and twenty-plus years later, Pearson is here at Well 80 transforming that same special liquid into old classics like Original Lager Year '64 and Original Dark '66. Both are rumored to be designed after original recipes from the now-defunct Olympia Brewing company. The '64 is a very mellow 16-IBU, 4.2% ABV pale-yellow beer that goes great with the brewpub's bacon, lettuce, tomato, and avocado sandwich and tasty black truffle/black garlic/Parmigiano-coated fries. But my favorite beer here on the narrow alleyway patio this warm spring evening is the more mature '66. It's a dark American lager, bolstered by roasted-malt notes and a pinch of chocolate, that has a bit more flavor than its slightly older counterpart, the '64. For those who want something a little more potent on their palate, Well 80 offers 80LBS of Hops IPA, a 6.5%, 40 IBU New England Style Hazy India Pale Ale and several other selections from its taps. This trendy little downtown brewery might be worth a stop in Washington's State Capital just to try the legendary water and take a trip down memory lane with the old local lager favorites.

There is something about stumbling on a discovery serendipitously that makes it extra special. Such is the case with **Barrel Mountain Brewing** in Battle Ground, Washington, roughly ten miles north of Vancouver. Owner/brewer Troy Steigman has put together an impressive lineup of beer, with options to please almost anyone who wanders in his front door. Bartenders Sierra and Hannah walk me through options ranging from a straw-colored lager to a midnight-black stout. Choosing a favorite is tough, so I'll highlight my three top picks, all award-winning beers at various competitions. This terrific trio includes the 5% ABV Silver Star Session, a remarkably mild all-night-long-drinkable ale for its 50 IBUS. The brewery's most decorated beer, the 6.6% ABV Starway Stout, is a bittersweet chocolate beer with an invitingly aromatic light-brown head that draws you back until it's time for a refill. The 9.3% ABV BackPacker Imperial Porter, with its smoked-malt vanilla notes, brings up the tail end of this short list. I'd call the deep-dark-brown top-fermented ale an after-dinner treat, since it isn't exactly sessionable unless you want that session to end with your head spinning. Although some of the locals rave about Barrel Mountain for its food, I'd make another the trip off the beaten path just to see what the creative Steigman will come up with next.

Josh King has been Head Brewer at **Sockeye Brewing**, a Boise, Idaho favorite, since 2002. Like most brewers, King is hard at work when I catch up with him at the brewery on a pea-soup-thick foggy morning in the Boise burbs. As we wander past stainless-steel tanks through the kitchen and into the bar, he tells me that Sockeye was originally started by a family that owned a fishing guide service in the area. That connection to the great outdoors is readily apparent. Many of Sockeye's beers are named after Idaho landmarks, like its Dagger Falls IPA, Angel's Perch Amber, and Lucky Peak Pilsner. My personal favorite catch of the day is the Dagger Falls, a bold, 100-IBU ale brewed with Simcoe, Bravo, Chinook, Cascade, and Idaho 7 hops. It would also make the perfect partner with anything from salmon to steelhead. The good news is that you don't need to travel far in these parts to make this near perfect nature- and man-made pairing.

Roughly 400 miles due northwest, **McMenamins** Edgefield, in Troutdale, Oregon, is a hot spot for those who enjoy draining pints in an enchanting atmosphere that includes several outdoor fire pits for contemplating the intricacies of craft beer. Located on the sprawling grounds of the former county poor farm, the hotel/resort has something for everyone, including its own brewery, distillery, and wine bar. Brian McMenamin shared a tray of delightful beers early one evening on my overnight visit. "Is this place haunted?" I asked him, working on a taster of Hammerhead pale ale. "Well, there are stories," he says with a wink. Just to be sure I would sleep through the night and avoid any uninvited guests at the foot of my bed, I gulped down a few pints of bitter, chocolatey Terminator Stout and its slightly sweet cousin, Black Rabbit Porter. I managed to make it to dawn without any unwanted interruptions from restless former residents dragging rattling chains. Regardless of your beer or alternative beverage preference (this cool place also has a winery and cider house), storybook-worthy Edgefield is a cool place to stop for a few beers or other adult beverages on a weekend getaway.

Portland has so many breweries popping up that I've lost count. There isn't enough space in this book to do all of the great breweries in the Rose City justice, but that hasn't stopped me from trying. Among my favorites is **Great Notion Brewing,** in the city's red-hot Alberta District, opened by three friends, Paul Reiter, James Dugan and Andy Miller in January 2016. I drop in on a partly sunny Saturday and plop down on the comfortable patio furniture for a few beers and an appetizer of waffle fries smothered in white and black beans, cheese, and pulled pork. Front-of-House Manager Sasha McHale takes good care of me, recommending a flight of beers that includes Blueberry Muffin (a fruited sour), Jammy Pants (another fruited sour), Juice Jr. (a hazy IPA), Hop Waffle (an India Maple Ale), and Double Stack (an imperial breakfast stout). Just for shits and giggles we add Blueberry Pancakes to the tray, but it's not what you might be imagining. This is a curious liquid-brunch blend of the Blueberry Muffin and Double Stack ales. Although these all turn out to be well-made beers, I'm crazy about the Blueberry Muffin (5.5% ABV), which smells like moist muffin tops straight out of the oven, but has a nice tart flavor, and Jammy Pants (7% ABV), a slightly more tart kettle sour loaded with a variety of berry, cherry, and other exotic fruit flavors. For those who aren't fond of puckering up during a craft-beer outing, there are fifteen other options on tap today, including a wide range of IPAs and a guest tap that sometimes includes mild pilsners among other selections. Turns out Great Notion is true to its name and one of those pleasant, serendipitous surprises that make exploring breweries, no matter where you happen to be in the world, so much fun.

After a day snowshoeing around the slopes of Mt. Hood, friend and fellow beer aficionado John Ortega joined me and photographer extraordinaire Lisa at **Base Camp Brewing** in Portland's east-side brewery district. At the brewery's more breathable fiftyish-foot elevation, we shared a twenty-four-ounce bottle of the brewery's Rye Saison, which won Base Camp a gold in the Specialty Saison category at 2017's Great American Beer Festival. It's a sneaky-potent, 7.6% ABV farmhouse ale with aromas of apple, herbs, and spices. The rye and brettanomyces (yeast) contribute to the crisp, slightly tart finish that climbs on the back end of each swallow. We also sampled the Bière de Mars, a French-style golden farmhouse ale combining wheat with lightly toasted malted barley. The fizzy carbonation and flavor reminded us of champagne. Just hearing about John's mountain trek had me famished and looking for something to pair with these wonderful beers. Lucky for us, Jangbo Sherpa from Sherpa Kitchen's on-site food truck brought us a generous helping of Nepalese-inspired MoMo (beef dumplings) and Bal Baht Tarkari (lentils, steamed rice, and curry with chicken). For those who aren't quite as adventurous but need sustenance to keep their energy up between curling pints, there are Mexican food options served truck-to-table by Poblano Pepper, Jangbo's neighboring food vendor, just outside the brewery's front door. You don't have to break a sweat to enjoy the many pleasures of this Base Camp.

Mere minutes away, off SE 7th, **Ground Breaker** serves its GABF gold medalist Dark Ale, a gluten-free brown beer brewed with chestnuts, lentils, and sorghum. You would swear you are tasting roasted malt in this wonderfully nutty dark ale, but that's the kiln-roasted chestnuts. Master Chef Neil Davidson attributes the similarity to an old Italian recipe discovered by James Neumeister, the brewery's founder and head of R&D. If you'd like to add a little kick to your pint, try the Imperial Darkness on nitro, which includes dark chocolate, vanilla syrup, and espresso beans. The protein in the lentils creates a wonderfully coffee-cream aromatic head that makes it worth the visit to Ground Breaker. PS: for those of you who miss bread, this beer might even trick you into believing you are back at the boulangerie. Mm good!

Nearby **Burnside Brewing** offers a range of quality craft beer to pair with food that goes well beyond the normal pub menu. When we visited, I tried the grilled octopus with crushed potato, chorizo rioja, espelette aioli, and marrow butter with the seasonally available Alt Star Beer, a German-style amber ale brewed with five different malts. Every time I've been to this place, rain or shine, it has been packed with happy people. Maybe that is because Burnside serves everything from hamburgers to fresh local trout for dinner and offers its staple ales and lagers along with a rotation of new beers. If you happen to be in the Portland anytime in the future, Uber across the Burnside Bridge and try the Too Sticky to Roll IRA, a 78 IBU American amber with Millennium and Centennial hops, or the 4.9% ABV Sweet Heat fruit/spice beer with apricot puree and imported Jamaican Scotch bonnet peppers.

Fifty miles south in Salem, **Santiam Brewing** is making noise in the local craft-beer community with its Real Ales. During a brief tour, co-owner Ian Croxall tells me that the brewery's Real Ales are unfiltered and unpasteurized beer that has been conditioned (undergone secondary fermentation) in the cask from which it will be served. When these ales are ready for Santiam's customers, they will be dispensed without additional nitrogen or carbon dioxide pressure. In addition to these flavorful beers, Ian and his partners Matt Killikelly, and Jim Smiley brew an award-winning coconuty Pirate Stout and moderately roasty Coal Porter. If dark beer isn't your thing, try the 1859, a 6.1% ABV German-style Maibock with Pilsner, Munich and Caramunich malts plus Czech Saaz and German Tetnang hops added for a little balance. Spitfire Amber, Edelweiss Hefeweizen, and Ecotopia IPA options were also on the tap list when I visited, and all proved well worth trying. Soak it all in with a baby back ribs and fries, a burger of the day, or one of the other tempting options on the pub menu. This place is worth a look if you find yourself in The Beaver State's capitol city near McNary Field (the city's airport).

There is a small brewery worth visiting in Corvallis, Oregon, home of the Oregon State University (OSU) Beavers. Just down the street from my writing loft on Madison Avenue is **Flat Tail Brewing**. Brewmaster Dave Marliave's selection of beers includes a Kölsch, a dry-hopped saison, an IPA, seasonal beers, and his Damn Wild Series of sours. Marliave has come up with a six-week process to brew sours, fermented with a proprietary strain of Brettanomyces and Lactobacillus Buchneri, that taste like they have been barrel-aged for months. The chemistry experiment has worked well enough that Flat Tail Brewing took home gold in GABF's American-Style Sour Ales category in 2017 with its DAM Wild: Hops and Lemon Verbena. This 6% ABV sour blonde is dry hopped with Citra and Simcoe and lemon verbena leaves. Those leaves combined with the

Citra hops deliver a refreshing tart flavor in an ale that even looks like a liquid lemon meringue pie. If you miss out, Flat Tail's Pink Lemonade and Marion Berries & Pink Peppercorns sours may also be available, depending on when you visit the little brick pub across the street from the Willamette River.

Oakshire Brewing in Eugene was packed when I arrived late one Saturday afternoon, and for good reason. The temperature was in the mid-seventies and the downtown brewery was providing much needed liquid refreshment in styles to meet most everyone's desire. I tried the Sun Made Cucumber Berliner Weisse, a 4% ABV sour beer with a touch of cucumber aroma in the background. India Pale Ale fans will appreciate the Citrafonix, a 6.3% ABV, 50 IBU Northwest-style IPA with hop-infused citrus flavors. On cooler days I might opt for more than a taster of the Nitro Overcast Stout, a dark, creamy, 5% ABV oatmeal espresso treat, but the beautiful weather dictated other choices. When an afternoon of beer tasting slips into the evening, there are food trucks on hand serving everything from thick-battered fried chicken to pizza and other options.

For you Belgian-style beer lovers, there is a little brewery just outside of Eugene, Oregon that will take you to the rolling countrysides from Flanders to Wallonia, without ever having to purchase a plane ticket. Brewmaster Matt Van Wyk, who left Eugene-based Oakshire Brewing in 2013 to start **Alesong Brewing and Blending** with brothers Brian and Doug Coombs, has something on tap to please most taste buds. My favorites at Alesong included the Terroir Pinot Noir (no, it's not a wine), a tarty farmhouse ale made with crushed and whole cluster grapes and aged in French oak barrels; Four Pirates, a spice-laden, Belgian-style quad that is a dark-fruit treat aged in Jamaican rum barrels, warm enough at 11.1% ABV that you may not need a jacket; and the Vanilla Rhino Suit, an 11% ABV imperial stout with silky smooth vanilla and cocoa notes that eliminate the need for dessert. The Touch of Brett Mandarina is a medal-winning French-style citrusy saison, dry hopped with Mandarina Bavaria hops, and probably my fourth-favorite beer at Alesong. For diehard hop-heads, Van Wyk has collaborated with brewers at Block 15 in Corvallis, Oregon to create a seven-hop 7.3% ABV IPA (while supplies last) that has absolutely no detectable levels of chocolate, vanilla, cinnamon, caramel, dates, raisins, figs, bananas, prune juice, brown sugar, bubblegum, Snickers, or anything else remotely sweet to foul your sensitive palates.

There must be a brewery on every block in Bend (okay, sometimes I've been known to exaggerate), and **Boneyard** is one worth winding through a hundred miles of mountain passes to visit. I recommend staying at a hotel like McMenamins Old St. Francis, a former school with secret rooms hidden in the walls and unending charm, including its own little brewery. Then you can visit Boneyard on foot, pub crawler bike, Uber or taxi. You big IPA fans will love the Notorious, an 11.5% ABV, 80 IBU beer that will turn a wallflower into a social butterfly in just a pint. If that isn't your style, try the Femme Fatale, a seductive sour ale fermented with raspberries that you'll fall for at first sip.

More than once, I've thought that this will be the most read chapter of the book. These short reviews cover some can't-miss breweries, at least in my book. **Crux Fermentation Project** is one of those worthwhile stops that is deserving of special mention. Looking out on stubborn snow-capped peaks from the Bend, Oregon "Fermentation Project" on a red-hot July afternoon, there is almost no place I would rather be in the world. Bartenders Spencer and Colin take good care of me. We talk about our favorite beers in the West, and I'm discovering a few of mine right here. As patrons soak up the sun, sip from a wide selection of ales and play cornhole in the grassy picnic area, I sample Half Hitch, a thirst-quenching imperial IPA. It takes me back to the grapefruit mom used to halve for us as kids, sans the sugar she would sprinkle on top. It's outstanding beer for cooling off in the 91°F weather.

The Crux logo is a set of intersecting arrows pointed in four directions, and the wide selection of beers available at the brewery, from Crux Farmhouse (a cloudy saison) to [Banished] Tough Love (an inescapably bourbon-influenced barrel-aged imperial Russian stout), provides something to satisfy every palate in every season.

The Deschutes River in Central Oregon is home to some of the best whitewater rafting you will find anywhere in the country. Just east of the ruggedly beautiful Deschutes in Redmond is **Wild Ride Brewing Company.** Wild Ride has made a name for itself around the state with its

Nut Crusher Peanut Butter Porter. This brown beer walks a fine line on my taste buds. Sip to sip, I alternated between hating the slightly sweet, 6% ABV porter to loving it. I guess love conquered hate in the end, since I finished the entire pint of the unmistakably peanut butter-spiked beer. But my favorite Wild Ride beer is the Belgian Cloak Dark Strong Ale, an 8.8% ass kicker. This summer seasonal root-beer-brown treat has a creamy salted-caramel flavor with hints of vanilla and brown sugar. There are many great breweries to visit in the Bend, Oregon area—just make sure that you make time for a whitewater river adventure and follow that bucket-list experience with a visit to Wild Ride. It won't disappoint!

Sunriver Brewing, south of Bend, Oregon, is making a name for itself with award-winning beers. The brewery is located in heaven on earth in the rain shadow of ski and hiking destination, Mt. Bachelor. Whether you are coming off the slopes, a hiking or biking trail, or from a whitewater rafting adventure, this is a good place to unwind and drink to a good time. The Fuzztail Hefeweizen, a gold medal winner at both the 2017 GABF and the 2016 World Beer Cup, is a 5% ABV hazy wheat beer, hopped to bring out the drop of lemon flavor you crave, without having to disturb near-perfection with a pulpy slice of fruit. I'm also crazy about the brewery's Vicious Mosquito, a five-hop, 7% ABV brew that had me itching for more after I voraciously drained a pint (like a hungry mosquito or two I've encountered in the nearby Cascade Lakes). The brewery also offers other styles, from pale ales to dark stouts, and a selection of hearty food (like a wild caught Alaskan Sockeye Sandwich) that will prepare you for the next day's adventure.

My windshield decorated with dead bugs courtesy of backroads and rural highways, I somehow managed to find **Klamath Basin Brewing** in southern Oregon. Since I was spending the night in Klamath Falls, had no interviews to conduct, and didn't feel like watching TV in my econo-style, shoebox room, this seemed like nice alternative. I'm guessing that my beer muse was at it again, whispering the suggestion in my ear. Klamath Basin brews enough liquid delights to fill a thirsty beer writer's tasting tray. Ales include the Defiance Double IPA, Rusty Axe IPA, Rebellion Red Ale, and Klamath Basin Blonde, my favorite of the bunch. The beer menu changes from time to time, but the Hard Hat Hefeweizen and award-winning Backroad Vanilla Porter are usually on tap too. It's easy to see why the locals sitting at the bar rave about the place. I'm sure more than one visitor has become a fan of this lively little brewery.

Due west in Ashland, Oregon, just off of the I-5, is another treat. **Caldera Brewing** sits in the foothills of the Siskiyou National Forest, and it's not too much to imagine oneself in a warm beer hall in the Bavarian Alps. Thankfully, there are a few hotels within walking distance of the brewery because the beer is worthy of seconds, thirds, etc. Caldera's claim to fame is that it has been canning its microbrews since 2005. That's great, but the real story here is its many European-styled beers. My focus is on the taster under my nose, a Rauch Ür Bock, a German bock lager with Hallertauer hops and smoked beechwood and cherry wood malts, reminiscent of Grandpa's cherry pipe tobacco. Caldera also serves Dark Lager, a malty, chestnut-brown German-style dunkel, Pilsener Bier, a 5.2% ABV, 33 IBU beer also flavored with German Hallertauer hops, and a Belgian-style dubbel made with Trappist yeast, Belgian candi sugar, and Munich malt. If you would like a taste of the Old World without having to find your passport, give this brewery and the beautiful alpine area around it a try!

Sierra Nevada, founded way back in 1979 by Ken Grossman and Paul Camusi, is still considered a craft brewery, even though it produces more than one million barrels of beer per year. Getting an inside look at one of the West Coast's legendary breweries is a special treat, well worth the long trek through small towns on windy country roads.

During a brief visit to Sierra Nevada's Chico, California headquarters, Grossman shares a little known fact with me: Something "very few people even know about our process that's really quite remarkable in this day and age, maybe, is that we're still bottle conditioning tens of thousands of barrels a beer a year," he reveals. "Even regular consumers of our beer don't understand that part of the brewing process is still the way we did it from day one. From our standpoint, we take all the care that we've always taken, and we've got more resources to do a better job today."

It's hard to dispute Grossman's commitment to the craft that he has helped refine into an industrial art form. "The brewing business was something I didn't get into as a get-rich-quick scheme," he shares. "I love the process of making beer, the alchemy of the brew house, and the wonders of fermentation. So that part of it has always engaged me, and I like the technology."

On a subsequent Engineering Tour, I get a behind-the-scenes glimpse of the technologically enhanced fifty-two-acre facility that Grossman alluded to earlier. In Chico, where temperatures can climb into triple digits in the summer, refrigeration systems are the life support system for the company's beers. The brewery's four 225-ton units, based on the cooling system used for a nuclear submarine, are capable of producing "a pyramid of ice cubes," according to my tour guide.

From the coolers, we make our way through a frigid warehouse that stores seemingly endless stacks of six-packs and on into the canning and bottling facility. Bottles hum through the packaging line at speeds that put curious visitors into a trance-like state. Watching the modern mechanization in action is mesmerizing, and I wonder if a younger Grossman ever dreamed that his little start-up brewery would mature into this state-of-the-art operation.

Eventually, we finish up inside, exit via a side door, and hop a ride on an eight-seat bike-bar for a quick cruise around the property on our way back to the parking lot. I abandon the group at that point and make a beeline for the on-site restaurant for a pint or two—hey, priorities! There are many choices on the menu, ranging from a mellow pilsner to a coffee-black stout . . . and plenty of hazy-to-golden options in between. But after a few samples, I settle on Sierra Nevada's flagship beer, Pale Ale. After all, the Magnum, Perle, and Cascade-hopped, 37-IBU American pale ale is a timeless classic. Although this golden beer helped define the style way back in 1980, its pine, grapefruit, and floral flavors continue to make it a contemporary favorite of the craft-loving masses, me included.

Placer County, California has a rich history of silver mining, but recently, one of its breweries struck gold. **Out of Bounds Brewing** in Rocklin won a GABF gold medal for its Hurly Burly Port Barrel Aged Barleywine. By the time I can make it to Rocklin for a tour and tasting, the microbrewery is completely tapped out of Hurly Burly. No worries.

Brewery Manager Bryan Crass sets me up with some of Out of Bounds' other unique craft beers, including the bizarre Powdered Toast Man Brown Ale. After a sip, I turn to Crass and ask, "Is there syrup in this beer?" He smiles and confirms my suspicion. This maple brown beer has a slight cinnamon aroma and leaves a syrupy sugar film on the palate that makes me crave a crisp, salty slab of bacon. "I've honestly never had anything like this," I tell Crass. "It's just weird, but I kind of like it." Before I catch a Lyft back to the hotel, he shares another treat with me that turns out to be my favorite. The barrel-aged stout smells like a bitter chocolate bar and delivers a cocoa flavor with a generous layer of bourbon. It's very smooth and goes down a little too easy for a 12% ABV beer, and tonight it makes a tasty dessert and the perfect way to end my short expedition to gold country.

On November 18, 1896, the Sacramento Bee reported an unidentified flying object, a light floating above the city that had narrowly missed a church steeple the night before. One hundred and twenty years and a handful of months later, I drifted into Sactown undetected and landed at **New Helvetia Brewing**. On this moderately chilly February afternoon, I wandered into the taproom and asked for a taste of Mystery Airship Imperial Chocolate Porter. New Helvetia's adult version of Oaxacan hot chocolate is an 8.3% ABV, double-chocolate porter flavored with cinnamon, Tahitian vanilla, pasilla peppers, and fresh ginger, then aged with cocoa nibs. Like a pedal-powered blimp cutting through the black night, a fiery kick burns through this dark, malty beer, and I welcomed the immediate but not overwhelming warmth with a smile. Apparently, the judges at the 2015 GABF agreed with me, awarding Mystery Airship a gold medal in its Experimental Beer Category. New Helvetia, which also serves a number of other tasty beers from lagers to hoppy IPAS, is well worth a stop the next time you find yourself in California's capitol.

North Coast Brewing Company, in Fort Bragg, California, has won more than a hundred national and international awards for its wide range of beers. President and cofounder Mark Ruedrich, who has been at this art and science since the craft-beer movement started, continues to produce high-quality beers like his Old Rasputin Imperial Stout. A consistent

favorite in the beer connoisseur community (attaining or flirting with a 100 rating on some beer review sites), this beauty, with its dark fruit, rich molasses, and other complex notes, will warm your soul if and when the fog rolls in during your visit to the coastal brewery. And while you might find the popular, 9% ABV, 75-IBU beer on tap in one of the forty-eight states that North Coast distributes to, it is well worth the trip through cathartically scenic Mendocino County to connect with Ruedrich's less ubiquitous ales and lagers. There are too many worthwhile options to cover here, but you might consider trying the fragrant, fruity PranqSter, a 7.6% ABV Belgian-style golden ale, or the dark-mahogany-colored Brother Thelonious, a more potent, boozy, 9.4% ABV Belgian-style abbey ale. In my opinion, anyone making the bucket-list journey in search of another of the region's fabled ales (see Pliny the Younger directly below), would double their pleasure by staying an extra day exploring the treasure trove of beer styles available along California's North Coast.

Speaking of which, by the time I roll into Santa Rosa to experience **Russian River Brewing Company's** much celebrated Pliny the Younger, it's late afternoon and 4th Street is packed. It is the second day that the famous triple IPA has been on tap, and a line of those waiting their turn for a few precious pints stretches to the end of the block. You see, Pliny the Younger is only available two weeks per year, starting the first Friday of February. This craft beer isn't bottled or canned, so it's developed a following of hopheads willing travel from all parts of the known world for a chance to sample the legendary winter seasonal.

Homebrewing beer nerd extraordinaire Mike Blakely, who has traveled here from the mountains of Colorado, and I are among the partying pilgrims in town for a taste of the storied 8-hop ale. I haven't quite convinced myself that it was worth the roughly 600 miles that I've driven from Oregon's Willamette Valley just to spend a few hours drinking double and triple IPAS. Then the star of the show arrives at our makeshift table.

Pliny the Younger, named after the ancient Roman magistrate and nephew of Pliny the Elder, is a 10.25% ABV hop volcano. The Simcoe, Warrior, Chinook, Centennial, Amarillo, CTZ, Comet, and Azacca hops

❮ Craft beer legend Vinnie Cilurzo of RUSSIAN RIVER BREWING COMPANY tests a pint of product at his Santa Rosa, California brewery

erupt in a feast of exotic fruit, citrus, and pine flavors. Even the spicy Mama Mia, a pepperoni, pineapple, and jalapeno pizza that I've paired with it couldn't get the upper hand on the 90-IBU palate dominator. Although there is probably a meal out there somewhere that is Younger's match, my recommendation is to just enjoy it on its own and savor the experience.

The memorable ale's predecessor, Pliny the Elder (first introduced in 2000), is just as worthy of an expedition to Russian River. In fact, this was my favorite among the brewery's wide range of hoppy and sour choices. Simcoe cones give Elder its piney backbone, its flavor enhanced by the citrus and floral notes exuding from the Amarillo, Centennial, and CTZ hops that are also part of Vinnie Cilurzo's perfected recipe. All in all, this is a worthwhile stop if you plan to be anywhere near Northern California Beer Country.

Just south of San Francisco along coast-hugging Highway 1 is the **Half Moon Bay Brewing Company**. It's little more than a keg toss away from the house that I once lived in near El Granada, California. The area is noteworthy for other reasons, including nearby Maverick's, where daredevil surfers take on mammoth waves. From the brewery, you can see Pillar Point, which overlooks the tempting swells of the Pacific. More tempting for me are brewer James Costa's IPAs. James learned the craft at Bear Republic, and he was apparently paying close attention. Alas, I wanted to try the pumpkin beer, since the area is covered in fields of orange every fall and hosts its own Pumpkin Festival, but the high-demand tap had run dry many moons ago. Oh well, that's just another good reason for another homecoming.

Just past scenic Santa Cruz, I visited **Corralitos Brewing Co.** in Freedom, California. Blink and you will race right through the fields lining Freedom and into Watsonville. Inside the welcoming countryside pub, I asked Owner Luke Taylor if he had anything on tap with fresh, local ingredients. He mentioned a chocolaty stout on the menu infused with local peppers. "Let's have a taste," I said, skeptical that I would like the spicy beer. But after allowing the beer a chance to check in and register with my taste buds, I swallowed the slightly malty, deep-brown liquid and was rewarded with a delayed hint of fire. Not bad at all, and it saved my sister Dawniele's reputation as a budding beer buff, since she highly recommended the place.

In Buellton, just south of San Luis Obispo in one of California's most scenic regions, I visited **Figueroa Mountain Brewing**. Fraternity brother Mike Duffy and his friend Anita Burns met me there to test the taps. This is a brewery that has its shit together, and I highly recommend the short detour off of Highway 101. Once there, you'll find colorfully named beers on the menu, like I Dunkeled in My Pants, a traditional Bavarian dark lager, and My Future Ex-wife, a barrel-aged imperial amber ale. As the three of us sat outside on the patio, I tried a taster tray of delicious beers that included most every hue on the color wheel. My favorite, though, was the Danish Red Lager, a gentle, 5.5% ABV, 23 IBU beer brewed with Weyermann Pilsner, Munich, and Crystal Malts. Inspired by the nearby Danish-style village of Solvang, this former GABF gold-medal winner is fermented with a European lager yeast and cold-conditioned for an extended period of time for a very clean profile. Duffy's go-to beer at "The Fig," as he calls the brewpub, is Lizard's Mouth Imperial Double IPA. This beer is too good for a lizard, with tropical fruit notes, and weighing in at an impressive 9.2%-I-will-kick-your-ass ABV. All too soon, it was time to head down the road, but I vowed to return to Figueroa Mountain and plan to make good on that promise soon.

With Matt Hoch, a Long Beach-based fireman who loves his lagers, I dropped into **Last Name Brewing** (formerly **Dale Bros Brewery**) in Upland, California. The brewery was very busy for a Tuesday night, definitely a good sign. In an effort to extinguish our thirst, we first tried the brewery's flagship beer, Pomona Queen amber lager. Her Majesty is a soft, 4.8% ABV, 13 IBU, slightly nutty jewel-of-a-beer (fitting the royal persona perfectly) that I could enjoy the company of late into the evening. But as fascinating as she was, my favorite beverage in this inconspicuous San Bernardino County-area office park is the Bl'oak, a barrel-aged dark that leaves a hint of sarsaparilla on the tongue—a lingeringly good, oak-kissed aftertaste. If you ever find yourself in the foothills region of the San Gabriel Mountains, stop by Last Name. Even those with a sketchy memory, fogged by too many barrels of beer over the years, won't have any trouble recalling its great beer after this worthwhile visit!

Beachwood BBQ & Brewing in Long Beach, California, has won so many medals at GABF (five golds since 2012) that they were hard to ignore. One of those is Foam Top Blonde, which took home gold in 2013. The 5.5% ABV blonde pours true to its name, with a nice, foamy white cap that is reminiscent of the nearby surf. Although it has been measured at just 10 IBUs, subtle citrus flavors peek out of the malt background in this lightly hopped beer. In almost direct contrast, my server brings me a coffee-black Mocha Machine Imperial Chocolate Coffee Porter with a tan head. The 9.2% ABV, 36-IBU beer is brewed with roasted dark beans from the nearby Portola Coffee Lab and aged with Ecuadorian cacao nibs. After the bittersweet chocolate flavor passes over the palate, each taste finishes with a nice, freshly ground roast retronasal aroma.

Garage Brewing in Temecula, California is a good place to park for beer when I-15 traffic slows to a crawl. Though this touristy town is known for its wineries and old western themes, many visitors have discovered this craft beer country outpost. Garage, with its bay doors that could accommodate broken-down cars if its beer wasn't such a popular product, is a combination quick-fire pizza parlor and taphouse. During a pit stop, I try the Golden Helles Lager, a refreshing 5.2% ABV Munich-style lager. The former GABF gold-medal-winning beer, a classic, slightly malty lager with a crisp finish, is the perfect coolant for the near ninety-degree weather one June afternoon. Other taste-test-worthy options are available, depending on when you drop by for a tune-up, include Belgians, IPAs, wheat ales, stouts, and other styles.

A little farther south, San Diego has long been known for its beautiful beaches and mostly magnificent weather. In the last twenty-five years or so, a growing group of passionate beer connoisseurs/entrepreneurs have given residents and visitors yet another reason to love California's southwest corner.

Just around the corner from **AleSmith** (see chapter 28) on Mira Mesa Boulevard is **Green Flash**. I have a mini-reunion there with fraternity brothers Bill Bergelin and George Bacon. Although Green Flash has a nice little patio/picnic area, we hang out at the bar in the tasting room. Our bartender Devin takes good care of us, serving several tasters of the brewery's fine beer. Since I tend to gravitate to the unique, a beer called

Le Freak immediately captures my attention. This crazy combination of a Belgian-style tripel and an American imperial IPA is an intriguing confluence of passion fruit and floral flavors spiked with Amarillo hops. It is a delicious, unexpectedly quaffable concoction that has a nice, dry finish. All too soon, our visit to Green Flash is coming to a close, and I decide to go out in style with a 9.5% ABV, 100+ off-the-charts IBU Palate Wrecker. This imperial India pale ale contains six pounds of Centennial, Columbus, and Simcoe hops (combined) per barrel. Although I love the bold, hoppy beer, I know that my taste buds have checked out for the afternoon. No worries, during my next trip to San Diego I'll be sure to visit Green Flash again and try another round of their very creative ales and lagers.

One of my favorite stops in Craft Beer Country was **Societe Brewing Company**, just off of I-163 in San Diego's Claremont Mesa neighborhood. CEO Douglas Constantiner and Brewmaster Travis Smith make a formidable duo when it comes to churning out consistently excellent craft beer. Smith spent time learning to brew under craft-beer legend Vinnie Cilurzo at Russian River, and the quality shows up in every pint. During my brief but memorable stop, I couldn't resist the Out West Series, which includes The Dandy (a citrusy, 6.6% ABV IPA), The Coachman (a super approachable, 4.7% Small IPA with fruit flavors layered over a light bitterness), and The Haberdasher (a classic, 5.4% ABV English IPA made with Goldings and Cascade hops). But my favorite ale at Societe is The Harlot, a 5.6% ABV Belgian blonde that combines classic Pilsner ingredients with Belgian yeast. Constantiner jokes that the idea for this Old World Series beer was born during a visit to the border region between Belgium and the Czech Republic. Be sure to carefully check your world map before booking a trip. A visit to Societe might be the more fruitful option.

Just a bridge and a bay away from downtown San Diego is Coronado Island, home of **Coronado Brewing**. The city, which translates to "crowned jewel" from Spanish, is home to the United States North Island base and one of the most magnificent hotels in the nation, the Hotel Del Coronado. The brewery is a short drive from the hotel and a stone's throw from the Navy base. On another beautiful day in Southern California, I slipped into the crowded brewpub and tried an Islander IPA. The brewery's original India Pale Ale is a 7.0% ABV gem with Centennial, Chinook, and Columbus hops, with fruity notes that are perfect match for one of the best beach towns in the West. Coronado Brewing's other regular selections include Seacoast Pilsner, Orange Ave. Wit, and Mermaid Red. There are plenty of other choices, including seasonal beers, and there is not a finer place on the West Coast to enjoy the world's favorite beverage!

When I step outside onto Orange Avenue, the last remnants of a beautiful sunset are fading away above the Pacific Ocean. All good things must come to an end. It's been a memorable journey exploring some of Craft Beer Country's best breweries and the multitude of characters who have pitched in to build this special industry, one that works together to bring people together. As this book ends, I'm already looking forward to beginning new chapters, discovering new places, meeting new friends, and searching for the best beers on the planet—pint by pint.

ACKNOWLEDGMENTS

Many people have gone out of their way to contribute to this Craft Beer Country book journey. Dozens of brewery owners, operators, brewmasters, marketing, and PR people took time to help me—from arranging and participating in interviews, to guiding tours, to fact checking and editing. I've come to learn that this type of collaboration and camaraderie is typical of the craft beer industry. As a journalist, I can't imagine a better group of folks to work with, and I hope that our paths cross again.

Beer has always brought people together, and it has been almost magical for me in that respect. It has generated opportunities to meet and compare notes with fellow authors at the PNWA Conference and the Beer Bloggers & Writers Conference. A night out drinking ales with Jeff VanDomelon and Alise Long at The Growler Garage & Tap House in Albany, Oregon, led to an idea that spawned the Craft Beer Country Club on Facebook, which connects people from around the world both virtually and in person.

I've reconnected with long-lost friends and developed many new friendships while writing this book, from old college pals to new taphouse chums and barstool drinking buddies who I've met in places like Albany's No Rails Ale House as well as a myriad of great pubs, festivals, and other beer-related venues. Thanks to all of you for sharing your tastes of your pints, your opinions on what I should try and who I should visit, and most of all, participating in good old-fashioned conversation.

Publishing a book is not for the faint of heart, and I had some serious help along the way, starting with sound advice and recommendations from my author coach, Jane Friedman. Special thanks to my patient-as-a-saint editor, Christopher Hoffmann at Grad Student Freelancers, who expertly polished my stories. Thanks also to talented photographers Rob Palmer of On Location Photography, Lisa Hoch Richardson of Catchlight Photography, and several other helpful contributors who provided such great images for the chapters and centerspread that they left me thirsty for more.

I found talented book designers Kevin Kane and Emma Hall, co-owners of The Frontispiece, just as they were moving from Kansas City to San Francisco to take on exciting new opportunities. The duo has taken my words and the pictures that we have selected and magically transformed those ingredients into a beautiful book.

Finally, thanks to Scott, Michelle, Daniel, Andy, Naren, and the incomparable team at Mascot Books for putting the finishing touches on *Craft Beer Country: In Search of the Best Breweries from the South Pacific to the Pacific Coast*. I made the right choices when it came to picking publishing partners.

Last, but far from least, thank you to my family for their support. Thanks to my mom Rose Richardson and father-in-law Harry Hoch for pushing me forward and my children Kelley and Michael for their support. Most of all, I appreciate my amazing wife Lisa. Without your steady encouragement and faith in me, this would never have fermented from just another wild idea to roughly 300 pages of entertaining reality. I'm looking forward to sharing many more Craft Beer Country adventures with you and everyone else here.

We hope that you, the reader, and other characters meet up with us on our future journeys. May good craft beer bring us all together!

ABOUT THE AUTHOR

Food and beverage writer Kirk Richardson lives in Oregon's pictur-esque Willamette Valley with wife Lisa, dog Tally, cat Louie, and two refrigerators full of craft beer. He enjoys those ales and lagers with good backyard barbecue and other delicious foods, at least when he isn't off somewhere meeting old pals and new friends while discovering some of the very best breweries in North America. You can reach Kirk at CRAFTBEERCOUNTRY@GMAIL.COM.